Political Learning,
Political Choice, and
Democratic Citizenship

Political Learning, Political Choice, and Democratic Citizenship

ROBERT WEISSBERG
Cornell University

PRENTICE-HALL, INC., ENGLEWOOD CLIFFS, NEW JERSEY

Library of Congress Cataloging in Publication Data

WEISSBERG, ROBERT.
    Political learning, political choice, and democratic
citizenship.

    Includes bibliographical references.
    1. Political science—Study and teaching—United
States.   2. Political socialization.   3. Political
participation—United States.   4. Children in the
United States.   I. Title.
JA88.U6W44   320'.07   74–630
ISBN   0–13–685008-1
ISBN   0–13–684993-8 (pbk.)

© **1974 by**
Prentice-Hall, Inc., Englewood Cliffs, N.J. 07632

10 9 8 7 6 5 4 3 2 1

Prentice-Hall International, Inc., London
Prentice-Hall of Australia, Pty. Ltd., Sydney
Prentice-Hall of Canada, Ltd., Toronto
Prentice-Hall of India Private Limited, New Delhi
Prentice-Hall of Japan, Inc., Tokyo

To my Parents

Contents

Preface

The basic purpose of this book is to suggest links between early political learning and political life. We do not mean explaining the actions of particular adults by their specific childhood experiences. The desirability of understanding the roots of an individual's political philosophy and behavior is clear, but such a goal remains beyond the capacities of contemporary research. Our argument is that the childhood socialization of Americans places broad constraints on what is politically acceptable or illegitimate within the realm of "adult" politics; that is, long before adulthood, Americans acquire beliefs about what is "normal" (and perverse) in politics. This argument does not require explicit connections between a particular individual's pre-adult experience and consequent adult behavior. We determine what young Americans in general learn about politics, and from these data we infer the types of policies that will be considered normal or legitimate as these children enter adulthood. We infer from an aggregation of childhood data to overall adult patterns, not from a particular child to a particular adult.

In exploring this link we have three major goals. At the simplest level we provide an overview of a vast number of political socialization research findings. Research on early political learning has currently reached explosive proportions, and by bringing many of these findings together we hope to provide a useful introduction to the field. As part of this introduction we also provide in Chapter 2 a brief foray into some issues and problems within the field of political socialization. However, an encyclopedic treatment of political socialization data and controversies is not our exclusive goal and thus, in a number of instances, we omit topics sometimes considered important in the field.

Much more important than reviewing a body of literature is our second goal of drawing out the broad political implications of political socialization research. The study of early political learning has its scholarly roots in anthropology, sociology, and psychology, and to a significant extent political scientists follow the perspectives of these disciplines. Though such inter-disciplinary reliance is absolutely essential, it is also nevertheless true that many of the broad *political* implications of this research have been given only limited attention even by political scientists. With few exceptions analyses of childhood politicization have emphasized findings more relevant to psychology or sociology than political life. This relative neglect of the political aspects of early learning has frequently led people to dismiss this scholarly endeavor as essentially nonpolitical. By emphasizing political implications where they have sometimes gone unstated, we hope to demonstrate that the study of early political learning is as relevant to understanding the political process as analyzing congressional voting behavior.

Our third goal is to show, if only in a limited way, the advantages of combining two types of analysis—normative and empirical—that have traditionally been viewed as distinct or even incompatible. By normative analysis we mean the formulations of statements about what is desirable (or valued); by empirical we mean assertions of fact. The bulk of our analysis is derived from empirical research, but in Chapter 9 we evaluate the overall pattern of these data against what *ought* to exist. Specifically, we shall consider whether the way we politically educate children is consistent with the demands of democratic citizenship. This is certainly not a novel question, and numerous answers have been advanced, but insofar as we make explicit our notions of "democracy" rather than using it as a catch-all concept for whatever is good in life, we hope to show that political philosophy has a valuable place in factually based research.

Most books reporting research findings confront at some point the problem of methodology, i.e., the methods and limitations of data collection and statistical techniques. Insofar as our analysis makes use of numerous separate studies, each with its particular sample of respondents, measures, and research goals, our problems of methodology are multiplied. No doubt many studies use identical concepts, e.g., "middle-class," but mean slightly different things by these labels. In addition, some of our data are from the 1940s while other information is relatively recent, but it is difficult (if not impossible) to know exactly how to treat such differences in time. Can we more or less assume that what was true in the early 1960s is also true in the mid-1970s? Of course, it would be preferable to use only current data, but this choice would exclude the vast bulk of socialization research. Moreover, our review of previous research must be, by the very nature of our enterprise, highly selective and this too raises problems. Some of the material we present represents only a miniscule portion of a study's data and the charge can always be leveled that our selectivity is biased. Our response to this problem has been wherever possible to cite the actual data. While not eliminating the problem of biased selectivity, the reader at least has more than our assertion of what another author said.

Our last methodological caveat concerns a point we consider in Chapter 2 in greater detail—the persistence into adulthood of early learning. By not analyzing the consequence of political learning for each individual's future behavior, we avoid perhaps the most difficult questions of learning persistence, but important questions still remain. Since learning theorists are not able to provide a precise solution to this problem, we must be perfectly frank and not claim that our basic theme —early political learning forecloses subsequent alternatives—can be conclusively demonstrated by our subsequent analysis. As we shall see, we are not so ignorant of the relationship between early socialization and adulthood that we must make uninformed guesses, but the reader should always remember that our assertion about foreclosed alternatives rests on a number of important assumptions about the relevance of early learning. Educated guesses to be sure, but guesses nevertheless.

Acknowledgments

As with most lengthy scholarly endeavors, this one owes its origins to a variety of sources and people. Mention must be made of my high school teachers who fortunately failed to socialize me into a normal, unquestioning student. Without their unwitting help, any serious attempt to go beyond conventional perspectives would have been impossible. On the more positive side, a few individuals deserve commendation. Brian Silver once again made his herculean effort to teach me how to write English and think clearly. Left to my own literary vices this book would have been twice as long and half as coherent. Don Pike and Ben Ginsberg read various parts of this manuscript and thus are to be named as accomplices (though each would today claim that he tried to stop me). Gertrude Fitzpatrick provided her usual deep insights into the clerical business and thus deserves a hearty thanks. Thanks is also given to the Jonathan R. Meigs Fund that provided financial assistance for research expenses and typing.

Political Choice and Political Socialization

Politics involves continual choice. There certainly are no universally agreed upon political methods or institutions that everyone accepts as inevitable. History suggests that the number of ways by which
any political question can be solved is virtually infinite. Almost every
political alternative has somewhere either been actually implemented
or suggested by leaders, theorists, or citizens. Political decisions range
in scope from the fundamental choice about giving primary loyalty to
a political community to the more mundane decision of whom to vote
for on election day. Whatever exists politically is a consequence of such
choices, be they conscious or unconscious, since the way citizens govern themselves is not biologically or physically preordained. Citizens
may view an existing political system as natural and virtually inevitable, but every detail represents a decision taken by individuals to do
things one way rather than another.

Politics may require continual choice, but obviously no citizens consciously engage in choosing among the multitude of competing alternatives. Perhaps only abstractly do citizens possess this total political freedom to choose. The image of a people freely selecting all the political rules governing their lives is a myth appropriate for the Declaration of Independence and the writings of social contract theorists such as Hobbes and Locke. Most Americans are free to make at least some important decisions about how they will live, who governs them, and on occasion what policies will be enacted; but even the most active, civic-minded individual is not concerned with more than a miniscule proportion of the possible choices. Many citizens in fact do not even participate in simple and accessible political decision processes such as voting. Politics may involve continual choice, but compared to what might be, there is little exercise of this power to select among alternatives.

Many explanations have been offered as to why the multitude of political alternatives remain undiscussed and un-thought-about nonissues. Obviously, few societies can function effectively if, at any given moment, every citizen were free to raise for consideration each and every political alternative. Life would be a gigantic debate in which nothing could be taken for granted even after a decision had been reached. Perhaps on Monday the political system would be based on the principles of equality and majority rule; by Tuesday others might argue that it was time for a change and demand a system weighted toward personal achievement and decisions made by technical experts. Official rules might even change hourly as circumstances changed. It would be as if everyone were a constitutional convention delegate charged with making all political decisions anew from the basic nature of the political system to detailed minor policy. Necessity clearly requires that at some point decisions once made would be beyond reconsideration. Continual making and re-making of all policy would be chaotic, difficult to imagine, perhaps, except at rare moments during major political crises.

Another reason suggested for the limited nature of political decision-making stresses the biases in any given status quo. Any set of governing arrangements benefits some people more than others, and those who benefit the most (and such people typically have great political influence) are not likely to encourage serious discussions of radical alternatives. More likely, they will insist that what exists is natural, appropriate, and difficult to change without great risk. We would hardly expect aristocrats to sponsor talks on the advantages of political equality. Even in some relatively free and open societies extensive powers of censorship and repression exist to protect existing arrangements from subversive influences. There has probably never been a government, no matter how tolerant and benign, that has never expelled or imprisoned some citizens for espousing alternatives to the status quo.

The impracticality of perpetual consideration of every political alternative and the use of political repression are not, however, the only explanations for why so many potential alternatives remain nonissues removed from thought and action. The problems inherent in a continual reexamination of all political possibilities are obvious, but it is unlikely that the average citizen refrains from entertaining the full range of alternatives merely because of the potentially disruptive consequences. Nor, at least in the United States, are most nonissues kept nonissues through the exercise of repressive state power. Critics of existing government policies may argue that some choices are kept out of bounds by the ruling elite, but few of these critics go so far as to claim that everything that now exists is a product of conscious and systematic coercion. It is highly unlikely that any political system's survival depends on a continual surveillance of citizens to stamp out subversive thought. The impracticality of continual decision-making and suppression of subversive alternatives undoubtedly contributes to the limiting of choices, but much more is involved.

What will be argued here is that this nonconsideration of all possible alternatives is largely due to citizens accepting most of the status quo as politically natural and thus beyond serious change. Most political alternatives are rejected because they never see the light of day as reasonable choices. For example, it is unnecessary to coerce Americans into accepting the idea that elections decided by majority rule are the best method of selecting leaders; nor do most citizens prefer majority rule elections only because deciding on something else would involve too much of a hassle. Of all the ways of selecting political leaders, virtually every American accepts voting by majority rule as *the* appropriate method and has little desire to debate the alternatives. Such alternatives as filling official positions by lottery (as was done in ancient Athens), or on the basis of heredity (as in monarchies) are not considered realistic or suited to the United States. Scholars viewing this question with detachment, however, are probably less willing to exclude certain alternatives as infeasible or impossible. Similarly, few Americans consider themselves coerced into membership of a geographically based nation-state though other possibilities (e.g., class based societies) have not yet had a fair hearing. Most of us view this loyalty as natural and historically inevitable. That primary political loyalty to a geographically based nation-state, as opposed to an ethnic or religious community, is historically a recent type of loyalty has little relevance for most Americans. Here again, the potential issue is a nonissue.

The somewhat arbitrary nature of American political institutions, procedures, and policies becomes much clearer when we examine how other political systems, past and present, deal with the problem of governance. The study of comparative government presents an enormous catalogue of political alternatives. Even nations with similar resources and experiences have chosen different ways of solving similar problems (compare, for example, the United States and Canada). It is interesting that many American institutions—e.g., an elected national executive, now widely viewed as almost an historical inevitability—were the results of close votes taken by mortal men hoping for the best.

We are not suggesting that all citizens unthinkingly accept everything as unchangeable and preordained. Such an argument is obviously false. Occasional riots and protests clearly indicate that not everyone accepts the status quo as desirable and impossible to change. A small minority even demands sweeping reorganization of American society. Even conservatives or reactionaries probably believe certain policies might be reevaluated and adapted to meet new circumstances. Moreover, there is not only talk of change, but considerable political change does occur. Obviously, the fact that few Americans wish to explore most alternatives to the status quo does not mean that no alternatives are considered and acted upon.

Nevertheless, compared to the range of choices that could be made, the number of choices that are even considered is very small. Even those demanding sweeping changes in the existing system accept many practices and institutions as givens. Cries for change typically revolve around such things as demands for new leadership, enacting new laws, reordering of national priorities, increasing our national commitment to certain social values. For the most part, the people making these demands unconsciously accept certain boundaries and assume that whatever the changes, certain communal and institutional patterns will remain more or less intact. Those seeking congressional reform typically call for more assertive leadership, abolishment of the seniority system, and greater responsiveness of public officials. There is little discussion of other ways, besides a body of elected officials, that this political function can be achieved. The persistence of Congress as a lawmaking institution is taken for granted. Indeed, the very idea of written laws is itself only one of a number of methods of political control; yet almost all Americans view legal codes as *the* primary method of social and political control. To be sure, such reforms taking place within a set of political givens are not perceived as trivial. For some these changes may be crucial for political survival or encourage extreme actions. However, the fever generated by such demands for change should not obscure the basic fact that compared to the full range of possibilities, the choices debated are relatively limited in scope.

It is crucial to realize that the elimination of most alternatives from the range of choices has significant political consequences. In many situations the elimination of eight out of ten alternatives can make the final choice between the remaining two relatively inconsequential. For example, every four years in the United States a fiercely contested battle for the presidency takes place. Though the outcome probably makes some policy difference, the fact that under the existing system we have a president rather than a hereditary monarch or an elected tyrant may be far more important than who is elected in a particular election. Similarly, the government's decision to send U.S. troops to Vietnam, though of obvious consequence, is relatively trivial compared to the continued decision of American leaders (and public) to place national goals ahead of transnational objectives. Merely because such standing decisions as having a presidential system and maintaining national sovereignty are not discussed and are consensually accepted does not make them unimportant. This situation can easily be likened to the role of managerial strategy in a baseball game —a manager's decision may be hotly debated and of clear consequence in a given situation, but ultimately far more important are the basic rules of baseball that all participants unquestioningly take for granted. Because in the short run the basic rules of baseball cannot be changed, they are a nonissue despite their obvious consequence.

The persistence of certain alternatives as nonissues or as standing decisions is clearly an important, though infrequently analyzed, dimension of American politics. With very few exceptions, political analysts focus on decisions among clear, well known, and immediate choices. Why the president introduced certain legislation or why a particular candidate won are typical questions that deal with concrete choices that actually happened. It is much more difficult, and less relevant to what most people consider politics, to focus on events that never happen no matter how important they may be. In some way, the very idea of a political analysis of choices that were never considered may strike one as absurd; it is far easier to take something that actually occurred and explain it than to account for a nonevent.

POLITICAL SOCIALIZATION AND NON-DECISIONS

Our concern for how millions of political possibilities are reduced to a mere handful or, in some cases, a single "inevitable" choice will concentrate on the early political socialization of American citizens.

We assume that each citizen was not born with existing political arrangements in his genes; political dispositions were learned, and this learning is the process of political socialization. The politically innocent child is willing to accept almost any political system, loyalty, method for settling disputes, or agenda of priorities as reasonable and legitimate, but by adulthood the vast majority of these possibilities are rejected as undesirable or impossible. Either on his own, or with a little help from his friends, the politically innocent child makes numerous decisions that will affect not only his life, but the lives of others. Compared to the activities of youthful rioters and demonstrators, such early decision-making may be undramatic and almost unnoticed. Nevertheless, as we suggested in our discussion of the importance of nonissues, this foreclosing of alternatives is of fundamental political significance.

These political decisions that are made during childhood and adolescence are not, of course, decisions in the usual adult sense of the term. There certainly is no conscious weighing of alternatives followed by a rational choice. Children make decisions only in the sense that they accept some things and reject others; there may not be any conflict or an awareness of the rejected alternatives (and this is typically the case), but this obliviousness and unthinking acceptance should not obscure the fact that some alternatives have been chosen over others. Though it is obvious that in many cases children's political choices are made for them by adults, this also does not make this early learning any less of a choice between competing alternatives. A young child may never even for an instant reject what he is told about what is preferable politically, but this obedience nevertheless results in accepting one position over another.

Plan of Analysis

The basic purpose of this book will be to understand how some, but not other, political alternatives become nonissues in the minds of Americans. We shall focus on early political socialization, the process by which citizens come to hold certain expectations about what is politically right and wrong and how the system ought to function. This analysis will be divided into four interrelated topics. First, we shall examine certain problems and issues in the study of early political learning. Such questions as what political socialization encompasses, the different ways children acquire their political orientations, and the persistence of early learning into adulthood are some of the questions we shall consider. The study of how citizens acquire their political orientations is not without occasional controversy, and before we can fully understand recent research findings, we must first have a general perspective on this field.

Our second question is central to our basic goal. Drawing data from numerous recent studies we shall present a picture of political learning as it occurs during the preadult years. The types of political learning occurring during this period are many; our description will concentrate on three general areas: attitudes toward the political system, its institutions, and leaders; orientations toward political participation; and finally, attitudes toward political decision-making and the regulation of conflict. Though certainly not inclusive of all important political issues, these three areas are undoubtedly crucial aspects of political life.

Our analysis considers such issues as the nature of citizen loyalty to the American community, evaluations of political leaders such as the president, attitudes toward ideologies such as democracy and communism, perceptions of the function of political conflict, beliefs about the role of law, and toleration for the civil liberties of minorities and dissenters.

Though our main purpose in describing this early political learning is to understand how certain possibilities are eliminated as reasonable alternatives, our findings are nevertheless relevant to political change. It may be true that once a young child learns that one thing is correct and another totally unacceptable, this learning lessens the probability of change. Nevertheless, it is also true that if changes are to be made, we must first understand the forces impeding change. For example, if it is true that attitudes toward political activism are acquired early in life and are very enduring ones, this suggests that reforms for increasing citizen participation by changing adult attitudes will encounter serious obstacles. In this situation reform directed toward changes in the institutional mechanics of political participation would be more efficient. Or, if one were committed to changing people rather than laws, an understanding of this early socialization would at least make reform efforts more knowledgeable—thus, knowing that political participation related attitudes were formed during childhood would prevent the mistaken investment of resources in trying to change the attitudes of adolescents.

Our third question involves a change in focus from *what* is learned to *who* does the teaching. Here we ask how important are such agencies of socialization as the family and the school in the acquisition of political orientations. The answer to this question not only contributes to our understanding of the socialization process, but, as for the second question, the answer is also relevant for political change. To a young child it may be irrelevant where he acquires his political values and behaviors, but it is of crucial importance for those desiring change, for not all agencies of socialization are equally susceptible to outside influence. Changing an attitude by modifying school curriculum, for example, is far easier to accomplish than influencing thousands of separate families. Not only are there fewer people in the education system to convince, but once changes are agreed to, it is much easier to supervise school programs than socialization taking place within intimate family situations. Moreover, especially in democratic societies, it is usually more acceptable to manipulate school than family factors.

The fourth and final question raises a different kind of issue. Our previous questions were concerned with describing political reality. We asked what children learned and from whom they learned it; whether what they learned was good or bad was irrelevant. This factual approach is typical of the research conducted on political socialization. As in all social science, the purpose of research is to account for what exists, not to make value judgments or argue for reform. Whether American children acquired humanitarian or evil political attitudes and behaviors made no analytical difference whatsoever.

There is, however, more to political analysis than mere stating the objective facts. Scientific political analysis does not require that facts remain unevaluated. As long as it is clear that the analyst is making a value judgment and not describing reality, there is nothing improper about considering certain objective facts as "good" or "bad," desirable or undesirable. Such judgment of reality in terms of one's own values is referred to as normative analysis; and this is the type of analysis that our final question involves. After our extensive review of what young Americans learn about politics we shall pass judgment on the desirability of this learning.

In making these evaluations we shall not simply state personal preferences. Such an evaluation would tell the reader little except my own political biases. Instead, we judge existing socialization according to standards that many theorists have claimed ought to be embodied in democratic citizens. Democracy and early socialization are frequently linked, and our analysis asks whether the various demands of democratic theory are met by reality. Each of these democratic demands provides a standard against which we can make judgments on the desirability of current political socialization. Because people disagree on what democracy means, our strategy will be to employ the ideals of different democratic theories as standards of evaluation. The end result of our analysis will not only help us understand how most of the political alternatives are eliminated from consideration, but also provide a judgment of whether such elimination of alternatives is consistent with democratic government.

In sum, this is a book about the political socialization of American citizens. We shall examine what young children learn about politics and from whom they learn their political lessons. Our interest in early learning derives from our desire to understand why, of all the millions of political alternatives available to citizens, only a few are commonly considered as reasonable or possible. In many ways the elimination of most of the alternatives is a crucial decision, yet it is a decision that is usually made without any awareness or discussion. Finally, when we examine the choices that are selected, we wish to evaluate the congruence between these selections and the goals of a democratic political system. It is not enough to describe what is and what is not; we must also judge what is against what ought to be.

2

The Study of
Political Socialization

Our goal of examining the process by which most political alternatives are eliminated from serious consideration requires that we focus on early political learning. We assume that well before reaching voting age Americans have come to perceive some alternatives as normal and desirable and others as impossible and objectionable. To determine what particular orientations[1] are deeply imbedded in people's political perspectives therefore necessitates a systematic review of research findings from the field of political socialization. Rather than plunge willy-nilly into the mass of data on political socialization, however, it will be helpful if we first set out a general (though brief) background

[1]Throughout this book we employ the concept "orientations" to encompass the different dimensions of political learning. We use orientations as a kind of shorthand notation for perceptions, including knowledge, beliefs, affect, and evaluations. Our purpose is literary insofar as we avoid repetitious lists of the variety of things learned.

to avoid many of the misunderstandings that frequently occur when first encountering data on early learning. So that subsequent research findings will be better understood, this chapter briefly considers the following: the historical emergence of political socialization research; differing conceptualizations of the subject; the sources of political orientations; and finally, the persistence of early political learning into adulthood.

HISTORICAL CONCERN FOR EARLY POLITICAL LEARNING

A concern for the citizen's early political development is as old as the study of political science itself. Since ancient Greece, philosophers and political theorists have argued about the right way to educate citizens politically. Both Plato and Aristotle, for example, wrote extensively about what is called today "citizenship training." Plato's *Republic* is in part an educational treatise asserting that the state's ultimate nature is closely dependent on child-rearing practices. Similarly, Aristotle in his *Politics* expounded at length on what constitutes the proper civic education, even claiming that the legislator's chief responsibility should be the proper education of the young. Other political theorists, such as the seventeenth-century Englishman Thomas Hobbes, anticipated certain modern socialization theories by drawing parallels between the exercise of family and of governmental authority.

The importance of early political socialization was also implied in nineteenth-century arguments for mass education in the United States. Advocates for free public schools argued that the preservation of freedom and the American way of life required mandatory mass education. The well-known educator Horace Mann stressed that unless young children were instructed in the values of self-rule and the ability to comply voluntarily with the laws of duty and reason, political freedom was impossible. Particularly when immigration had reached tidal wave proportions in the late nineteenth century and the absorption of diverse ethnic and religious groups posed major problems, early political indoctrination was frequently viewed as the means to the goal of Americanization. The vestiges of this concern still lingers on in the many state-required civics and history courses originally designed to Americanize foreigners.

Though the study of political socialization dates at least from Plato's time, much of this analysis remained quite limited until relatively recently. The arguments put forth by Plato, Aristotle, Hobbes, and others were typically arguments for particular political goals and were based on limited, nonsystematically collected evidence. By the standards of modern political science, most of these older treatments of political socialization are only suggestive of possibilities, not verified conclusions. Plato and Aristotle may, of course, be correct in their assessment of early political education, but we do not know for sure. It is one thing to recognize the political importance of early learning; it is quite another to demonstrate adequately the nature of this relationship.

With the emergence of modern social science, our capacity to understand the political significance of early learning advanced significantly. Disciplines such as anthropology, sociology, and psychology have all focused on the processes by which young children develop their adult personalities and acquire characteristics making them members of particular political and social groups.[2] Though most research in these disciplines have not dealt explicitly with political factors, they have provided a large number of theories, concepts, and methods relevant to specifically political learning.

Despite the fact that sociologists and anthropologists used the concept socialization over one hundred years ago, the field of *political* socialization as a specific research focus is a recent innovation. As recently as 1950 the political science profession listed no specialization called political socialization. Most political scientists rejected the political relevance of early learning and consequently most of the early research on the area was conducted by psychologists, sociologists, and educators.[3] The field of political socialization was probably born in 1959 with the publication of Herbert Hyman's *Political Socialization.*[4] In the space of a relatively few pages, Hyman (a sociologist) summarized most of the research findings from over fifty years of scholarship. Within the last five years the research on political socialization has been enormous, but its emergence as a scientifically based field of scholarly endeavor is only a recent event.

[2]The emergence and use of socialization in various disciplines are further described by John A. Clausen, "A Historical and Comparative View of Socialization Theory and Research," in *Socialization and Society,* ed. Clausen (Boston: Little, Brown and Company, 1968), pp. 22–52.

[3]A conspicuous exception to this neglect was Charles E. Merriam, *The Making of Citizens: A Comparative Study of Methods of Civic Training* (Chicago: University of Chicago Press, 1931). Even here, however, there was little emphasis on empirical research.

[4]Herbert H. Hyman, *Political Socialization: A Study in the Psychology of Political Behavior* (New York: The Free Press, 1959).

DEFINITIONS OF POLITICAL SOCIALIZATION

As could be expected with such rapid scholarly growth, no universal agreement exists on what political socialization means or what the research priorities ought to be. Like the proverbial blindfolded wisemen, each holding a different part of an elephant, disagreements arise over what is being examined. In some instances these disagreements merely reflect trivial semantic emphases, but in others there is a more serious disagreement on what is relevant in the study of early political learning. Though there are probably as many definitions of political socialization as books on the subject, the following conceptualizations indicate the range of thinking:

> [Political socialization consists of] those developmental processes through which persons acquire political orientations and patterns of behavior.[5]
>
> [Political socialization is all] political learning, formal and informal, deliberate and unplanned, at every stage of the life cycle, including not only explicit political learning but also nominally non-political learning of politically relevant social attitudes and the acquisition of politically relevant personality characteristics.[6]
>
> Political socialization [is] the process, mediated through various agencies of society, by which an individual learns politically relevant dispositions and behavior patterns.[7]
>
> Political socialization, then, will be defined as the learning of politically relevant social patterns corresponding to societal positions as mediated through various agencies of society.[8]
>
> Political socialization refers to the learning process by which the political norms and behaviors acceptable to an ongoing political system are transmitted from generation to generation.[9]

All these conceptions of political socialization acknowledge that political attitudes, knowledge, values, and behaviors are learned; thus the study of political socialization involves the study of individual learning. This much everyone agrees on. However, when we proceed

[5]David Easton and Jack Dennis, *Children in the Political System* (New York: McGraw-Hill Book Company, 1969), p. 7.

[6]Fred I. Greenstein, "Political Socialization," *International Encyclopedia of the Social Sciences* (New York: Crowell-Collier, 1965), p. 551.

[7]Kenneth P. Langton, *Political Socialization* (New York: Oxford University Press, 1969), p. 5.

[8]Louis Froman, "Personality and Political Socialization," *Journal of Politics*, 23 (1961), 342.

[9]Roberta Sigel, "Assumptions About the Learning of Political Values," *The Annals*, 361 (1965), 1.

to *what* learned political orientations should be the focus of research, important differences in emphasis emerge. Two such definitional approaches can be distinguished. One perspective (illustrated by Easton and Dennis, Greenstein, and Langton) focuses attention on the process by which *any* political attitudes are acquired. Within this perspective some researchers (e.g., Greenstein) specifically spell out various ways political learning takes place, while others (such as Langton) are less precise. But what is common to all of these researchers is that no political learning is excluded from the political socialization process. No prejudgment is made on whether learning is functional or disfunctional for the survival of the existing political system. In the United States, for example, one may learn to be anti-American, anti-democratic, and unalterably opposed to obeying laws, yet such learning, despite its potentially disruptive consequences, is considered political socialization.

This inclusion of all political learning into the study of political socialization, however, is rejected in the second approach. In Sigel's definition, for example, political socialization is not merely the learning of any political attitude or behavior, *but only those attitudes and behaviors that contribute to the basic stability of the existing political system.* This second approach views the socialization process from the perspective of the political system's requirement, i.e., political socialization helps maintain the status quo. While a researcher employing the first approach might ask, "What do American children learn about politics and who teaches them?" someone approaching political socialization from the second perspective would ask instead, "How do children in the United States learn to become good citizens?" Though answers to these questions would overlap somewhat, major differences in data collection and interpretation would occur reflecting the initial differences in focus.

Both approaches are valid and have their relative advantages. The first approach, with its emphasis on individual learning of any political orientation, is well suited for accounting for adult attitudes and behaviors. If we were interested in explaining American political values and patterns of political activity, the first type of definition is more appropriate for our research. If, on the other hand, our goal is explaining how present political institutions survived, the second approach is more suitable.[10]   In each instance, some aspects of political learning are

[10]Actually, the second approach with its emphasis on making young children into "proper" members of the community has been of little utility in socialization research in modern political systems where change is so rapid that the "proper" political role is continually shifting. Though certain authors like Sigel espouse this perspective, actual research rarely, if ever, follows this perspective. No doubt potential socialization research in more stable societies would find this second approach more relevant.

ignored and others emphasized; but this is essential in any investigation since examining everything is impossible and undesirable. Depending on the types of questions we are interested in, these approaches are complementary, not conflicting.

LEARNING ABOUT POLITICS

Acquiring one's political orientations, like all learning, is an extremely complex process. Why some people learn faster than others or how learning actually happens are difficult, complicated questions to answer. The learning process is one of the most researched areas in psychology and education, yet our knowledge is far from complete. Our purpose here, however, is not to discuss the mental processes by which children acquire their political orientations. Rather, our basic concerns are the much simpler ones of (1) where does early political learning occur and (2) what types of nonpolitical learning have political implications. We begin by considering four different situations in which children may acquire political attitudes, knowledge, and behavior.

Formal Political Instruction

When most people think of early political socialization, they probably first think of the formal school instruction usually known as civics or citizenship training. In the United States most states legally require that national and state history courses be taught to both grade school and high school students. The kind of politics taught in school civics courses is usually so bland, nonpartisan, and noncontroversial that it may not even be considered political. Nevertheless, the consensual and nonpartisan nature of this instruction should not blind us to the fact that these children are indoctrinated with only one version of historical and political truth. Many of the so-called facts about the American Revolution, for example, are not so much uncontroversial non-political truths as speculative interpretations of incomplete bodies of information that reinforce particular political positions. Though few Americans desire highly politicized schools where controversial matters are openly discussed, this is indeed what occurs in American history and citizenship courses. Because virtually everyone agrees on what is true in these controversies, few citizens perceive their children as being politically brainwashed.

Formal political education in the schools occurs in other areas besides history and civics. Instruction in geography, reading, English, and even art can have specific political content, though, due to its noncontroversial nature, it may not be recognized as such. Frequently only an outsider or a dissenter recognizes the implicit political message in ostensibly non-political subjects. The common portrayal of non-Europeans as backward, quaint, and folksy in world geography is one common illustration of such political communication. Similarly, until fairly recently it was not unusual for "non-political" books teaching reading skills to picture America as populated only by white, middle-class suburbanites untouched by unemployment, poor housing, and racial and religious discrimination. In such instances, facts not taught were perhaps more significant than what was described.

Non-school organizations also perform important political socialization functions. Groups like the Boy Scouts and some church-related youth groups frequently engage in explicit political education and though political socialization typically comes under the heading of character building or leadership training the goals are clearly political. Obedience to established authority, respect for the nation and flag, and the obligations of "good citizens" are perhaps the most common political themes in such organizations. The United States armed forces likewise engage in extensive formal political education. Both college R.O.T.C. programs and basic training reflect a concern that American soldiers know how to defend our way of life against subversive propaganda. Formal political education need not, of course, be used only to defend the status quo. The Communist Party of the United States has a long tradition of educational meetings for resocializing recent members to the officially correct party ideology. Radical organizations such as the Black Panthers have also recently engaged in activities quite similar to explicit classroom political instruction.

Informal Political Learning

Political education obviously involves much more than attending classes or explicit indoctrination programs. Equally, if not more important, than formal political socialization is the more informal political learning that people just seem to pick up without being very aware of it. Such casual learning can take place almost anywhere—in school, at home, with friends, or from the mass media. In the home, for instance, a young child can be influenced merely by overhearing his parents continually complain about "all the corrupt politicians" or how the Republican party causes depressions. Children need not be interested in politics to be the recipient of a steady stream of political messages. Watching television, attending John Wayne war movies, reading comic books, hearing people discuss war protesters, and participating in a Fourth of July celebration may all influence an individual's political development. In each instance something is learned, but unlike the formal socialization discussed above, there is no organized formal educational program.

Informal political socialization is an individualistic process. No two people share identical experiences or interests; hence many individual differences occur in learning. In some homes, for example, politics may be a central issue; in others political topics may be taboo. Similarly, some children thrive on comic books, movies, and adventure TV programs while others spend their time practicing the violin. Since even young children exercise some choice over their interests, one cannot argue that merely because certain political stimuli are present in an environment they will necessarily be learned. The mass media may, for instance, provide a biased picture of American foreign policy, but this does not mean that everyone who watches TV acquires these beliefs. Some children have no receptivity whatsoever to the subject. Though all American children have considerable exposure to informal political socialization, it is very difficult to say exactly what any one person has been exposed to.

The Structure of Authority

Our discussion of the different ways people acquire their political attitudes and behaviors has so far concentrated on the transmission of explicit political messages. Such transmission may have been highly organized or informal and subtle, but some political information was conveyed. Attitudes and behaviors are not only influenced by *what* is being transmitted, but also by *how* messages are transmitted. Indeed, it is entirely possible that political learning may occur where nothing political is taught; it is the *way* something is taught that has the political consequences.

The importance of the transmission process becomes clear when we realize that many political questions (e.g., the limits on governmental power) involve rules about the exercise of authority and all social situations similarly involve the exercise of authority. Almost from birth people are immeshed in complex webs of authority relationships. Every type of interpersonal activity—from learning to be a well-behaved child to sports—requires learning a relationship to established authority. In each situation, sets of acceptable behaviors, ways these rules can be modified, and penalties for infractions are acquired. Some of us learn, for example, that all rules must be obeyed regardless of one's own opinion, that authority cannot be challenged, and that disobedience brings inevitable and harsh consequences. Others learn that all regulations are flexible, rules are decided on by common consent, and punishment for wrongdoing can be negotiated.

Some scholars argue that exposure to authority patterns in non-political situations creates expectations about the proper use of authority in political situations.[11] Analysis of the congruence between early authority experiences and subsequent political attitudes and behavior is frequently (but not always) formulated in terms of authoritarian and democratic authority relationships. The argument suggests that where families, schools, and organizations stress unthinking acceptance of non-negotiable rules handed down by higher authorities, citizens will thus prefer a political system where decisions are similarly made and implemented. The key assumption is that people seek congruence between their own personal authority experience and its relationship to broader political authority. Hence, democracy in the larger political system begins with democratic political socialization (and autocratic systems similarly begin with autocratic political and non-political learning).[12]

Experiences with Political Authority

A fourth way political orientations are acquired also involves experience with authority, but in this case the experience is directly political. That is, an individual learns about politics by actually interacting with public officials. The idea of children having direct political experiences may seem strange to those perceiving political activity as something that begins with voting, but even before age eighteen, preadults can have numerous experiences with public officials such as policemen, postmen, court officials, and, of course, school teachers (who are, after all, state officials). Such political experiences are particularly common in adolescence where young men confront the selective service system and the car culture opens up vast opportunities for contact with law enforcement officials. Moreover, everyone encounters the bureaucracy when taking a driver's license test, registering for Social Security, or using the state employment service for a summer job. This political behavior perhaps seems inconsequential when compared with voting for president or writing a letter to a congressman, but in

[11]See, for example, Harry Eckstein, *Division and Cohesion in a Democracy* (Princeton, N.J.: Princeton University Press, 1966), pp. 240–41.

[12]Perhaps the most famous argument linking early authority patterns to the exercise of authority in the political system is the one attributing nazism to the authoritarian German family. In effect, the argument asserts that Germans wanted leaders reminiscent of their strong fathers. Such arguments are advanced by Bertram Schaffner, *Father Land: A Study of Authoritarianism in the German Family* (New York: Columbia University Press, 1948); and G. M. Gilbert, *The Psychology of Dictatorship: Based on an Examination of the Leaders of Nazi Germany* (New York: The Ronald Press, 1950). The validity of these arguments will be explored in Chapter 8.

terms of sheer frequency, they provide a great opportunity for political learning. Indeed, for most people the vast majority of their directly political activities consist of contacts with such public officials as police, tax officials, and other bureaucratic functionaries.

Because these political experiences are typically relatively routine and trouble free, they may pass largely unnoticed. To realize the significance of these experiences, imagine one's reactions if most contacts with minor officials were negative. Rather than the neighborhood policeman giving friendly advice, for example, he would instead suspiciously demand to know what you were doing, where you lived, and then search you if you objected to this questioning. What if the local licensing officials informed you that it was impossible to obtain a permit without a bribe. Few people have not, at one time or another, experienced exasperating moments with governmental officials, but these usually turn out to be exceptions soon forgotten. In such instances, the positive experiences do not teach us anything new but instead reinforce existing favorable dispositions. It is perhaps only when incongruities exist—e.g., a supposedly competent government makes a mess out of a draft deferment request—that the learning is new; but this does not mean that a consistent, reinforcing experience is without consequences.

Though our discussion of political learning has emphasized children as recipients of numerous political stimuli, we must also realize that socialization is not an assembly-line process over which individuals have no control. There are, no doubt, many political orientations that few Americans can avoid acquiring, but this does not mean that political socialization is predetermined by what parents, schools, the mass media, and other socialization agents decide are appropriate. People can ignore or reject political messages directed at them. It is entirely possible, for example, for a poor black child to draw his own conclusions from his experience and thus be unimpressed by glowing descriptions of American life. Individuals have goals and may themselves choose to be socialized in certain ways to achieve these goals. It has been noted that political careerists consciously choose environments conducive to developing the characteristics required for future political activity. Such an individual is not socialized into political activism by his environment, but rather selects his environment on the basis of his goals.[13]

---

[13]This process of consciously choosing one's socialization experience to achieve future goals is referred to as "anticipatory socialization." The extent of this process among politicians is described in Heinz Eulau and John D. Sprague, *Lawyers in Politics* (Indianapolis: Bobbs-Merrill Co., Inc., 1964), pp. 56–64.

Non-Political Learning
with Potential Political Consequences

Our discussion of political socialization has thus far focused on the transmission of explicit political orientations. Even where the acquisition is indirect—as in the role of authority structure, for example—the individual learns something that is clearly political in content. It is clear, however, that not all politically relevant learning is explicitly political in content. Obviously, any kind of learning can, under certain circumstances, have political implications. A strong dislike for red hair may appear politically irrelevant, but if a presidential candidate just happens to have red hair, this dislike becomes politically relevant. It is probably impossible to find any nonpolitical socialization that will never, under some set of conditions, have a political consequence.

At the same time, however, we must also realize that some non-political dispositions are potentially more politically relevant than others. In the above illustration, for instance, though a red hair phobia is in this one instance relevant to politics, most of the time it is less relevant than attitudes toward Negroes. Though it is impossible to discuss in detail every type of learning with potential political consequences, some forms of nonpolitical learning deserve more careful attention. Our discussion focuses on four such nonpolitical factors: personality traits, social roles, skills, and social and personal identifications.

The relationship between personality and politics has been well documented. Personality characteristics such as ego-strength, self-esteem, authoritarianism, ambition, need for power, feelings of control over one's environment, and sociability are all related to political attitudes and behavior.[14]   Because personality traits such as these and other politically relevant ones are a complex result of thousands of experiences, one can imply that every aspect of one's overall development is therefore politically relevant. For example, the development of ego strength—an important factor in political participation—may result from early parental encouragement, the emotional atmosphere at home, relationships with brothers and sisters, the types of school friends or one's academic and social successes. Each one of these experiences thus becomes politically significant. When we consider that a trait such as ego-strength is but one of many politically relevant personality characteristics, and the processes related to personality devel-

---

[14]A significant portion of this vast personality and politics literature is briefly described in Fred I. Greenstein, *Personality and Politics* (Chicago: Markham Publishing Company, 1969), pp. 154–84.

opment are themselves numerous and complex, the scope of socialization research would have to be all encompassing.

However, while the importance of personality factors in politics must be acknowledged, it is counterproductive to suggest that the entire process of personality development be viewed as an integral part of the political socialization process. To be sure, it would be immensely informative to understand the origins of politically relevant personality traits, but this far-reaching task is better left to psychologists and sociologists specializing in child development and personality theory. Even if we could adequately describe the emergence of traits such as ego-strength, in most instances the relationship between personality and political orientations is so complex and indirect that the immediate political relevance is not commensurate with the research costs. It is difficult enough, for example, relating authoritarianism to political behavior without first determining the roots of this disposition.

There is another type of nonpolitical, but potentially politically relevant learning that presents many problems similar to those in considering personality traits. Throughout life one acquires a variety of roles to be played on certain occasions. Young girls, for instance, usually learn that in most situations they are expected to play a female role that traditionally has emphasized passivity, charm rather than intellect, subdued ambition, and concern for physical appearances. Individuals also learn to play many group-related roles. Some elementary school children may demonstrate a particular predilection for being leaders; others adopt roles such as passive follower, task-oriented organizer, or social charmer. Such roles as passive unambitious female or dynamic organizer obviously have political implications, though the roles themselves originate from nonpolitical learning. Many areas of political life resemble nonpolitical life, so it is not surprising that nonpolitical roles affect political attitudes and behavior. It is frequently argued, for example, that training young girls to play the role of the housewife, who leaves important decisions to her husband and is unconcerned with the outside world, probably also discourages greater political activity among women.

A third type of nonpolitical, but occasionally politically relevant, learning is the acquisition of skills. Many political activities require specific skills, but few of these abilities are unique to political activity. We could not expect an illiterate who has difficulty speaking in public to organize a mass letter-writing campaign. Nor could we expect citizens to critically evaluate their government's policies if they are unable to question what they are told. Literacy, public speaking skills, and critical thinking are thus politically relevant though not political per se.

Like personality development and the learning of nonpolitical roles, the acquisition of skills that have potential political significance may be defined as an integral part of the political socialization process. That an individual flunked college chemistry is important if that person becomes a violent bomb-building revolutionary. Should American politics become increasingly more violent, skills like marksmanship will become politically relevant. Nevertheless, as was the case for personality traits and politics, it is one thing to acknowledge the potential political relevance of this learning, quite another to include it explicitly as part of political socialization. There are too many nonpolitical roles and skills with potential political relevance to consider. Analysis of each learned role and skill requires an encyclopedic treatment of human development. In addition, as we suggest in our illustrations, predicting which roles and skills acquired in childhood will be politically relevant for adults is no simple matter. Rather than attempt such predictions and describe the many roles and skills that children acquire, subsequent analysis considers only those roles and skills that are explicitly political.

The last type of nonpolitical learning we shall consider is an individual's social and group identifications. With maturity children receive themselves as members of social communities larger than their immediate families. They learn that they share important characteristics such as ethnicity, religion, race, region, and social class with other people. Such group loyalties, by themselves, are not necessarily political. There is nothing explicitly political about being a Catholic or a southerner. However, group identities typically play very important political roles. In 1960, for example, while not all fellow Catholics voted for the Catholic presidential candidate, numerous Catholics did vote on the basis of religious identification. Religious identification can also influence foreign policy position as witnessed by strong Jewish support given to United States efforts to help Israel.

In considering these nonpolitical group identifications we face many problems comparable to those encountered in analyzing other nonpolitical learning with political implications. First, in many situations it is not self-evident which of a person's nonpolitical identifications are politically relevant. People belong to numerous social groups simultaneously, and it is not easy to predict which identity will be most salient. For example, what identity is politically most significant for a lower-class, urban, Catholic, northerner, whose parents migrated from Eastern Europe? Individuals sharing the identical characteristics may even react differently to the same group-related political stimuli.

This problem of isolating the social group identities with the greatest political relevance is fundamental insofar as we cannot hope to look at the learning of all group identifications. The situation is even more complicated since political scientists disagree on what constitutes the politically most important group loyalties. Should we include region, religion, social class, ethnicity, race, sex, local community, or even generation? Each of these factors may be politically significant in some situations, but in other instances they may be irrelevant.

Our solution to this issue of which identities are relevant to the political socialization process is to limit ourselves to those explicit political identities such as national identity. There are many nonpolitical identities with a demonstrated impact on attitudes and behaviors, but to incorporate the acquisition of nonpolitical group loyalties as an integral part of the socialization process presents, at least for our purposes, more costs than benefits. The learning of religious affiliation may be potentially politically relevant, but to initially assume that it *is* politically relevant is unwarranted. If the United States were a theocracy, or politics were organized around religious conflict, religion would then become an explicitly political loyalty.

THE PERSISTENCE OF EARLY POLITICAL SOCIALIZATION

Thus far we have implicitly assumed that early political learning effects adult attitudes, knowledge, and behaviors. This is a crucial assumption. If early learning were soon forgotten or greatly modified as individuals entered the real (adult) political world, our subsequent analysis would be politically irrelevant. This assumption of the persistence of early political learning is not completely shared by everyone.[15] The concern for preadult political education dates from Plato and Aristotle, but not everyone agrees that early political socialization has a specific influence beyond childhood. In fact, until recently, most political scientists did not even examine early political learning's subsequent impact; its existence was deemed irrelevant.

Though considerable research has focused on the relationship between childhood and adulthood, important questions remain only par-

[15]See, for example, David Marsh, "Political Socialization: The Implicit Assumptions Questioned," *British Journal of Political Science*, 1 (1971), 456–64. A recent empirical examination of a portion of the persistence assumption is reported in Donald D. Searing, Joel T. Schwartz, and Oldin E. Lind, "The Structuring Principle: Political Socialization and Belief Systems," *American Political Science Review* 67 (1973), 415–32.

tially answered.[16] Anthropologists, child psychologists, sociologists, and psychiatrists, among others—all must deal with the influence of early experiences on later life, but little (if any) consensus exists on exactly how childhood affects adulthood. It is not difficult to understand our lack of precise knowledge on this crucial question. Relating childhood experiences to adult behavior would, ideally, require two measurements separated by a sufficient time difference. Unfortunately, rarely can a researcher analyze childhood characteristics and then wait twenty years and measure the same characteristics in the adult. Frequently a few years interval is all that is possible and this hardly permits measuring the relationship between adulthood and childhood. One common alternative to this time problem is adult recall of childhood feelings and experiences. Though more practical than overtime studies, few of us can accurately recall our childhood, and post-childhood experiences undoubtedly color and distort early memories. Even if accurate recollection were possible, a single viewpoint on what had occured twenty years earlier may be an incomplete description of events. Parents and children differ on perceptions of many facts (e.g., how family decisions are made) and relying on a single viewpoint can lead to inaccuracies.[17]

Nevertheless, while no precise, systematic framework exists connecting early political socialization to specific adulthood characteristics, at least some consensus exists among scholars on what types of early learning, at what point in childhood, are relatively more important for influencing adult political orientations. It is useful to begin our discussion by posing two alternative positions on this question of persistence. The first, which we may refer to as the primacy argument, asserts that fundamental and enduring attitudes, values, and behaviors are formed *early* in childhood. Young children are not miniature adults, but the basic developmental framework is asserted to be more

[16]Among others, see Benjamin S. Bloom, *Stability and Change in Human Characteristics* (New York: John Wiley & Sons, Inc., 1964), Chapters 3–5; Jerome Kagan and Howard A. Moss, *Birth to Maturity* (New York: John Wiley & Sons, Inc., 1962); and Jerome Kagan, "The Three Faces of Continuity in Human Development," in *Handbook of Socialization Theory and Research,* ed. David A. Goslin (Chicago: Rand McNally, 1969), 983–1002; Jeane N. Knutson, "Long Term Effects of Personality on Political Attitudes and Beliefs," unpublished paper presented at the American Political Science convention, 1973; and Jeane Knutson, *Personality Stability and Political Belief* (San Francisco: Jossey-Bass, forthcoming).

[17]This point is dramatically made by Niemi's comparison of children's and parents' perceptions of political preferences and family interactions. Niemi finds that only reports of demographic characteristics are consistently accurate. See Richard G. Niemi, "Reliability and Validity of Survey and Non-Survey Data About the Family," paper presented at the American Political Science Association Convention, 1971.

or less formed by the age of ten. Proponents as diverse as the Jesuits and Sigmund Freud emphasize the crucial and determining role of early learning in the development of the adult personality. The underlying reasons for the primacy argument vary greatly, but agreement exists that early childhood socialization places enormous constraints and predispositions on subsequent development.[18]

On the other hand, some scholars subscribe to what can be labeled the recency argument. That is, the closer a learning experience is to adulthood, the greater its influence and political relevance.[19] Much of this argument derives from the elementary, but important, fact that young children are intellectually incapable of acquiring many kinds of attitudes, knowledge, and skills. We may want to instruct every young American in his constitutional rights, but even a bright five-year-old is intellectually incapable of grasping these concepts. Because much of politics involves complex skills and concepts that are probably incomprehensible to most children, this recency argument has considerable appeal. In addition, the post-childhood period presents ample opportunity for important socializing experiences and recent occurrences may be more salient than earlier learning.

Both the primacy and recency arguments have much to recommend them as valid descriptions of political learning. Research exists to support both positions. However, a serious conflict need not exist between these two perspectives for each may be correct, though in different areas of political learning. Certain political orientations are learned very early in life and are highly resistant to change while different political orientations may be susceptible to continual modification with recent learning being most important. As a way of simply portraying the varied patterns of persistence that different political orientations exhibit, let us describe three general models depicting the relationship of early political learning to subsequent adult attitudes and behaviors. We shall then briefly describe how these models appear to fit certain political orientations. Figure 1 illustrates these three models:

[18]Political scientists emphasizing the primacy argument are (among others): Fred I. Greenstein, *Children and Politics* (New Haven: Yale University Press, 1965), pp. 56, 79–81, passim; Richard E. Dawson and Kenneth Prewitt, *Political Socialization* (Boston: Little, Brown and Company, 1969), pp. 41–48; Gabriel Almond, "A Functional Approach to Comparative Politics," in *The Politics of Developing Areas*, ed. Gabriel Almond and James S. Coleman (Princeton, N.J.: Princeton University Press, 1960), p. 28; David Easton and Jack Dennis, *Children in the Political System* (New York: McGraw-Hill, 1969), p. 6.

[19]See, for example, M. Kent Jennings and Richard G. Niemi, "Patterns of Political Learning," *Harvard Educational Review*, 38 (1968), pp. 443–67; and Gabriel A. Almond and Sidney Verba, *The Civic Culture* (Princeton, N.J.: Princeton University Press, 1963), pp. 371–72.

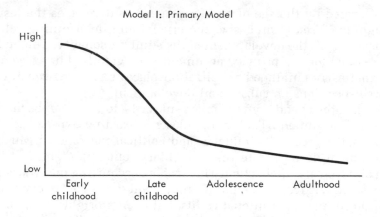

Model I: Primary Model

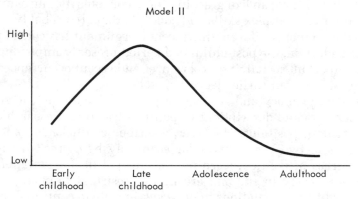

Model II

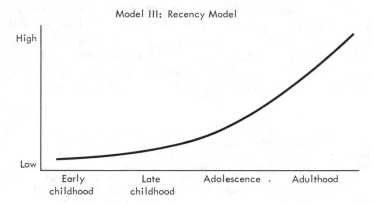

Model III: Recency Model

FIGURE 1
Relevance of political learning for adult political
attitudes and behavior.

Model I depicts the primacy argument; political learning acquired in early childhood, though susceptible to future modification, sets powerful limits on adult attitudes and behaviors. One type of political orientation that seems to fit this model quite well is basic political attachments and identifications. The primary object of loyalty and identity can vary considerably, but regardless of its focus it seems to be acquired very early in life (probably even before age five) and endures with little change. Such loyalty can also include attachments to more specific political institutions, customs, and symbols. In the United States basic political loyalty encompasses such institutions as the president, symbols such as the American flag and Constitution, and celebrated historical figures (e.g., Abraham Lincoln). These attachments probably form the core of an individual's political identity, and although the intellectual justifications for one's political attachments become more sophisticated and complex with age, the basic attachments themselves remain stable. The great difficulties encountered in creating a new sense of political identity among people in the newly developing nations illustrate the tenacity of these early loyalties once they are formed.

The Model I primary pattern also seems to be particularly relevant in the area of general ideological identities and evaluations. Most young children cannot understand the differences among such value systems as democracy, communism, or socialism. Nevertheless, as in the case of basic political attachment, a lack of knowledge does not prevent the formation of relatively enduring evaluations. Many an American knows, for example, that democracy and free enterprise are much better than communism long before these concepts are understood. Needless to say, citizens of the Soviet Union probably feel the same way about communism versus capitalist enslavement.

The Primary model is also descriptive of the acquisition of consensually held factual knowledge. In every political system there exists a body of facts (or more accurately, myths) that young children are exposed to and that everyone accepts without question. For example, how many of us accept the image of the early colonial settlers as staunch supporters of freedom? How many believe that the United States never initiated a war? Though much of the political information acquired during childhood is transformed as children come into contact with civics courses, the mass media, and adult politics, some of these early facts linger on. Frequently, few people question consensually held political beliefs, and those who do may become the objects of scorn and incredulity. The persistence as valid facts of political myths acquired early in life seems particularly appropriate where the evidence is ambiguous or where questioning the validity of a fact might be inter-preted as a sign of political heresy.

We are not arguing that these early orientations remain forever unchanged. Any political identity, loyalty, evaluation, or myth can undergo radical change at any point in a person's lifetime. Rather, we claim that this early learning acts as a filter and sets broad limits on subsequent learning. It is likely (but not predetermined) that with maturation and increasing political sophistication new information and experiences modify, but do not replace, earlier socialization; de-tails, but not the basics, are changed. In some ways the relationship between early and later learning in the areas of basic political loyalty and identity and general evaluations of government and ideologies can be compared to the relationship between genetic and environmental factors in human development—genetic factors provide general limits and direction to growth, while environmental conditions affect growth within these broad limits.

Though many of the broad outlines of an individual's political world may be formed early in life, much remains to be learned. For some political orientations the pattern in Model II is most relevant: changes can occur during adulthood, but the bulk of enduring attitudes and behaviors seems to be acquired between early childhood and adult-hood. This latter description seems appropriate in the area of learning about political participation. Particularly from about the age of ten onward, children can develop many skills relevant to future participa-tion, such as being able to communicate effectively and socially manip-ulate others. In addition, it is after early childhood that opportunities exist for taking part in such adult political activities as discussing partisan issues or political campaigning. It is also during this period that children develop the mental ability to understand many of the concepts and processes associated with political participation. Social-ization in this period does not fix forever one's level of political activity; but as subsequent analysis will show, the fact that most attempts to increase participation among students are relatively unsuccessful un-derlines the importance of late childhood political socialization.

Evidence also suggests that the pattern of Model II is a good de-scription of most citizens' acquisition of general political information. For the very young child the political system is a rather diffuse concept defined by a few salient authority positions, simple rules, and concrete symbols. With intellectual development and greater exposure to politi-cal stimuli, the broad outlines of the political world are filled in and made comprehensible. By eighth grade, authority figures such as the president and senators are no longer vague and distinct figures whose personal qualities are inseparable from their official positions. By early adolescence political leaders can be separated from their official positions and judged apart from the more general political system. The formal, legalistic relationships between authority figures also become much clearer and some notion of the function of abstract laws in regulating these officials also occurs during this age period. By thirteen or fourteen an individual is hardly politically sophisticated about his environment, but the textbook knowledge of politics he carries is much closer to that of an adult than a young child. Important details remain unknown, but essential positions, rules, and obligations are understood.

Model II also is relevant to the learning of general policy preferences, especially partisan preference. As was true in the case of learning about specific authority roles and their interrelationships, it is only after early childhood that certain political phenomena can be intellectually comprehended. A six-year-old cannot understand the concept of civil liberties (though he knows that freedom is a good thing), but by thirteen he has most likely formed an opinion on freedom of the press and toleration of dissent. Considerable evidence also indicates that identification with a political party also must wait until after early childhood. At a very broad level, opinions formed on such topics as foreign involvement, civil rights, and the government's economic role may have their roots in this period. We are not suggesting that specific adult issue positions are all formed before the age of twenty-one, for this is clearly not true. Rather, as was the case with basic political attachments and loyalties, in certain broad issue areas individuals tend to operate within bounds set by earlier political socialization. For example, an individual socialized as a strong supporter of Negro civil rights may experience doubts as an adult, but it is unlikely (though far from impossible) that he will exchange positions with someone socialized to the opposite set of beliefs.

When we move away from more general political attitudes and behaviors into specific issues and actions characteristic of day-to-day political conflict, we find the strongest support for the Model III pattern of political socialization. Positions on specific current issues, perceptions of candidates for office, strategies of political influence in specific circumstances, and similar attitudes and behavior are all choices greatly influenced by events and experiences occurring during adulthood. In some cases, socialization during adulthood could not be otherwise: we could hardly expect, for example, a middle-aged voter to have formed an attitude about a current candidate thirty years before the candidate ran for office. In other instances this adult socialization is the consequence of greater adult involvement in political life. With maturation frequently comes the awareness of how political decisions affect one's life and this leads to a greater exposure to the day-to-day politics and hence greater detailed learning. Along with this greater awareness comes a greater sophistication and hence ability to learn more politically. Events and experiences that preadults cannot grasp or interpret, e.g., the passage of a specific bill by Congress, may be important socialization experiences for adults. In short, as we move away from broad political issues, loyalties, and orientations to the specific policies and activities generating conflict in the adult political world, we find that post-childhood socialization becomes more and more relevant. This general relationship between when certain political orientations are acquired and their scope is summarized in Fig. 2.

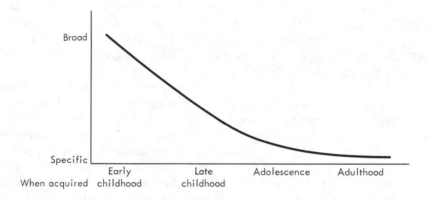

FIGURE 2
Scope of political orientation.

Let us recapitulate our analysis of the persistence of early political socialization into adulthood. The whole question of the relationship between early learning and subsequent development is a complex issue for which no universally accepted answer exists. Nevertheless, among scholars examining this problem many agree that early learning involving broad attachments, loyalties, and identifications is particularly enduring though not immune to change. This early political socialization acts as a filter for considerable subsequent learning: many adult choices between conflicting issue positions or activities are made in a previously determined context. This suggests that if we wish to examine the tenacity of broad political orientations removed from day-to-day political conflict, the preadult years (particularly early childhood) are more relevant for analysis. On the other hand, the closer we move to the detailed, more complex issues characteristic of adult politics, the greater the relevance of post-childhood socialization. Thus, if our concern is for the details of on-going politics rather than unquestioned givens, the appropriate focus is more recent political learning.

This completes our brief overview of some of the problems and issues of the political socialization process. Our goal in this chapter has been to raise these issues rather than provide a final answer. The next step in our analysis is to examine what American children learn about politics and how this political socialization may ultimately affect American political life. We shall begin with an examination of basic loyalties and attachments to the existing political system.

3

The Political Community,
Authority Roles,
and Evaluating Government

For most adults political decisions focus largely on electoral conflict and current controversies: which party to support, who to vote for, what position to take on a current issue, and perhaps whether to be politically active. At least in the United States, few people seem to seriously question the broad framework in which this daily political conflict occurs. The existing political community and institutions ostensibly appear to be, with rare exception, noncontroversial givens beyond serious reconsideration. We may vigorously debate the qualification of a presidential candidate, but we rarely (if ever) ask whether the institution of the presidency itself (as opposed, say, to a prime minister) is worth preserving. Tempers flare over the proper global role of the United States, but there is little movement toward disbanding the American nation in favor of a broader world-wide political community. As suggested in Chapter 1, such nondecisions, though scarcely debated, nevertheless represent choices among alternatives that are of crucial political significance. Important as the day-to-day political issues may be, they are relatively trivial compared to these longstanding choices that provide the framework for such daily decisions.

Are these crucial nondecisions permanent and unchangeable? Is the institution of the presidency so deeply ingrained that it is beyond reevaluation and modification at least for the present and immediate future? More generally, are the broad communal and institutional givens of the existing political system open to reevaluation and change? We cannot answer this question merely by examining what exists politically. Because customs and institutions are presently unchallenged does not mean that they will remain so. Political systems undergo violent revolutions and whole constitutional orders can suddenly change. We cannot unquestionably extrapolate from the present to the future. If what existed were inherently enduring, we would obviously never have moved beyond the Stone Age.

Determining the durability of these givens requires an analysis of how citizens view these longstanding decisions and institutions. We assume that where citizens accept certain alternatives as wise, legitimate, and beyond change, they will be less likely to change than if these choices are viewed as undesirable, inappropriate, and disastrous. Citizen feelings about political institutions are not the only factor affecting their persistence. Many a widely accepted and treasured institution has been replaced against popular desire. Military defeat, economic disaster, and coup d'etat, among many other factors, can destroy popularly supported national communities and institutions. The widespread popular acceptance of certain political features as beyond question is a necessary, but not sufficient condition, for their continued persistence. Nevertheless, without such acceptance of certain things as beyond debate, a political system's givens quickly become just another set of policies and thus open to debate and possible change.

The American political system is exceptionally complex. We obviously cannot examine whether citizens accept each and every feature of it as legitimate and worth preserving. Our analysis must be selective and emphasize what is most fundamental. Following David Easton's characterization of political systems, our analysis will be divided into two broad sections: orientation toward *political community* known as the United States of America, and orientation toward those *political institutions* that govern this community.[1] In each section our basic question is the same: does the early political socialization of citizens encourage the acceptance of existing political phenomena as legitimate

[1]David Easton, *A Systems Analysis of Political Life* (New York: John Wiley & Sons, Inc., 1965), Chapters 11 and 12. What we refer to as "political institutions" is labelled "regime" by Easton.

and beyond serious reconsideration? Do decisions made well before voting age effectively foreclose even the possibility of seriously evaluating political alternatives? Or, on the other hand, is it possible that numerous features of the present system are viewed merely as one among many reasonable choices?

SENSE OF POLITICAL COMMUNITY: LEARNING TO BE AN AMERICAN

According to Easton, a political community is a collection of individuals sharing a division of political labor.[2] Political communities may range in size from a dozen to a billion, but their essential characteristic is an acceptance among members of the community that they are to be governed together. We can say, for example, that people belong to the German political community when they view political decisions made for Germany as applying to themselves. These people have in common a sense of political identity that is typically reflected in a "we" versus "they" relationship to the rest of the world. It is important to realize that this sense of political community is not necessarily dependent on geographical proximity. People living near one another need not be members of the same political community. Similarly, individuals separated by thousands of miles may consider themselves as political compatriots. There are many areas today such as the Middle East and parts of Africa where people in close proximity to one another disagree violently about what political community should exist.

It can be argued that it is virtually impossible for people not to develop some sense of collective identity and political community. We should realize, however, that while this drive to form a political "we" may be almost biologically inherent, there is certainly no predetermined way this drive expresses itself.[3] A political community may be formed on the basis of an almost infinite number of shared characteristics. Similarities of language, religion, race, ethnicity, and experiences can all provide the basis for political community. The criteria that will bind people together are frequently matters of violent controversy. Consider, for example, the history of East Pakistan. In 1947 the criterion of religion dominated and the Moslem Bengalis sought political unity

[2]Easton, *A Systems Analysis of Political Life*, p. 177.

[3]Some of the historical manifestations of basic political loyalty are considered by Morton Grodzins in *The Loyal and the Disloyal* (New York: World Publishing Company, 1966), pp. 8–11.

with their fellow Moslems in West Pakistan despite a thousand-mile physical separation and major differences in language, tradition, and ethnicity. A generation later, however, a common religion became meaningless as a characteristic binding East and West Pakistan together. With the aid of Hindi India—once the archenemy of Moslems —East Pakistan severed the communal tie with West Pakistan and formed the new political community of Bangladesh based on a common ethnicity rather than common religion.

The contemporary world abounds with loyalties and identities that could form the basis of a political community. Marxists have traditionally viewed common relationship to the ownership of the means of production as the natural basis of political community. That is, a worker in Pittsburgh has more in common politically with a worker in Leningrad than with a Pittsburgh boss and hence they should be governed together. Another alternative has been offered by "nativists" who demand the exclusion of all nonwhite, Anglo-Saxon, Protestants from our shores much in the same way that the Nazis envisioned a German nation based on "pure" Aryan descent. The racial criterion for organizing the political community has similarly been advocated by Black Muslims who demand their own territory and separate state. Quite obviously, exactly what is the natural political community is an open question.

Given all the possible alternatives for membership in a political community, the evidence overwhelmingly suggests that citizens living within the physical boundaries of the United States accept America as the primary political community.[4] Though each citizen undoubtedly identifies with other communities, e.g., religious groups, life style groups, social class, or age groups, none of these seem to prevail significantly over the nation-state as the fundamental *political* unit of membership. Contrary to what exists in other parts of the world, primary identification with a geographically defined nation-state is not secondary to the family, village, or tribal identity. Someone may be a Southerner, a Baptist, white, middle class, and from Georgia, but none of these loyalties compare in strength to being an American.

The tenacity of this choice among alternatives becomes evident when we examine the emergence of feelings of nationalism. Studies of the development of Americanism among young children indicate that this sense of political community is perhaps one of the earliest learned political orientations. Even among preschool children possessing only

[4]Donald J. Devine, *The Political Culture of the United States* (Boston: Little, Brown and Company, 1972), pp. 91–95 offers a variety of data on this point.

the most limited political understanding, membership in the American community is acquired almost as if it were an integral part of becoming a social being. Few children are unaware that they are Americans long before contact with school programs about our country; and from the youngest to the oldest child there is little disagreement that "America is the best country in the world."[5] Studies among adults confirm the endurance of this particular allegiance—there are probably few citizens who despite dissatisfactions with particular officials and policies can reject their allegiance with their fellow citizens.[6] When we consider the diversity of social groups comprising the American people that could be the basis of alternative political communities, the pervasiveness of this acceptance of a single geographically defined political community is remarkable.

This early attachment to the existing political community is apparent when children are asked to select the most attractive national flags. Strictly speaking, there is no objective method to determine beauty among national flags. Aesthetic judgments reflect value judgments, so these choices provide an insight into what children hold in esteem. As we might expect, numerous studies confirm the great preference for the American flag as most attractive. Lawson found, for example, that among kindergarten to twelfth grade students about 70 percent in each grade ranked the American flag in the top five (of twenty choices) in terms of beauty. Significantly, the Liberian flag, which is very similar to the U. S. flag, suffers a sharp decline in attractiveness among older respondents. Further evidence of the political nature of these aesthetic choices is provided by the very low ratings given to flag of the Soviet Union. Even among Kindergarten students, only one in ten rates the Soviet flag among the top in terms of its physical attractiveness.[7]

The attachment to one's nation is not a universal phenomenon among children in all countries. Particularly in the developing nations where national identity may be a recent occurrence or may coexist with more provincial political allegiance, the national political community has only limited appeal. This possibility is well demonstrated by Reid Reading's study of school children in Colombia, South America. Table 3.1 compares Colombian and American children's responses as to whether their country is the best in the world.

[5]Robert D. Hess and Judith V. Torney, *The Development of Political Attitudes in Children* (Garden City, N.Y.: Doubleday Anchor Books, 1968), pp. 30–32.
[6]See, for example, Robert E. Lane, *Political Ideology* (New York: The Free Press, 1962), especially pp. 166–67.
[7]Edwin D. Lawson, "The Development of Patriotism in Children: A Second Look," *Journal of Psychology* 55 (1963), 279–86. Also see E. L. Horowitz, "Some Aspects of the Development of Patriotism in Children," *Sociometry* 3 (1941), 329–41.

TABLE 3.1 Perceptions of Nation among Colombian and American Children, by Grade

	"Colombia is the best country in the world."						"America is the best country in the world."				
School grade	Very true	True	Don't know	False	Very false	School grade	Very true	True	Don't know	False	Very false
3	62%	14%	18%	4%	1%	2	70%	14%	9%	4%	2%
4	44	25	31	0	0	3	62	22	9	5	22
5	34	26	32	6	2	4	60	23	8	6	2
I	19	30	33	16	2	5	66	20	7	5	2
II	17	24	26	27	6	6	65	21	7	5	1
III	18	11	28	37	6	7	68	21	7	4	1
IV	12	16	28	35	9	8	70	21	5	3	1

Source: Reid Reading, "Political Socialization in Colombia and the U.S.," Midwest Journal of Political Science 7 (1968), 361. (The U.S. data were collected by Hess and Torney.)

Colombian and American children are alike in the earliest grades, but this similarity quickly passes. Even before they reach adolescence a majority of Colombian students do not perceive their country as the best in the world while only a very small proportion of Americans express this view. It is particularly interesting to note that the proportion of American responses in the "very true" and "don't know" categories remains fairly constant with age. Apparently, exposure to the virtues of other nationalities and possible defects of their own countrymen has little effect on the certainty of these convictions.[8]

While the roots of this membership in a political community reach back to children's earliest years, and usually remain undisturbed for a lifetime, the justifications for the choice change with age. A four-year-old and an adult have both made the same decision, but each offers a different reason why this choice is the best one. Very young children have a difficult time providing logical and concrete rationales for their membership though there is no vacillation in their convictions. Symbols such as the flag and the Statue of Liberty help focus their attachment to America, but the most frequent explanations are on the order of "I am one" or "It is my country." There is no awareness of the implications of this one particular alternative vis-a-vis other possibilities or understanding of future costs and benefits. Consider one second-grader's response when he was asked why it was better to be an American than an Englishman:

> Well, I wouldn't like to be an Englishman because I wouldn't like to talk their way, and I'd rather be an American because they have better toys, because they have better things, better stores, and better beds and blankets, and they have better play guns, and better boots and mittens and coats, and better schools and teachers.[9]

Among older children this justification becomes more sophisticated, but the conviction does not wane. It is particularly significant that one's attachment to the national political community becomes wedded to support to the political apparatus that governs the community. Although many Americans have difficulty distinguishing between America and "the government," this separation can easily be made as witnessed by the capacity of many patriotic Frenchmen to reject the existing government as illegitimate. This ability to separate

---

[8]We are not, however, suggesting that American children exhibit unqualified ethnocentrism. When American children are compared with children of ten other nations (or ethnic groups), they score the lowest on ethnocentrism. See Wallace E. Lambert and Otto Klineberg, *Children's Views of Foreign People* (New York: Appleton-Century-Crofts, 1967), p. 190.

[9]Quoted in Hess and Torney, *The Development of Political Attitudes in Children*, p. 32.

the government from attachment to the political community is dramatically illustrated by Almond and Verba's data on national pride. When asked what they were most proud of, 85 percent of the Americans answered their government and political system; this contrasts with 46 percent of the Englishmen, 7 percent of the Germans, 3 percent of the Italians, and 30 percent of the Mexicans.[10]

Group Differences in Accepting the Existing Political Community

An important question that must be raised here is whether some social groups, even a small minority, do not accept America as the primary political community. Perhaps certain United States citizens do not see the American political community as relevant to their political needs and aspirations. Such citizens might peacefully accept their status but nevertheless hope for their own separate community; or, perhaps like the French Canadian separatists in Quebec, their self-conception as a distinctive linguistic and cultural community leads to demands for political partition. As many bloody civil wars and communal riots demonstrate, such lack of a collective sense of political identity can have profound consequences even where the majority accepts the existing political community as an untamperable given.

What citizen might reject the existing American political community? In some countries (e.g., Northern Ireland), strongly felt religious differences exacerbate division over the basic political community. Particularly where religious groups with very different life styles are a minority, a tendency exists for them to de-emphasize the importance of the larger political community. Prior to World War II eastern European Jews were much more conscious of themselves as a community of Jews governed by religious laws than as citizens of Poland or Romania. Another group that could reject the existing community is that benefiting the least in society. It is plausible to expect members of the lower class and Negroes to hold the weakest attachments to America. After all, why should one strongly support something in which one always gets fewer of the available benefits?

On the whole, it does not appear that significant groups of citizens reject America as the basic political unit. Certain religious sects and

---

[10]Almond and Verba, *The Civic Culture*, p. 102. This identity of the political community (i.e., Americans) and the political structure is also evidenced by the very infrequent choice of nonpolitical attributes such as the characteristics of the people, contribution to the arts, or the physical beauty of the nation. Jennings' 1965 data on high school seniors depict a very similar pattern: when asked what they like best about the United States, about 75 percent mention aspects of the political system. M. Kent Jennings, *The Student-Parent Socialization Study* ICPR codebook (1971), variable 117.

political extremists may consider themselves outsiders, but these are limited in number and appear more interested in being left alone than in violently establishing an independent community. The United States contains a multitude of ethnic and religious groups, but it is a very rare, German-American or Roman Catholic who considers his German or Catholic identity as coming before his American political identity. Nineteenth-century fears that Catholics would owe their first loyalty to the Pope, or that Chinese would always remain loyal to China, have proven groundless. Evidence also suggests that working-class children are no less American than those reaping greater economic benefits.[11]   The Marxist slogan "Working men of the world unite, you have nothing to lose but your chains" has made no headway in the United States. Many lower-class adults are among the staunchest opponents of any ideology stressing the common international brotherhood of workers against the capitalist bosses.[12]

What about blacks? Do young black children learn that the American political community is strictly for the white man? Is there widespread support for a separate black political community responsive only to black people? The evidence here is limited, but the data do not indicate a widespread racially related rejection of the American political community. In his study of white and black Philadelphia children, Edward Greenberg found that while older children were less idealistic about the virtues of America than younger children, racial differences were relatively small. Greenberg found that there was 11 percent difference between black and white seventh- and ninth-graders in their appreciation of the American flag; 76 percent of the blacks compared to 87 percent of the whites selected the American flag as the best flag in the world. Similarly, the proportion of black seventh- and ninth-graders agreeing with the statement "Sometimes I'm not very proud to be an American" was only 6 percent higher than among whites.[13] These data generally show some racial differences in support for the existing American political community, but we certainly do not have a picture of blacks rejecting this community as not their own. Differences are a matter of degree, not of racial polarization.

[11]Hess and Torney, The Development of Political Attitudes in Children, p. 150.

[12]Lane, Political Ideology, especially Chapter 4.

[13]Edward S. Greenberg, "Political Socialization to Support of the System," (unpublished dissertation, University of Wisconsin, 1969), p. 108. A different image is conveyed by Billings' study of black high school students. Billings presented political activists and nonactivists with Eldridge Cleaver's statement—"We live today in a system that is in the last stages of breaking up on a worldwide basis" and reports that 65 percent of the activists and 55 percent of the nonactivists agreed with it. This suggests that while most blacks accept the existing political community, they also expect changes in it. Charles E. Billings, "Black Student Activism and Political Socialization," paper presented at the 1971 American Political Science Association annual meeting.

Mexican-Americans are another distinct group that could be expected to exhibit reservations about the existing political community. Not only does this group share some of the disadvantages experienced by blacks, but the existence of Mexico as an alternative community might certainly undermine their American allegiance. Nevertheless, data collected by Gutierrez and Hirsch on seventh- through twelfth-grade students in a small South Texas city suggests that while some alienation occurs, this is not the majority sentiment.[14] Only between a fifth and a quarter of students in grades seven through twelve believe that "If you are poor or not white, you can never achieve freedom in America." These Chicano adolescents also exhibit considerable chauvinism and a willingness to blame individuals for problems rather than the system. As in the case of the black data, support appears to be more qualified than among whites, but these qualifications are a very long way from rejection.

Two important points emerge when we consider this early socialization to be an American. First, this decision to be a member of a geographically defined collectivity is made without any consideration of the alternatives. This choice may be desirable for the persistence of the nation-state, but this does not mean that it is also beneficial to every individual. One may reasonably argue that cross-national social class political loyalty has more to offer the working man than Americanism. The possibility that a political community of all the world's poor people may be more peaceful and humanitarian than one of separate nation-states cannot be dismissed out of hand as ridiculous. Nevertheless, these and other alternatives are beyond the pale of serious consideration. It is not that they are discussed and rejected; rather, the issue never even arises. Children and adults alike know that only fools would not want to be Americans, and those who might give their primary political loyalty elsewhere (e.g., social class, religious, family, or ethnic group) are treated contemptuously.

A second feature of the acceptance of America as the basic political collectivity is the noncontingent nature of this decision. A major theme underlying the Declaration of Independence and the rhetoric of the American Revolution is the contractual tie between the individual and the political community. That is, the individual joins the community because it benefits him and when the costs exceed the benefits, the contract is voided. The decision of the colonists to secede from England in 1776 was essentially justified in terms of nonfulfillment of a contract.

[14]Armando G. Gutierrez and Herbert Hirsch, "Political Maturation and Political Awareness: The Case of the Crystal City Chicano," unpublished paper.

When we examine the content of political learning it is clear that few, if any, children learn that their continued membership in the ongoing community is contingent on their getting something (e.g., freedom, protection of property, a good life) in return. Loyalty is, in effect, given with no strings attached. We are not saying that individuals will never withdraw from the American community. Rather, the individual does not begin his involvement with an expectation that if some agreed-upon condition is not met, he is free to resign his membership. American children do not learn, for example, that the right to particiapte politically is a contractual part of being an American and that if one is denied this right one can then go elsewhere. The right of political participation and loyalty to the American community are both learned, but each is learned independently of the other. Whatever agreement exists between the individual and his fellow citizens is made without any understanding of consequences, without any expectation, and is usually executed before the age of five.

SUPPORT FOR POLITICAL INSTITUTIONS

Orientations toward the Government

As important as membership in a political community may be, many equally important decisions remain to be made. Even after the basic political community has been established and accepted, particular institutional patterns must be adopted. Without some formal structure providing for leadership roles and channels for settling conflict, political life would be chaotic: policy questions would be decided on an *ad hoc* basis by whoever momentarily could command attention or physical force. Even in the smallest political systems, political life must be routinized and organized to some extent. Just what kind of routinization Americans grow up believing is the appropriate way of conducting the business of politics will be our focus in this section.

Analysis begins with what children learn about the government. This concept, according to Easton and Dennis, plays a crucial role in the learning process. The government is a relatively simple concept and can thus be grasped by even the youngest children. As such it provides an early link between the citizen and the political system. More important, however, the government being a broad concept provides a framework in which subsequent learning takes place. This framework not only allows the child to integrate diverse political authority roles and institutions into some coherent whole (as part of the government), but also provides a way of comprehending new political figures as they appear.[15]   For example, authority figures like Cabinet officials and Supreme Court justices are readily comprehensible to someone who already knows about the government. An early positive (or negative) evaluation of the government can thus influence evaluation of a wide range of political objects once these new objects are associated as part of the government.

We should realize that no necessary logical relationship exists between loyalty toward the political community (i.e., America) and support for political roles and institutions. It is entirely possible for someone to be highly supportive of one but not the other. Such a condition at one time existed in France where many citizens considered the government as beneath contempt and tolerated drastic changes in political regimes while remaining good, loyal Frenchmen. The opposite pattern is also conceivable—political authorities are held in great esteem despite very little sense of political community. In many newly independent nations charismatic leaders can sometimes hold together a highly heterogeneous people with little or no collective identity. We cannot automatically presume that the high regard for America previously described leads to similar evaluations of the government and other political objects.

What do young Americans think about their government? As we found in the development of sense of community, awareness begins early: even very young children know that something called the government exists. Easton and Dennis report that about three quarters of the second-graders claimed to understand what government meant. With age the child's image and knowledge of government naturally change. When asked to select figures that best represented the government, the younger children selected George Washington or a picture of the current president. By eighth grade the government's meaning changes, and Congress and voting become more symbolic of government. Within six years it is transformed from a highly personalized institution to a more institutionalized concept with a large component of citizen participation through voting.[16]

It is significant that despite this great transformation in the government's image there is little variation in perceptions of the government's importance. From the very beginning, Americans see the exercise of political power as important—the government affects people's lives and provides essential services. Such a belief appears natural to Americans, but in many nations people are only dimly aware of the central government's existence, and it is certainly not considered per-

[15]Easton and Dennis, *Children in the Political System,* pp. 111–12.
[16]Easton and Dennis, *Children in the Political System*, pp. 113–16.

sonally relevant. Until very recently most of the world's people knew the government as an occasional tax official or army recruiter far less significant than family or religious authorities. Long before they have any direct contact with their government, Americans clearly know that their government is not an irrelevant and inconsequential phenomenon that society could perhaps do without.[17]

Americans begin their political lives not only believing that government is essential, but also knowing that the existing government is exceptionally knowledgeable, helpful, and rarely in error. In grades four through eight the number of children who claim that the government does not know much, frequently makes mistakes, and is unconcerned for their welfare is miniscule. It is significant that this perception of virtually infallible benevolence undergoes only moderate change with increasing age and political sophistication. Other children acknowledge the existence of some defects, but this disenchantment is only a matter of degree. For example, Easton and Dennis report that while only 13 percent of their eighth grade respondents believe that the government "never" makes mistakes, just 2 percent think the government is in error "often" or "usually."[18] Other data suggest that adolescents and adults give a more qualified vote of confidence to the government, but it is unlikely that these earlier, and highly positive orientations completely erode. It would probably take a protracted crisis and years of bumbling, incompetent governmental behavior to overcome the many years spent believing in the government's virtue and wisdom.[19]

As in our previous analysis of support for the political community, the social uniformity of this early socialization pattern must be examined. Recent events suggest that one group that might hold very different beliefs about the government are black Americans. It would not be surprising if we found that young blacks perceived government to be more fallible and less generous than their white counterparts. Again relying on the Philadelphia data collected by Edward Greenberg, we find that black-white differences in this area of socialization are either moderate or nonexistent. When asked whether the government "cares about us," "makes things better for most people," "is helpful," and "knows a lot," positive responses generally declined with age, but race

[17]Easton and Dennis, *Children in the Political System,* p. 132.

[18]Easton and Dennis, *Children in the Political System,* p. 133.

[19]More recent evidence on adolescent perceptions suggests that perhaps the Vietnam War and its domestic consequences have undermined this previous high regard. For example, Weissberg in his 1969 study of University of Wisconsin freshmen reports that evaluations of the federal government are only lukewarm and the state government is perceived negatively. Robert Weissberg, "Adolescents' Perceptions of Political Authorities: Another Look at Political Virtue and Power," *Midwest Journal of Political Science* 16 (1972), 147–68.

related differences among the oldest respondents were less than five percentage points. One exception to this pattern was the question of trust in government, but even here among the ninth-graders 11 percent fewer blacks than whites expressed "high trust."[20]

When viewing the acquisition of these beliefs about government we must realize that, as in so many other areas of political learning, there is little, if any, reality testing. It is possible, of course, that the government *is* virtually infallible, highly knowledgeable, and greatly concerned for each and every citizen, but a ten-year-old is hardly in a position to judge the factual validity of these arguments. Yet he nevertheless accepts them as true. When an individual becomes sufficiently sophisticated to judge these arguments for himself, previous socialization undoubtedly discourages impartiality. More likely, most people would either continue to not question these facts or, if the issue were considered, an answer would probably be heavily biased toward confirming what one already knew. In short, American children accept one version of how the government functions, and while this acceptance is qualified with age, this choice of belief tends to be a longstanding decision.

Another important area of political learning concerns the scope of the government's power, i.e., whether we should have a big or a little government. The Founding Fathers clearly preferred limited government for they believed that the basic purpose of any government was to do only those things people themselves could not do. Big government, particularly powerful national government, was thought to be inherently evil and tyrannical. This aversion to extensive government intervention in people's lives has supposedly been a longstanding and integral part of the American character. In recent years conservative spokesmen such as Barry Goldwater have reiterated the importance of individual initiative as opposed to government paternalism as being the basis of national greatness. Is an aversion to big, paternalistic government still a basic, integral part of our national character?

An analysis of early political socialization clearly indicates that whatever the previous support for rugged individualism, this mentality is not converged in the political socialization process. Americans do not begin life supporting limited government and then succumb to the lures of collectivist big government. As the data in Table 3.2 indicate, Americans learn to be advocates of big government early in life.

[20]Greenberg, "Political Socialization to Support of the System," pp. 294–309. However, data for adults indicate that racial differences in trust in government have grown more significant. Whether this adult pattern will prevail over the earlier childhood pattern is an open question. Adult comparisons are presented in Joel D. Aberbach and Jack L. Walker, "Political Trust and Racial Ideology," *American Political Science Review* 64 (1970), 1203–4.

TABLE 3.2 Attitudes Toward Role of Government

GRADE	The government is getting too big for America % agree	N	The government meddles too much in private lives % agree	N	The government has too much power % agree	N	The government usually knows what is best for the people % agree	N	The government ought to give money and food to people out of work % agree	N	The government should have more power over the people % agree	N
3	16	113	28	108	36	116	80	69	70	69	22	69
4	14	125	21	118	19	122	77	119	84	119	33	129
5	10	118	17	116	22	118	87	117	80	117	24	117
6	7	146	19	145	10	146	84	145	78	143	13	145
7	13	143	19	139	12	139	91	139	71	139	20	138
8	11	149	14	148	15	147	84	147	77	145	19	145

Source: From Children in the Political System, by David Easton and Jack Dennis. Copyright (1969 McGraw-Hill Book Company), p. 130. Used with permission of McGraw-Hill Book Company.

These data suggest that whatever sense of political individualism Americans may have is acquired in adolescence or adulthood, if at all.[21] The lack of fear that big government will necessarily undermine individual liberty would probably appal James Madison and Thomas Jefferson, let alone modern libertarian conservatives like Goldwater. At the same time, however, this collectivist spirit does not extend to making government bigger and bigger. As the answer to the question of whether the government should have more power over the people indicates, at every age only a small minority favor more government. In a sense these children are conservative collectivists—they accept big government but simultaneously reject further changes in it.

Orientations Toward Political Leaders

The American people may have unqualified admiration for America and the government, but when we focus on orientations toward political leaders, we find considerable ambivalence. Numerous studies and everyday impressions suggest that many Americans can't decide whether our leaders are a bunch of politicians out for themselves or hardworking statesmen deserving our greatest respect.[22] A majority of Americans doubt whether political leaders can ever remain honest —yet these same people simultaneously grant great prestige to such political roles as mayor, senator, and Supreme Court justice. Nor is it unknown for people to one day chide the president as our leader whom everyone should stand behind whether one agrees or disagrees with his policies.

Does this hostility to politicians and dirty politics begin at an early age? This is an important question for, if American children do acquire such a tainted image, we would suggest that existing political authority is less secure than its historical longevity indicates. Demagogic appeals to get rid of the corrupt politician, straighten out the system, or run the country dictatorially above politics would thus not fall entirely on deaf ears. Particularly in periods of national crisis and disorganization, such deep-seated hostility might very well rise to the surface and even support a radical or reactionary mass movement to "clean up the mess in Washington" or destroy the system. A lack of

[21]Considerable evidence suggests that even a drift toward rugged individualism during adolescence or adulthood is rare. Though most Americans abstractly reject socialism, they are more than willing to accept government intervention on their behalf. Among others, see Lane, *Political Ideology*, Chapter 12, and H. Lloyd Free and Hadley Cantril, *The Political Beliefs of Americans* (New York: Simon & Schuster, 1968).

[22]See, for example, William C. Mitchell, "The Ambivalent Status of the American Politician," *Western Political Quarterly* 12 (1959), 683–98.

such deepseated hostility to existing authority structures, however, would provide a reservoir of toleration for existing authority arrangements particularly during periods of critical reexamination of national goals and priorities. Adults might complain about crooked politics, but such mumblings would be of a superficial and perhaps therapeutic nature rather than genuine hostility that could be politically mobilized. Let us begin our analysis with orientations toward the president; subsequent analysis will focus on evaluation of leaders occupying less exalted positions.

The president has been the major focus of research on children's images of political authority, with good reason. For one, despite the intentions of the Constitution's separation of powers, the president has clearly become the leading political figure in American government. His political importance thus makes popular regard for him of much greater significance than, say, orientation toward a mayor or congressman. Besides his role as chief executive, the president also occupies a highly symbolic position. Like the king in a monarchy, the American president stands for much more than a single leader.[23] In many respects he personally embodies the whole spirit of government so that a dynamic, vigorous president can easily create the image of a dynamic, vigorous government. How people relate to him may easily spill over, or generalize, to other positions of authority even though the other positions are in fact independent of the presidency.

When American children first become aware of the presidency, it is viewed in highly personalized terms. The president is a very important *person* who leads the country and provides useful services. In a sense he is much like one's father except on a grand scale. Particularly among younger children, there is little appreciation of the institutionalized nature of the presidency. The constraints on the president's power and scope of authority are beyond the grasp of most children.[24] In many ways the president appears as an almost godlike person with vast duties and omnipresent powers. The following excerpts from interviews with New Haven children illustrate the child's perception of the president's capabilities and responsibilities:

[The president] deals with foreign countries and takes care of the U.S. (eighth-grade boy)

[The president] gives us freedom. (eighth-grade girl)

[23]This phenomenon has been commented upon by numerous observers of American politics. Among others, see Fred I. Greenstein, "The psychological Function of the American President for Citizens," in *The American Presidency: Vital Center,* ed. Elmer E. Cornwell Jr. (Chicago: Scott, Foresman and Company, 1966).

[24]Easton and Dennis, *Children in the Political System,* pp. 200–201.

[The president] makes peace with every country but bad. (fifth-grade boy)
[The president] worries about all the problems of all the 48 states. Takes care of threatening wars by holding peace conferences. (seventh-grade boy)[25]

In having such duties as taking care of the United States and giving us freedom, the president is also endowed with considerable power. Especially to younger children, the president is perceived as being able to punish almost everyone. Like an absolute monarch, his desire becomes an obeyed command. With increasing age, however, the power to punish becomes more restricted as children realize there are some people beyond presidential power. Easton and Dennis find, for example, that by eighth grade only 37 percent of their national sample believe that the president can punish anyone or almost anyone. Nevertheless, it is only a relatively small minority at this age who view the president as having little power. The president's perceived power, though diminished, remains considerable.[26]

Significantly, this power is not seen as leading to corruption or tyranny. Lord Acton may have been correct when he said that power corrupts, and absolute power corrupts absolutely, but in the minds of young Americans, power and evil are not connected. It is inconceivable to a child that the president of the United States would use his power to do anything but take care of the country or make peace with the good countries. As is the case in evaluations of the government, Americans today are not socialized to accept the Founding Fathers' belief that good government is limited government. In a word, the president is a benevolent leader, not someone to be feared or to be avoided.[27]

Together with this benevolence there exists a high respect for the president's capabilities. There is no logical reason why goodness and competence should be associated. Historically, it is not uncommon to find leaders with hearts of gold, but without the capabilities to match. Indeed, some evidence would suggest that the American presidency has not always attracted the brightest and most knowledgeable people. Nevertheless, few children seriously question presidential compe-

[25]Quoted in Fred I. Greenstein, "The Benevolent Leader: Children's Images of Political Authority," *American Political Science Review* 54 (1960), pp. 939.

[26]Easton and Dennis, *Children in the Political System*, p. 181.

[27]An alternative explanation of this highly positive image is that questions typically asked of young children contain many more positive than negative alternatives. Hence, ignorant children who gamble on their answer inflate the positive image. This is well demonstrated by Kolson and Green's study showing that most children say they like "Thomas Walker," a nonexistent person. See Kenneth L. Kolson and Justin J. Green, "Response Set Bias and Political Socialization Research," *Social Science Quarterly* 51 (1970), 527–38.

tence. When questioned on whether the president makes mistakes and how much he knows, it is a very rare child who can impute any degree of incompetence to the president. Even by eighth grade, when we would expect children to be more realistic in their judgments, only 3 percent say the president makes mistakes "often" (and no one chooses the "usually" or "almost always" category). Likewise, only 1 percent of these children believe that the president knows less than many people.[28] Such data are consistent with the views of many adults who assume that leaders, particularly the president, should be given the benefit of the doubt by virtue of their special competence.[29]

Another widely perceived and politically relevant characteristic of the president is his personal responsiveness. The president may be viewed as a godlike individual, but he is not an aloof, distant divinity. Despite a position of power barely comprehensible to a child, the president is not beyond anyone's reach. Even older children assume that their letters to the chief executive would be taken seriously and if the president's help were needed, it would be forthcoming.[30] The president, in a sense, becomes a democratic god—powerful, benevolent, but also responsive to popular desires. Here again, as in many other political beliefs, there is little (if any) empirical reality testing. Like the efficacy of prayer, one can never be sure about responsiveness for there are always ambiguities and extenuating circumstances. One can easily write letters to the president and still believe that they are taken seriously regardless of the consequences. Indeed, it is quite possible to believe in presidential responsiveness even where the president acts contrary to a public majority—the president obviously had secret information that if it were publicly known would change the minds of citizens.

The picture we have so far drawn of young children's attitudes toward the president depicts a heroic figure using his vast power and ability for good while paying close attention to the wishes of all citizens. As in our previous analysis, the question arises of whether these perceptions are equally shared by all citizens. Do some children learn

[28]Easton and Dennis, *Children in the Political System*, pp. 180–81. However, a recent study by Howard Tolley reports considerable questioning of Nixon's competence and honesty among children aged 7 to 15. Less than a third of the survey children believed that Nixon did the right thing in Vietnam, and only 29 percent believed he always tells the truth about the war. Howard Tolley, Jr., *Children and War* (New York: Teachers College Press, 1973), p. 65.

[29]The public's deference to presidential action, even when the action is clearly contrary to public opinion, is documented in Roberta S. Sigel, "Image of the American Presidency—Part II of an Exploration into Popular Views of the Presidency," *Midwest Journal of Political Science* 10 (1966), 127.

[30]Hess and Torney, *The Development of Political Attitudes in Children*, p. 48.

that the president is not their great friend and protector? Theoretically, there are a number of groups in which we might expect evaluations of public leaders to be somewhat less positive. Our analysis, however, for theoretical reasons and due to the availability of data focuses on three such groups—Appalachian whites, Chicanos in a small South Texas city, and urban black children.

The Appalachian region that extends from New York to Georgia has long been noted for its hostility to political authority, particularly national authority. For decades federal programs designed to help Appalachians have experienced difficulty in eliciting popular cooperation since many Appalachians prize their independence more than government assistance. The Chicano (Mexican-American) communities in the Southwest do not have this tradition of hostile independence, but for a variety of reasons we also could expect them to be less favorable toward political authority. Particularly at the local level, established authority has acted more as an agent of repression than as a benevolent provider. Both these environments thus provide an excellent test of the generality of political socialization toward national leadership positions. To determine whether young Appalachians and Mexican-Americans were different from their counterparts elsewhere in the United States, samples of rural schoolchildren in Knox County, Kentucky, and Crystal City, Texas, were asked the same questions about the president as were Chicago children in a previous study.[31] Table 3.3 presents the responses to these questions.

Clearly, to these rural Appalachian and Mexican-American preadults the president is not quite the hero he is in Chicago. Both these subcultural groups are likely to view the president as less hardworking than other men, less knowledgeable, and not as good a person as other men. Given the fact that the Chicago study was done during the Eisenhower period and the Crystal City, Texas study during the Nixon ad-

[31]Because of differences in when these questions were asked and age variations among the three groups, subcultural differences should be treated cautiously. Specifically, the Chicago children were responding to Eisenhower, who was an exceptionally likeable figure. On the other hand, the Appalachians had Lyndon Johnson as the referent and the Mexican-Americans were responding to Richard M. Nixon. No doubt, differences in the public images of these men help account for part of the overall differences. (One wonders, for example, what the Chicano response would have been if Robert Kennedy had been president instead of Nixon.) Moreover, both the Appalachian and Chicano samples are older than the Chicago sample (with the Chicano group being the oldest), and research indicates that older children, regardless of social characteristics, are less positive toward the president. Also, since older children are better able to distinguish between the role occupant and the institution, and since Nixon is hardly a heroic figure among Chicanos, the likelihood that group differences are partially an artifact of sampling and time of study is further increased. In sum, subcultural differences are probably exaggerated by these data.

ministration might partially account for this difference. On the other hand, these data can indicate that the presidency is not as revered among disadvantaged subcultures as it is among privileged groups. If this latter explanation is correct, we might expect increasing demand for basic institutional patterns as groups like the Chicanos become more politically aware.

TABLE 3.3   Children's Evaluation of the President within Three Sub-Cultures (Grades Five through Eight)

Question	Response	Texas Chicanos	Appalachia	Chicago
1. View of how hard the President works compared with most men	harder	49%	35%	77%
	as hard	27	24	21
	less hard	24	41	3
		100%	100%	101%
	N =	48	128	214
2. View of the honesty of the President compared with most men	more honest	*	23%	57%
	as honest	*	50	42
	less honest	*	27	1
			100%	100%
	N =		133	214
3. View of the President's knowledge compared to most men	knows more	41%	45%	82%
	knows about the same	42	33	16
	knows less	17	22	2
		100%	100%	100%
	N =	62	124	212
4. View of the President as a person	best in the world	11%	6%	11%
	a good person	63	68	82
	not a good person	26	26	8
		100%	100%	101%
	N =	37	139	211

*   Data not reported
Source: Appalachian and Chicago data reported in Dean Jaros, Herbert Hirsch, and Frederic J. Fleron, Jr., "The Malevolent Leader: Political Socialization in an American Sub-Culture," American Political Science Review 62 (1968), p. 568; the Mexican-American data are reported in Herbert Hirsch and Armand Gutierrez, "The Socialization of Political Aggression and Political Affect: A Subcultural Analysis," unpublished paper.

In our previous analysis of race related variations in patriotism and attitudes toward the government, differences tended to be very moderate or insignificant. In attitudes toward the president, however, we find larger and more consistent differences, with black children usually being less impressed. For example, Greenberg reported that among very young Philadelphia school children racial differences in ratings of the president were minimal. With increasing age, however, a significantly larger proportion of blacks saw the president as not knowing as much as other people and not working as hard. The pattern of increasing divergence with age suggests that social differences will be greatest during adulthood. We should not, however, get the impression of extensive black alienation from existing political authority as represented by the president. For one, black-white differences are not extreme (rarely greater than 20 percent) and second, Greenberg also found that a greater proportion of older blacks than older whites say they like the president.[32] Thus, though more blacks than whites generally have reservations about the president, in some orientations blacks may be more supportive of political authority.

Our analysis thus far indicates that most (but certainly not all) young children perceive the president as virtually all-powerful and beyond reproach. It is an unanswered question, however, whether this imagery can survive growing sophistication. It is also important to determine whether political figures such as senators and Supreme Court justices who emerge in the child's political world subsequent to the president also share the image of power and benevolence. Our examination of these questions begins by first considering what happens to the president's image as children mature.

The most prominent feature of children's changing perceptions of the president is the depersonalization of authority. Recall that to very young children the president is a figure with enormous *personal* power and goodness. With age, however, children come to understand the difference between the man who occupies the office (i.e., the president) and the office itself (i.e., the presidency). That is, power and benevolence are not inherent individual attributes, but instead derive from the position one occupies.[33] At least to older children the president is not a divine person whose powers and virtues, like those of the Japanese emperor, remain with him under any circumstances. Even a relatively uncharismatic and unforceful individual partakes of the aura of the presidency once elected. In a word, the presidency becomes an institution rather than a person.

---

[32]Greenberg, "Political Socialization to Support of the System," pp. 315–21. Tolley also reports a significant racial difference in the president's credulity on the Vietnam War. Tolley, *Children and War*, p. 72.

[33]Easton and Dennis, *Children in the Political System*, p. 271.

This separation of the man from the office is a crucial process. As children become more knowledgeable and sophisticated they increasingly become more sensitive to partisan and policy considerations in evaluating occupants of the presidency. Easton and Dennis find that judgments of an incumbent become more and more dependent on partisan affiliation as children approach adulthood—young Democrats are less willing to see a Republican president as virtuous than are young Republicans.[34] The president also increasingly becomes identified with more specific programs (e.g., civil rights) than such broad policies as helping citizens or making peace.[35] To the extent that these more specific policy areas are more controversial, evaluations made on these bases will undoubtedly cause greater disenchantment than previous policy associations. A very young southern white, for example, might have only the vaguest notion that John Kennedy strongly advocated the Negro cause; by age twelve or thirteen, however, the association of Kennedy with civil rights would be much clearer and hence possibly lead to a less favorable presidential image.

However, because the man is now separated from the role, these less positive evaluations do not necessarily affect perceptions of the presidency. As long as this distinction between the man and the institutionalized role is maintained it is possible for an individual to have a relatively low regard for an incumbent while simultaneously strongly favoring the presidency as an institution. The particular role incumbent may be judged imcompetent, but this hostility need not spill over into a questioning of the leadership system that allowed an incompetent to become a national leader.[36] Dissatisfaction is thus easily channeled into replacing the man, not the institution. This is not the case in all political systems. In some nations dissatisfaction wth a particular leader may well become dissatisfaction with the very *system* of the leadership, so that dissatisfaction with a particular prime minister might lead to replacing him with a dictator or a president rather than selecting a new prime minister.

What about other political leaders? Do attitudes toward senators, mayors, judges, and other less prominent officials follow a pattern similar to that of the president? Or, do these relatively more mundane

[34]Easton and Dennis, *Children in the Political System*, p. 195.

[35]Roberta S. Sigel, "Image of a President: Some Insights into the Political Views of School Children," *American Political Science Review* 62 (1968), 216–26.

[36]Recall the data on the low esteem given the president among seventh and eighth grade Mexican-Americans. Though a majority perceived him as not a good person, it seems unlikely that these students want to replace the president with a prime minister. More likely, they would prefer to replace Richard M. Nixon. We would not make this inference if respondents were in second or third grade where the institution and the particular role incumbent are far less distinguishable.

authorities suffer from being mere politicians while the president and the presidency tower above them in statesmanlike glory? To a significant extent, largely due to a lack of specific data, answers to these questions are fragmentary. Nevertheless, though considerable research remains to be done, we can venture some observations.

First, these less-prominent officials are not viewed with the same high regard as the president. To be sure, they are perceived positively, but they are certainly not godlike figures. Moreover, there does not seem to be a uniform, age-related pattern of change across all authorities. In some instances, such as with senators, a relatively small but consistent decline occurs in favorable evaluations with increasing age. For the Supreme Court, however, some types of judgments become slightly more favorable with age while others decline slightly.[37] Evidence also suggests that evaluations of lesser political leaders may occasionally depend on specific local conditions and personalities. In New Haven, Connecticut, for instance, where a highly visible and dynamic mayor *personally* visited every school classroom once a year, the mayor's image almost rivaled that of the president.[38] Considerable variation exists on the salience of state and local political figures and so we would thus expect evaluations of congressmen, city councilmen, and state legislators to show considerable variation.

The general conclusion that we may draw is that most American children do not grow up seriously questioning these lesser political leadership roles though some political figures are seen as not very extraordinary. As we saw in evaluations of the presidency, maturation brings a qualification of support, not a rejection of politicians as crooks. If we assume that earliest impressions are enduring despite subsequent and perhaps contrary socialization, the decline of idealization of a senator may be less important than the many previous years spent believing that the government and our leaders (which subsume particular lesser figures) are powerful and benevolent godlike figures. That is, despite an adult's hostility toward politicians, earlier learning lingers on so he nevertheless unconsciously believes the very same things young children believe—leaders will take care of us, know more than we, and in a jam can be counted upon.[39] This argument finds some support in public reactions to American leaders during national crises (e.g., the Bay of Pigs invasion), when political figures once more become the saving heroes they were during earliest socialization.

[37]Easton and Dennis, *Children in the Political System,* Chapter 12.
[38]Greenstein, "The Benevolent Leader," pp. 939–40.
[39]This is suggested in Greenstein, "The Benevolent Leader," p. 942.

Finally, though the data are limited, there seems to be no evidence that the development of more qualified impressions of less prominent political leaders undermines institutionalized patterns of authority. The pattern appears to be similar to the one found for the presidency: the incumbent is separated from the role so a very low evaluation of the office holder is not incompatible with unquestioningly taking the office itself for granted. This duality no doubt helps people to believe that particular leaders are dishonest while simultaneously having little desire to change the existing system.

EVALUATING THE POLITICAL SYSTEM: AMERICA AND DEMOCRACY

The appropriate relationship between citizens and leaders has long been a subject of debate. Political theorists have written extensively on the proper role of citizens in political decision-making and the relative virtues of democracy, monarchy, and aristocracy were even debated by the Founding Fathers when they set out to design a new political order. Even today the debate over the political power the average citizen should have continues in controversies over community control of local schools, the lowered voting age, and leaders' responsibility to public opinion. At the same time, much of the focus of this debate has shifted from the question of how much power *should* citizens possess to how much power *do* they have. Few people today would deny the common man a significant political role; the issue is whether this role does in fact exist.

We must realize that the extent of citizen political influence is an empirical question. That is, an answer can be reached only by the analysis of facts. One can assert with no evidence whatsoever that government *should* be based on the popular will, but empirical analysis is absolutely essential before one may claim that government *is* based on the popular will. On an issue as controversial and complex as popular political influence scholars are by no means of one mind. Vast differences of opinion exist and range from the firm belief that the average citizen has no influence to exactly the opposite view.[40] Nor is it likely that further research will eventually produce a definitive answer to this question. The whole issue is so clouded with numerous controversies, that someone seeking a true answer will find himself increasingly bewildered and overwhelmed with conflicting conclusions.

[40]A sampling of this seemingly endless debate is found in Nelson W. Polsby, *Community Power and Political Theory* (New Haven, Conn: Yale University Press, 1963).

Despite all the problems in reaching a conclusion about citizen influence in government decision-making, young Americans exhibit little difficulty in forming definite opinions on the subject. Questions viewed as almost unanswerable by experienced scholars are irrelevant to young children—to them the answer is obvious and needs no further inquiry. Just as we all know that the earth is round and the sun rises every morning, so children learn that in the United States the government listens to the people and acts accordingly. Citizen rule is not something that can be observed and confirmed; it is much closer to an article of faith than an hypothesis to be demonstrated. How do Americans come to accept the assertion that the people tell the government what to do? Is there any attempt to question this relationship? What might be some of the political consequences of blindly accepting their article of faith?

To understand how Americans come to know that in the United States the people tell the government how to act, we must examine the emergence of democracy in the minds of young children. Like so many political concepts, democracy emerges during the earliest school grades. When children have only the vaguest notions of what democracy means. It is highly significant that despite this ignorance, it is a highly valued concept. Young children may be baffled when asked to explain its meaning, but one thing they do know is that they wouldn't want to be without democracy. Equally as important, democracy is closely identified with America.[41] For young children democracy is America and America is democracy and that's that. Other countries may have this democracy but for a variety of inarticulatable reasons, other people's democracy is not as good as the American version.

With age democracy becomes a more complex and more political concept. From being almost a synonym for America, it begins to stand for popular influence in government. Between fourth and eighth grade, the proportions stating that "democracy means the people rule," "all grown-ups can vote," and "all have equal chance" rises dramatically to 75 percent or more.[42] The political demands implied by "the people rule" and other similar conceptions are obviously more difficult to meet than those implied in the tautological "democracy is America" and vice

[41]Hess and Torney, *The Development of Political Attitudes in Children,* p. 30. Not only is democracy closely identified with America, but Zeligs' study of sixth-graders suggests that democracy embodies virtually everything that is desirable in life. For example, when asked do they practice democracy in school, children gave answers such as "I am practicing democracy by learning to obey the teacher," "I don't fight with my brother and I run errands for my mother," "I take good and bad luck as they come, and do not give up trying when things are hard," and "I try very hard not to chew gum in the room but sometimes I just can't help it." Rose Zeligs, "The Meaning of Democracy to Sixth-Grade Children," *Journal of Genetic Psychology* 76 (1950), 262–81.

[42]Hess and Torney, *The Development of Political Attitudes in Children,* p. 75.

versa. One might even hypothesize that as conceptions of democracy become more sophisticated and demanding the close association between America and democracy would weaken or at least be reexamined. This does not seem to be the case. Rather, the association of America and democracy now becomes "America is where the people rule, everyone can vote, and all have an equal chance." Given the consensual nature of these beliefs as well as their flattering implications, it is more than likely that they persist unquestioned into adulthood. Once made, the virtual identity between the existing political system and popular rule is difficult to break; all that changes is the way the connection is made. Needless to say, the validity of these assertions remains a controversial empirical question, not something decided by faith.

This learning virtually by definition that in America the people rule is politically significant. Historically, the demand for popular rule has been one of the most explosive and persistent political issues. The present system was founded on that desire and throughout the contemporary world the issue still vigorously survives. Within American politics today, despite a very few shrill cries for "all power to the people," the issue of popular rule is a dead one. This is clearly not due to a lack of desire for popular rule; rather, the issue is already settled —the people *do* rule. Militant demands for real or true democracy are thus viewed as redundant, not wrong or un-American. In this way a potentially explosive question is defused into a nonissue. Moreover, the nonempirical nature of this belief in popular rule suggests that rather serious violations of the public must occur before this nonissue is opened for debate. Such would not be the case if Americans were socialized to believe that public control of government was an open question demanding continual empirical analysis. In this situation, a significant departure from popular rule would immediately be noticed by a citizen who did not take democracy as an article of faith existing by definition. It is difficult to imagine almost anything short of a massive suspension of elections and the dissolution of legislative bodies that could force many Americans to ask whether their political system really is based on the popular will.

CONCLUSIONS

If politics involves a choice of alternatives among different ways of organizing and governing political life, and each individual begins life with the full array of choices before him, we can readily see that by adolescence most Americans have narrowed down the range of political alternatives. Because virtually all of these choices are non-controversial they may appear to be less important than the current issues of the day. Only rarely are there newspaper exposés, protest marches, congressional investigations, and public outcries about the early political education of American children. Almost without notice, political socialization goes on and as it happens one alternative after another becomes politically unreasonable and impossible. Americans are born with no innate political loyalty or institutional preferences, but within a relatively short time, most of them know that the basic features of the existing political life—the primary of America as the political community, the government, the president and other institutionalized authority positions—are beyond serious reconsideration. There is nothing inherent about this process, but as we have seen, the socialization process in the United States does a thorough job.

The political consequences of these choices are enormous. Political conflict thus becomes restricted to a relatively narrow range of issue positions. One does not raise questions about abolishing America as a country, substituting decentralized communes for a national government, and having a hereditary monarch instead of elected officials. It is more reasonable and acceptable to speak of what America's foreign policy ought to be or who should be president. For many people these latter questions are the real political issues while the former possibilities are perhaps more in the realm of fantasy. It should be clear from our illustrations that these broader issues make the day-to-day issues look minor by comparison. To repeat an analogy proposed earlier—the political choices made by adults are like the immediate tactical decisions in a basketball game, while it is during childhood that the decision is made to play basketball.

It should be understood that removing fundamental choices from serious reexamination is neither inherently desirable nor undesirable. It all depends on what is to be maximized. One can reasonably argue that no political system could survive unless certain fundamental decisions, once made, were at least in the short run beyond reconsideration. Unless this were so, political life would be paralyzed by a never-ending debate on every conceivable issue with the likely result that little could be actually accomplished (or the pressing agenda would encourage quick, unscrutinized decisions). One would first decide on whether one wanted a president (or a king or a dictator, or any other kind of ruler) and on the selection system before one even approached the more mundane decisions of who should govern. Obviously, if political continuity and consideration of only a few issues at a time are to be maximized, it is highly desirable that young children learn to accept longstanding decisions as givens that should not be tampered with.

On the other hand, one could also argue that since fundamental political decisions have such a great impact, they are too important to be placed out of bounds through early political socialization. Situations change and an institutional framework that might have been perfectly fine in 1800 may be totally out of date in 1980 so citizens should be able to raise more basic questions than minor points of day-to-day policy. If in addition one also posits that *all* political policies ought to be *consciously* chosen by those who have to live with them, it then becomes almost mandatory that basic political alternatives of political loyalty and institutional structure be kept open for discussion rather than transformed into givens. To be sure, one might have to suffer a certain degree of chaos and uncertainty in choosing this path, but this is a necessary price for allowing people to decide their own political fates.

Regardless of the merits of the respective positions, however, there seems to be no real choice to be made. The fact is that most young Americans, with little or no consideration of the alternatives or analysis of the evidence, make important decisions on their political community, authority roles, and descriptions of this system. Many children undoubtedly make choices that are not in their own self-interest though they probably would not have it any other way. Once made, these decisions are rarely, if ever, reexamined. Whether this early, largely unconscious process is to be applauded or condemned depends on one's values.

4

Political Participation

Political systems vary not only in their institutions and authority structures, but also in their levels and forms of citizen participation. Just as there is virtually an infinite number of alternative choices regarding forms of political community, the nature of government, and the exercise of power, so there is no single, predetermined, or inevitable pattern of citizen participation. In some political systems, like that of ancient Athens, it is customary for all citizens to be deeply involved in every aspect of civic life. At the other extreme are political systems in which all but a few citizens are excluded from power. An absolute monarchy where citizens unquestioningly obey every command illustrates this possibility. Between these extremes of total involvement and complete apathy are literally thousands of gradations of popular involvement.

Political participation not only varies in its quantity, but also in its focus and method. In the Soviet Union, for instance, citizen activism in detailed administrative implementation is emphasized; in other countries the focus of involvement is the formulation of broad, general policies, not administrative detail. The techniques employed in participation also evidence considerable variation. In some areas assassination, bombing, and other forms of violence are standard ways of making one's opinion heard; in other nations such tactics are considered unthinkable and are rejected in favor of voting, petitioning or letter writing. In view of all this diversity we cannot maintain that political involvement of American citizens must be of a certain quantity, focus, and technique.

Our approach to the political participation of American citizens is identical to our previous approach to citizens' support of the political system. Just as we assume that at birth an individual faces a bewildering array of alternatives of political community and institutions from which to choose, so we shall argue here that similar choices are faced in the area of political activism. Differences between apathetic and active citizens are acquired differences, not genetically inherited characteristics. As each individual becomes politically socialized, some attitudes, skills, and behaviors are learned and others are rejected or ignored. The end result of this socialization process is that by maturity certain political behavior options are open and others are virtually foreclosed. While one citizen is convinced that it is right to leave politics to an elite and to obey unthinkingly their dictates, another may adhere to precisely the opposite position. In both instances early learning has reduced an initially immense number of behavioral possibilities to only a handful or even a single one.

We are not asserting that a citizen's future participatory behavior is determined once and for all by early learning. Any explanation of adult behavior must go beyond individual characteristics and preferences and must consider such factors as environmental conditions (e.g., the existence of laws prohibiting certain types of activity) and specific events encouraging participation.[1] It is doubtful, for example, whether a poor Mississippi black during the 1950s would have been a political activist regardless of his prior socialization. As noted in Chapter 2, socialization occurs at all ages, so the acquisition of new behavior

---

[1]The crucial importance of nonindividual factors in political participation is widely documented. See among others Angus Campbell, Philip E. Converse, Warren E. Miller, and Donald E. Stokes, *The American Voter* (New York: John Wiley & Sons, Inc., 1960), Chapter 11, "Election Laws and Political Environment"; and Stanley Kelly, Jr., Richard E. Ayers, and William G. Bowen, "Registration and Voting: Putting First Things First," *American Political Science Review,* 61 (1967), 359–79.

patterns also remains a possibility. Our position is more modest: our argument is simply that the available behavioral options are constrained or limited, but not completely determined, by early political socialization. Early learning creates possibilities (and nonpossibilities), not absolute certainties. For example, it would be quite a shock if a poor, traditionally minded peasant trained to accept his status as unchangeable emerged suddenly as a political revolutionary. Nor would we expect someone lacking political skills to metamorphose into a dynamic leader. To be sure, such transformations are possible, but they are not likely. Our basic problem emerges: given their early political education, what types of participatory behavior are reasonably open to adult Americans? The emphasis should be on reasonably open, not on what specific action will be taken by each and every individual.

Participation-related socialization is an exceptionally complex phenomenon. Such learning involves far more than motivation or specific skills, and to make matters even more complex, almost all of one's personality development may, in some way, be relevant to one's civic involvement.[2] We cannot make our analysis of participatory options identical to an analysis of all human development. Instead, let us consider only four general areas of early socialization particularly relevant to future behavior: (1) orientations toward the political system; (2) the norm of political activism; (3) skills and knowledge necessary for effective future participation; and (4) preadult protopolitical activity.

ORIENTATIONS TOWARD THE POLITICAL SYSTEM

As we have seen in the previous chapter, with few exceptions young Americans view their political system and leaders very favorably: institutions and authorities are perceived as highly benevolent, wise, capable, powerful, and deeply concerned for the public welfare. Leaders, particularly the president, are almost Superman-like heroes

[2]In addition, there is no single definition of what political participation is. It can be reasonably argued that almost any kind of behavior is, in some way, political if it has public consequences. Thus, the decision of the local grocer to raise his prices becomes a political act when dissatisfaction with food prices becomes a public issue. In the Soviet Union showing up for work drunk is a political offense; in the United States it is merely a personal problem. When we begin asking about political motives in such crimes as tax cheating, draft evasion, and rioting, the question of what is political participation becomes incredibly complex and confusing. This problem is further elaborated in Lester W. Milbrath, *Political Participation* (Chicago: Rand McNally & Company, 1965), Chapter 1, "Conceptual Problems of Political Participation."

dedicated to the triumph of good over evil dutifully awaiting calls from the distressed. The responsiveness of political authorities, despite their power and position, is widely believed regardless of age. Indeed, most children believe that the president himself would personally help them if necessary. The Jeffersonian position that the people must be eternally on guard lest government tyrannize finds little support; the government takes care of us, rather than tyrannizes us.

Such images of political authority are not unique to the United States. Many a politically unsophisticated peasant in a tradition-oriented authoritarian society also views distant leaders as godlike heroes protecting them from evil. The situation characterized by leaders looking out for popular interests while citizens defer to the greater expertise of officials is commonly referred to as paternalism. The appropriate citizen function in a paternalistic system is passive obedience to edicts made for his benefit but without his influence. To be sure, on occasion leaders can go to great lengths to ascertain popular opinion, and it may be perfectly acceptable for citizens to grumble occasionally about their lot, but actually letting citizens decide significant questions is certainly not the norm.

Whether the existing government functions paternalistically is a complex question. We would have to examine the behavior and beliefs of public officials to answer the question. It is clear, nevertheless, that many Americans have been socialized to accept beliefs broadly consistent with a paternalistic political system.[3] When we realize that political activism requires expenditures of time and effort, it would not be unreasonable for citizens to leave government in the hands of benevolent experts. No doubt the occasional cry for government run by experts above politics echoes this paternalistic sentiment. While a Jeffersonian democrat would argue that only continual citizen involvement can keep the government working for the people rather than for a leader's interests, many of today's citizens might very well argue that only by leaving the government alone can the interests of the people

---

[3]The persistence of the willingness to defer to the greater capabilities of our leaders becomes apparent when citizens are confronted with a conflict between mere citizen opinion and the desires of leaders. For example, Roberta Sigel found that 75 percent of a Detroit sample supported a president's decision to dispatch troops to a foreign war *in spite of public opposition to this policy.* See Sigel, "Image of the American Presidency," pp. 123–37. A similar conclusion is reached by Nadel in his analysis of opinion poll data before and after presidential action. See Mark V. Nadel, "Public Opinion and Public Policy," in *American Democracy: Theory and Reality,* eds. Robert Weissberg and Mark V. Nadel (New York: John Wiley & Sons, Inc., 1972), p. 539.

be served. Because leaders are good men, the link between involvement and government responsiveness is broken.[4]

The existence of attitudes and beliefs consistent with paternalistic, minimal citizen involvement does not, of course, settle the question of participatory possibilities available to Americans. We have described only a single tendency in one direction, not the only factor affecting future behavior. Despite beliefs in government responsiveness independent of citizen action, it is entirely reasonable that many other orientations exist that run counter to the creation of an apathetic public. To determine whether our findings so far are typical let us consider another set of participation-related attitudes and beliefs.

THE NORM OF POLITICAL PARTICIPATION

One of the minimal requirements for political activism is the belief that such activity is legitimate and acceptable. We could hardly imagine people voting, criticizing public officials, organizing political groups, or engaging in any other political action if it were widely believed that these things "just weren't done." In some political systems this type of norm pervades political life—no matter what happens, one just does not get involved. One learns to accept things, not question or try to change them. Politics and government are for other people and the average citizen would no sooner get involved in these matters than decide questions of religious faith or meddle in the laws of physics. The normative legitimacy of political action is not activity itself, but certainly an important prerequisite for participation.

Studies of early socialization clearly show that almost from the beginning of grade school the norm of political activity gains wide acceptance. Perhaps due to the popularity of classroom elections as a method of deciding everything from blackboard monitors to most likely to succeed, and the frequent occurrence of elections in American

[4]The reader should be aware of an argument reaching the opposite conclusion. That is, where public officials are believed to be good men genuinely interested in the masses, people will be encouraged, not discouraged, from active involvement. No doubt this argument is valid in the extreme case of totally corrupt, insensitive authorities. Other than attempts to replace such leaders, political participation in this situation would be futile. We suspect that a balanced, realistic view of public officials rather than either a highly positive or negative image is most consistent with the goal of maximum citizen participation. For the argument that perception of responsiveness encourages activism see David Easton and Jack Dennis, "The Child's Acquisition of Regime Norms: Political Efficacy," *American Political Science Review,* 61 (1967) 25–38.

politics, children quickly grasp that political activity is perfectly normal and acceptable. In his study of New Haven children, for example, Fred Greenstein found that virtually all children claim that they will vote once legally able.[5] Just as it is perfectly normal for people to have jobs and raise families, so young children take for granted the right of citizens to take part in civic affairs.

The development of children's orientations toward political activity is made clear by the data in Table 4.1 showing judgments on what constitutes good citizenship. In the earlier grades, when children are still acquiring rules of social conduct and discipline, there is a greater emphasis on nonpolitical activity as the mark of the good citizen: one fulfills civic obligations by obeying the law and helping others. With increasing age, however, a noticeable shift in emphasis occurs toward more politically active conceptualizations of citizenship so that by eighth grade interest in political affairs and getting out the vote are the most popular choices. Considering our previous discussion of the possibility of political paternalism, it seems significant that by later years two characteristics of a good citizen frequently associated with paternalistic political systems—hard work and obedience—are not commonly accepted as the citizenship role. Thus, we see that it is possible for Americans to be socialized to the belief that the government is responsive and benevolent while simultaneously accepting the legitimacy of citizen participation in politics. The goodness of the existing system may not require citizen involvement, but it is also true that Americans are not trained into accepting civic passivity as an ideal.

At the same time we must also realize that despite an acceptance of this participatory norm, there are aspects of this learning that place major limitations on future possibilities. It is one thing to believe that it is acceptable for citizens to play a political role; it is quite another to take for granted extensive political activism in all spheres of civic life. While the citizenship role learned by young Americans is hardly that of a subject in an absolute monarchy, the role stops considerably short of total activism. These inhibiting factors are not so much explicit prohibitions against political activity as they are omissions and matters of emphases that encourage behavior into limited channels.

When we move beyond asking whether a norm of political activism merely exists and consider the nature of the activism, it becomes clear that participation is limited to voting, some campaign activities, and being informed. There is, especially among older children, an awareness of nonelectoral forms of political participation, but in no way do these rival voting and elections as appropriate channels of

[5]Fred I. Greenstein, *Children and Politics,* p. 36.

TABLE 4.1   Perceptions of Qualities of Good Adult Citizens, by Grade

Grade level	Works hard	Everybody likes him	Votes & gets others to vote	Helps others	Interested in way country is run	Always obeys laws	Goes to church	Don't know
4	13.5*	7.0	26.4	47.8	28.2	44.3	23.6	2.0
5	11.3	8.5	29.8	42.1	41.8	42.0	20.6	.6
6	10.7	9.0	35.8	35.4	50.5	37.4	16.0	.6
7	11.1	8.3	35.9	34.2	52.7	32.7	14.6	.2
8	10.0	8.1	44.6	26.3	65.0	29.0	11.8	.7

* Percentages indicate proportion of children choosing each alternative. More than one choice was allowed so percentages add to more than 100 percent.
Adapted from Hess and Torney. The Development of Political Attitudes in Children, *p. 46. Sample is a national one and the number of respondents per grade varies from 1780 to 1674.*

citizen political power.[6] Thus it becomes entirely possible to fulfill one's civic duties by being informed and casting an occasional vote. Other forms of political activity—joining interest groups, overseeing administration, running for office, and raising public issues—are not associated with bad, or prohibited behavior; rather, they are never emphasized as an integral part of the citizen role. There is no learning that specifically prohibits citizens from engaging in these activities, but at the same time, unlike voting, these are not the types of things one naturally engages in. Needless to say, as important as voting and being informed are, this conceptualization of customary, expected political activity effectively closes off many important modes of citizen influence. American politics would be drastically different if most citizens accepted economic boycotts and mass demonstrations to be as respectable and normal as voting.

Another belief relevant to political participation is one's conception of politics. Some scholars define politics as an all-inclusive phenomenon—wherever there is conflict or there are choices to be made, there is politics. Thus, according to this broad conception, politics not only happens in the government, but in the home, in school, on the job, and wherever else decisions affecting people's lives are made. Politics can, however, be construed much more narrowly to include only the behavior of public (particularly elected) officials. Used in this way, politics is virtually identical with formal government or attempts to attain formal positions of power, and thus becomes considerably re-

[6]Hess and Torney, *The Development of Political Attitudes in Children*, p. 77.

moved from the realm of daily activity. While in the former conceptualization politics can no more be avoided than social interaction, the latter approach views politics as a phenomenon that rarely impinges on one's life unless one specifically desires otherwise.

The importance of holding differing conceptions of what politics includes is apparent when we consider that two individuals may both believe strongly in political activism; but their actual behavior can vary considerably if one thinks politics involves only formal government activities, while the other views politics more broadly. Hence, merely knowing that an individual considers it normal to be politically active tells us relatively little about the kind of activities in which a person is likely to participate. An activist with a broad conception of politics might, for example, consider it perfectly appropriate to become involved in such public areas as schools, the local police force, social welfare, bureaucracies, large corporations, military institutions, hospitals, and wherever else decisions are made affecting public life. On the other hand, someone with a narrower conception of politics would probably view such decisions as nonpolitical and out of bounds of citizen interference.

What is the conception of politics acquired by young Americans? Is politics a pervasive part of life or merely something involving elections and formal government? The evidence, though speculative and impressionistic, suggests that current socialization encourages the former perspective.[7] That is, while most children embrace the norm of political activity, it is a norm applicable only to a relatively narrow range of activities, particularly those associated with elections and elected officials. The good citizen should be politically involved, but this involvement excludes major areas of civic life, regardless of their public impact, that are not formally part of government. For example, corporate decisions are not viewed as political in the same way that local government decisions are political even though corporate decisions may enormously affect the entire community. Moreover, this emphasis on elections and elected leaders also tends to minimize the importance of administrative decision-making. Though the public bureaucrat is as much a part of government as an elected official, the norm of citizen participation does not seem to require public involvement in bureaucracies despite the great relevance of these officials' decisions compared to actions taken by the local city council. This acquisition of a relatively narrow conception of politics simplifies a citizen's civic

[7]Fred M. Newman, "Political Socialization in the Schools," *Harvard Educational Review* 38 (1968), pp. 536–45; and Byron G. Marsialas, "American Government: We Are the Greatest," in *Social Studies in the United States: A Critical Appraisal,* ed. Charles B. Cox and Byron G. Marsialas (New York: Harcourt, Brace and World, Inc., 1967), p. 177.

obligation by eliminating numerous responsibilities, but it also minimizes the options for influencing decisions affecting one's life.

Another important participation-related area of political socialization deserving attention is toleration for divisive conflict. If political action is to be more than ritualistic playacting during which nothing ever happens despite enormous noise and commotion, significant divisive conflict must be present. Unless everyone agrees on everything— an obviously rare occurrence—conflict suppression or avoidance undoubtedly means that political choices are inconsequential ones between tweedledee and tweedledum alternatives. Besides eliminating meaningful choices, conflict avoidance is an excellent means for suppressing demands for radical change. Where an unwillingness to face divisive conflict prevails, anyone seeking major changes is quickly labelled a trouble-maker or out to rock the boat and therefore is readily dismissed with little serious attention to his substantive demands. Alternatives thus become nonissues, not through rational consideration, but rather through a psychological unwillingness or inability to face conflict-laden situations.

Despite the obvious necessity of some toleration of conflict in order for meaningful (rather than playacting) political participation to occur, most American children fail to develop this orientation. Little doubt exists that Americans are overwhelmingly trained to prefer harmony and consensus to conflict. For example, many children show a genuine interest in elections and campaigns, yet nevertheless view any conflict between candidates as injurious to the nation. Even as children become politically more sophisticated, this aversion to conflict remains essentially unchanged.[8] Children are deeply committed to the desirability of electoral contests, but the differences between the contestants—and hence the election's significance—must be kept to a minimum. This intolerance of controversy even distorts perceptions of existing conflict. Hess and Torney note that although children begin acquiring party loyalty during grade-school years, few children will distinguish between Republicans and Democrats in terms of their contribution to the national welfare. That is, one may prefer one party over another, but this choice does not ultimately mean very much since both are equally

---

[8]Hess and Torney, *The Development of Political Attitudes in Children,* pp. 88, 94. Adult data on the desirability of sharp conflict suggests that these earlier orientations are highly persistent. For example, in his study of support for the American political party system Jack Dennis found that while most citizens accept the existence of parties and elections, they also believe that parties artificially create conflict, and the country would be better off if the parties disagreed less. Jack Dennis, "Support for the Party System by the Mass Public," *American Political Science Review* 60 (1966), 600–15, and Dennis, "Support for the Institution of Elections by the Mass Public," *American Political Science Review* 64 (1970), 819–35.

devoted to everyone's welfare. A similar underplaying of conflict occurs in evaluating candidates, though here many older children at least realize that differences exist. Once again, however, a few find these conflicts desirable.[9]

If this aversion to political conflict persists unchanged into adulthood, it undoubtedly encourages a ritualistic and substantiveless form of political activism. People might get highly emotional and deeply committed, but the political significance of this behavior would be virtually nil. Campaigns would thus be more like sporting events than an opportunity to make real choices. Spectators would yell, applaud, and occasionally even run on to the playing field, but everyone would know that nothing of real consequence was to be decided. At worst, one might feel momentary displeasure and frustration when one's team lost, but one would be consoled simultaneously by knowing that the outcome did not actually matter that much. Political participation hence functions more as a therapeutic outlet and legitimizing activity than as a means of deciding among meaningful alternatives. At the expense of having substantial choices highly relevant to people's lives, one would instead have the psychological comfort of knowing that whatever happened would have minimal consequences.

When we consider these participation-related orientations, we must be careful to distinguish between what is functional for the existing political system's survival and what is best for certain individuals. No doubt, learning that activism largely means electoral activism, politics is limited to formal government, and divisive conflict should be avoided insures a political system free from the stresses and strain of massive, highly pervasive and emotional activism. Imagine the problems faced by authorities where sharp conflict over highly controversial issues continually pervaded all decision-making. The system would be perpetually in a state of crisis, not too dissimilar, perhaps, to the early 1930's in Weimar Germany or certain periods in post World War II Italy. No sooner would a public decision be contemplated than would highly animated public reaction confront the decision maker. The problem of coping with such a politicized public would undoubtedly make life extremely difficult for officials interested in a smooth running government.

At the same time we must also realize that by limiting these stresses and strains we also suppress the interests of those disagreeing with the status quo. The exclusion from consideration of significant

[9]Hess and Torney, *The Development of Political Attitudes in Children,* p. 92. For an attempt to account for why children do not learn to deal with divisive conflict, see Stanley E. Ballinger, "The Social Studies and Social Controversy," *The School Review* 70 (1963), 97–111.

political alternatives in many areas means that groups possibly desirous of such alternatives, e.g., blacks, women, poor people, are politically defeated before an issue ever arises. Their demands for fundamental change are met by charges that an issue is not a political one, that one should work within normal political channels, i.e., voting and elections, and that the demanded change would cause too much conflict (stir things up). Since many of those potentially benefiting from consideration of these alternatives hold the same norms and beliefs about proper political participation, their charges of changing the status quo are even further reduced. In short, when young Americans implicitly (and unconsciously) choose one set of political participation-related orientations over another, they not only choose the scope and content of involvement, but also affect the political outcomes of all interests, whether they affirm or oppose existing policies.

LEARNING TO PARTICIPATE EFFECTIVELY

Learning about political involvement obviously demands more than acquiring norms and beliefs about the desirability and nature of citizen political activity. One can be totally committed to all-inclusive activism, yet the end result could be zero. In any complex modern political system, the desire to participate is not enough; one must also know *how* to participate. Without the appropriate skills and knowledge, the motivation and opportunity for participation are superfluous. Even a relatively simple act like voting for president requires some analytical thinking and understanding if it is to have any meaning. A prospective voter must, at a minimum, know how to register, when to vote, and perhaps something about one of the candidates. When we consider nonelectoral participation such as organizing and joining groups, writing letters, and speaking out on issues, the necessity of having certain skills and abilities in addition to the appropriate attitudes is obvious.

Political Knowledge

At the simplest level, effective political participation requires adequate factual knowledge of the political system. One must be acquainted with, among other things, where political authority lies, the rules governing the exercise of power, and the relationships between institutions. Knowing, for example, that Congress, not the president, is the primary legislative agency may appear to be a trivial fact, but its acquisition is essential to any group seeking new legislation. Unless facts such as who is primarily responsible for lawmaking are learned, the energy spent trying to change existing laws will probably be wasted. The immense complexities of modern bureaucratic government makes such information a virtual prerequisite for political action.

American schools spend considerable time and effort trying to teach the basic facts of political life. From the earliest grades onward children sit through numerous state-prescribed courses describing the evolution and present structure of existing government.[10]   By high school, with its own set of history and civics courses, most Americans have been exposed to such facts as what the three branches of government are, elementary rules of parliamentary procedure, the how and when of elections, how bills become law, and some of the other pieces of information known as textbook knowledge. Though considerable evidence exists that much of this effort makes a limited impression or is soon forgotten upon leaving school, young Americans entering adulthood appear to possess at least the minimum rudimentary formal political awareness.[11] They may not know who their congressman is or how the Supreme Court functions, but they are not totally baffled by terms such as "legislation" or "interest group."[12]

At the same time, this instruction in the basic facts of the existing system omits much important information. The stress on structural characteristics, e.g. separation of powers, checks and balances, and such legalistic treatments of policy-making as how a bill becomes a law, gives the highly misleading picture of government operating as a neutral, mechanistic processor of the public will. Such an image ignores the role of interest groups, propaganda, the manipulation of laws in their enforcement, the passage of purely symbolic laws, and all the less formal features of government essential to an understanding of the political process. To be sure, most students are exposed to the idea of pressure groups and may even learn something about sinister interests,

[10]The characteristics of early civics education are further described in Frank J. Estvan, "Teaching Government in Elementary Schools," *The Elementary School Journal* 62 (1962), 291–97. The sheer magnitude of this educational effort is described in George Z. F. Bereday and Bonnie B. Stretch, "Political Education in the U.S.A. and the Soviet Union," *Comparative Education Review* 7 (1963), 9–16. Bereday and Stretch suggest that American schools expend greater effort on political education than do Soviet schools when you include all the politically related subjects.

[11]For a review of adult knowledge of politics see "The Polls: The Informed Public," *Public Opinion Quarterly,* 26 (1962), 668–77.

[12]The minimal nature of political awareness of most students deserves further clarification. There is little doubt that even after the completion of civics courses, many high school seniors are ignorant of the most elementary political facts. For example, Merelman, in his study of two California communities, found that 38 percent of high school seniors could not name the three branches of government. See Richard M. Merelman, *Political Socialization and Educational Climates* (New York: Holt, Rinehart, and Winston, Inc., 1971), p. 86. Other studies provide essentially similar conclusions.

but such exposure is a long way from detailed understanding of how political interests actually manage to get their way.[13] We could not expect someone to influence the passage of a law unless he were generally aware of the nature of congressional influence, possible resistance from other interests, and other informal, but very real, political considerations. Even when dealing with issues much closer to home, e.g. influencing the local school curriculum, one must understand far more than the formal structures and laws if one is to be an effective political activist.

The simplistic and naive version of the political process acquired by most children becomes clear when they rate the relative political influence of different groups. Hess and Torney find that as children mature they give increasing political weight to the influence of the average citizen. By eighth grade, only the president and labor unions exercise more power than the common man. Rich people, newspapers, and large companies are all viewed as less influential.[14] Perhaps in some ultimate sense this imputation of great political power to the average citizen is factually correct. At least in the daily struggle of who gets what in government, most political scientists would probably agree that direct citizen influence unaided by organization plays only a minor role. To accept a picture of the political process where common men outweigh newspapers and corporations is to accept an image clearly dysfunctional for subsequent effective participation. Here again, political beliefs providing psychological satisfaction simultaneously limit the effectiveness of participation.

The inadequacy of existing political socialization for training citizens to participate effectively also manifests itself in the schools' ten-

[13]Litt, in his analysis of ninth-grade civics books employed in three Massachusetts communities, found exceptionally few references to the exercise of power and clashing interests as determinants of policy. The impression subtly conveyed is that public policy, perhaps like the weather, just seems to happen. It is politically significant that lower-class students are considerably more likely than middle-class students to accept this sanitized version of reality. See Edgar Litt, "Civic Education, Community Norms, and Political Indoctrination," *American Sociological Review* 28 (1963), 69–75. Also see Fred M. Newman, *Harvard Educational Review* 38 (1968) 536–45. No doubt the controversial nature of describing the informal, less-aboveboard aspects of American politics discourages a more realistic treatment. Imagine what might happen in many communities if teachers even suggested the possibility that some aspects of foreign policy were greatly influenced by a few oil producers.

[14]Hess and Torney, *The Development of Political Attitudes in Children*, p. 76. This exaggeration of individual power probably persists into adulthood. Many Americans seem to see themselves as part of a slumbering Gulliver who, when the occasion warrants it, will rise up and strike down the Lilliputian sinister interests. Because individual power is largely *potential*, no contradiction exists between it and the effective machinations of special interests. For analysis of adults' view of the individual's political power see Lane, *Political Ideology*, pp. 141–44.

dency to emphasize the learning of objective facts instead of the development of analytical thinking. Teaching about the American Revolution involves learning the names of prominent leaders, historical dates, major issues, and the contents of documents. Unfortunately, there is little, if any, attempt to provide students with the means to acquire and evaluate these facts. The implicit assumption is that understanding history and politics merely involves knowing what happened and when it happened.[15] The impression is frequently conveyed that to know something all one must know is where to look it up in some totally objective compendium. Thus, the argument goes, when we obtain all the factual details of an issue we will have everything needed to decide our own position and behavior. Political disagreements arise because of unequal factual information—once all the facts are known, conflict disappears.

While this emphasis on acquiring facts does not inherently discourage political activism, it certainly does not foster intelligent participation. Politics is always changing and what was an objective fact ten years ago, may now be obsolete. Without learning the methods of collecting and analyzing factual data, one can continue to function with an inaccurate picture of how the world operates. Consider, for example, the enormous recent growth of bureaucracy at all levels of government to the point where many crucial decisions are now made administratively. Knowing that all laws are made by legislators might lead to misguided action.

Even if we knew all the relevant facts, the facts themselves are no guide to one's own political behavior. Perfect factual information does not tell what side of an issue to pursue or what behaviors are consistent with personal political values. Without an ability to understand one's own interests, and relate these interests to concrete issues, the consequences of political activism are likely to be more symbolic and expressive than real. In such situations one can easily fight for programs that have no meaning while ignoring issues highly relevant to our self-interest.[16]

Sophisticated Political Thinking

When we speak of sophisticated political thinking, we imply more than an accurate knowledge of how government works. If such knowl-

[15]This argument is one of the standard criticisms of civics and history courses. See, among others, John R. Palmer, "American History" in *Social Studies in the United States: A Critical Appraisal,* ed. C. Benjamin Cox and Byron G. Massialas (New York: Harcourt, Brace & World, Inc., 1967). Also see Ballinger, "The Social Studies and Social Controversy," pp. 97–111.

[16]The pervasiveness of this type of public response to political events is brilliantly discussed in Murray Edelman, *The Symbolic Uses of Politics* (Urbana, Ill.: University of Illinois Press, 1964).

edge were the only requirement, we would be able to turn out competent political analysts at the age of ten or eleven. Sophisticated political thinking means the ability to conceptualize, organize, and evaluate political phenomena so they make coherent sense. Without these abilities the would-be participant is lost and confused in a world of unique, unrelated phenomena. Although an individual might know the detailed facts of every situation, an inability to place events into a coherent framework would make him more a collector of encyclopedic information than an effective participant. It would be as if a seven-year-old child prodigy having memorized every Civil War battle were suddenly placed in a graduate seminar on the Civil War; despite his vast knowledge, immense confusion would be the likely result.

Thus ability to conceptualize coherently not only affects the individual, but can also influence the quality of political life in general. Consider the probable results if leaders faced a public able to comprehend only the simplest, most concrete arguments. At best, issues and programs would have to be stripped of their complexities and made into easily understood, but undoubtedly distorted, catch phrases (e.g., policy X is good because it helps the working man). At worst, leaders would be able to manipulate opinion through the clever use of appealing slogans and deceptive arguments. In either case, the quality of political life would not be conducive to effective and meaningful citizen involvement. Even those able to think systematically and coherently about politics would be a frustrated minority unable to communicate with their fellow citizens.

The emergence of the capacity for systematic, complex thinking in children is one of the major questions in socialization research. Particularly in the field of child development, considerable attention has been focused on the stages by which very young children gradually come to grips with complex concepts and events. Scholars such as Piaget and Kohlberg have spent lifetimes carefully documenting the growth of cognitive ability among young children.[17] Despite this wealth of information, an answer to the question of whether Americans develop the capacity for sophisticated political thinking is not clear. As in so many other areas, a judgment one way or the other depends on what research one accepts. Let us consider some of the major arguments and their supportive data.

[17]See, for example, Jean Piaget, *The Moral Judgment of the Child* (New York: The Free Press of Glencoe, 1965); Barbel Inhelder and Jean Piaget, *The Growth of Logical Thinking,* trans. Anne Parsons and Stanley Milgram (New York: Basic Books, Inc., 1958); Lawrence Kohlberg, "The Development of Children's Orientation Toward a Moral Order." *Vita Humana* 6 (1963), 11–33; and Richard M. Merelman, "The Development of Political Ideology: A Framework for the Analysis of Political Socialization," *American Political Science Review,* 63 (1969), 750–67.

There is little disagreement that a young child lacks the mental capacity necessary for complex political thinking. As we have seen, young children view complex institutions and processes as persons rather than as abstract patterns of interaction. For example, just as his father might command him, so the young child conceives of the president ordering the mayor around. This personalistic thinking also extends to judgments about alternative policies. Children are hedonists who view policy largely in terms of its impact on them personally, not its larger social consequences. In a word, a young child is egocentric—the political world revolves around him. The use of abstract principles, other than this hedonistic egocentrism, is minimal.

The young child is also unable to think abstractly. Early thinking is concrete—phenomena are perceived as discrete, specific entities, although they may share much in common or even emanate from the same source. When asked the purpose of government, young children enumerate specific services (e.g., build parks) rather than describe government's function more abstractly. Future-oriented thinking also seems to be beyond the reach of most young children. Preferences are a here and now matter with little awareness of a decision's future consequences or realizations that subsequent conditions and possibilities are partially determined in the present. Finally, young children evidence many difficulties with cause and effect thinking. When confronted with such questions as why poverty exists or why there are wars, very few children can link diverse facts together into some coherent explanation. More typical are merely listings of possibly related facts or simple one factor causes (e.g., poor people are lazy).[18]

We can thus see that the young child's mental ability hardly allows him to be a sophisticated political observer or participant. We may now ask whether these characteristics remain essentially unchanged. Do Americans, at least by their late adolescence, have the capacity for coherent, non-egocentric, analytical thinking? Or, on the other hand, are adults no more advanced in their thinking than a very knowledgeable ten-year-old?

One answer is provided by Adelson and O'Neil's study of children's solutions to political dilemmas.[19] Using a sample of 120 children drawn from the fifth, seventh, ninth, and twelfth grades, Adelson and O'Neil asked each child to imagine himself on a Pacific island with the

---

[18]This picture of childhood thinking is further elaborated in Joseph Adelson and Robert P. O'Neil, "Growth of Political Ideas in Adolescence: The Sense of Community," *Journal of Personality and Social Psychology* 4 (1966), 295–306. Also see Joseph Adelson, Bernard Green, and Robert O'Neil, "The Growth of the Idea of Law in Adolescence," *Developmental Psychology* 1 (1969), 327–32.

[19]Adelson and O'Neil, "Growth of Political Ideas in Adolescence," pp. 295–306.

task of deciding how the community was to be run. To gauge the child's mode of thinking, numerous difficult and ambiguous political dilemmas were posed. For example, children were asked what to do if people without children objected to paying taxes for community schools.

Consistent with other child development research, Adelson and O'Neil find a clear development of more complex, analytical thinking between the ages of eleven and eighteen. While the eleven-year-old's social perspective is largely limited to his own world, an eighteen-year-old is cognizant of a larger society with its collective needs. Policy decisions were now made from a broader, less egocentric, more public perspective. In addition, with greater maturity comes the capacity to conceptualize alternative policies in terms of their consequences. Choices are thus no longer simply evaluated on whether they are good or bad, right or wrong, but also in terms of relative costs and benefits and long-term social implications. When asked to justify compulsory education, for example, an eleven-year-old is likely to speak in terms of education being necessary for you to know more. Seven years later compulsory education's justification shifts to arguments such as society's need for trained people or the preservation of the existing community. Finally, and perhaps most important, the eighteen-year-old's thinking is marked by a degree of coherence and orderliness almost totally absent in an eleven-year-old. Principles and abstract concepts replace a grabbag of uncontested slogans and sentiments. To be sure, even the most thoughtful respondents in Adelson and O'Neil's sample were a long way from possessing totally integrated political perspective; they nevertheless demonstrated a capacity to organize issues and events in a lasting and meaningful fashion.[20]

Do Adelson and O'Neil conclusively demonstrate that Americans are socialized to sophisticated, complex political thinking? Not necessarily. Other researchers using different approaches have reached somewhat different conclusions. For example, Jennings in his 1965 national study of high school seniors measured political sophistication in terms of an ability to perceive political party differences in broad ideological terms. While Adelson and O'Neil focus on how children think about policy dilemmas, Jennings asks whether eighteen-year-olds have the capacity to interpret important political phenomena (e.g., political parties) in sophisticated ideological terms. To the extent that this task is closer to reality than solving hypothetical issues in an imaginary community, it is perhaps a more politically relevant method of measuring sophisticated thinking.

[20]Adelson and O'Neil, "Growth of Political Ideas in Adolescence," p. 306.

TABLE 4.2 Ideological Perceptions of Political Parties among High School Seniors*

Perception of Party Differences:

Accurate, broad definition (correctly matches ideological labels "liberal" and "conservative" to party and can provide broad, abstract meaning to ideological concept) 24%

Accurate, narrow definition (correctly matches party and ideological label but can only offer narrow, e.g. spend more money, meaning to ideological concept) 10%

Some Error (cannot match party and ideological concept) 13%

No definition of ideological terms 16%

No differences between parties 37%

100%

* For additional discussion of this approach to measuring ideology and specific comparisons with adult responses see Philip E. Converse, "The Nature of Belief Systems in Mass Publics" in *Ideology and Discontent,* ed. David E. Apter (New York: The Free Press of Glencoe, 1964), especially pp. 219–40.
Source: M. Kent Jennings, The Student-Parent Socialization Study, ICPR edition code books (1971), variable 317, p. 177. Data made available through the Inter-University Consortium for Political Research.

In Table 4.2 we see the proportion of these high school seniors capable of varying political conceptualizations. In evaluating these findings we must realize that since we are dealing with seniors, these data probably exaggerate the level of ideological perception since it is doubtful whether high school dropouts would do equally well or better than seniors. In addition, answers to these questions were coded very generously to give individuals the benefit of the doubt and thus place them in the highest category possible.[21] Even with these exaggerations, the evidence does not present a very flattering picture. What may seem like an obviously simple feat for a politically attuned college student—describing the Democrats as more liberal, the Republicans as more conservative, and providing some broad, abstract meaning to these labels—cannot be accomplished by the vast majority of these seniors. Even when we combine the broad and narrow conceptions of ideology, only about a third can be considered as sophisticated political observers. For the majority, phrases such as "Republicans are becoming more conservative" convey little meaning. Thus, if we use this test

[21]See Converse, "The Nature of Belief Systems in Mass Publics," *Ideology and Discontent,* p. 220, where the coding procedures employed by Jennings are further detailed.

as our measure of sophisticated thinking, the results are less impressive than those reported by Adelson and O'Neil.[22]

Can these two differing analyses be reconciled? Do American adolescents approach political issues in a sophisticated manner as suggested by Adelson and O'Neil or are Jennings's data closer to the truth? To a certain extent an answer is indeterminate since neither study is a comprehensive analysis of the problem. Sophisticated political thinking is not a concept that everyone agrees upon and other investigations would probably produce yet other differences.

Assuming that both studies are accurate portrayals of different, though related, phenomena, we can conclude that while most adolescents are capable of complex, coherent political thinking *if pressed,* far fewer actively attempt such thinking on their own. The potential for sophisticated thinking exists but perhaps the low salience of politics in most people's lives provides insufficient motivation for this potential to be actualized. We suspect that if Jennings more forcefully pressed his subjects the same way Adelson and O'Neil encouraged their respondents, a greater proportion could offer more sophisticated ideological descriptions of partisan differences. Does this mean that existing socialization practices equip individuals for sophisticated, complex political analyses? Even assuming that this potential does not atrophy with continued non-use, it is difficult to argue that citizens are trained for sophisticated political analysis when the end product seems to be a widespread inability (or unwillingness) to engage in this type of thinking.[23]

[22]Additional studies, too complex to discuss in detail, using yet other measures of political conceptualization, also cast doubts on the capacity of young adults for sophisticated political thinking. For example, Merelman relying heavily on Piaget formulates nine dimensions of thought important for what he terms policy thinking. Using a small sample of above average intelligence, middle-class respondents, Merelman finds that between eighth and twelfth grade there is a statistically significant development on only three of these nine policy thinking dimensions. However, because of the very limited nature of this sample and the way the data are presented, an answer to the question of whether most Americans acquire the capacity for complex, systematic thinking remains inconclusive. See Richard M. Merelman, "The Development of Policy Thinking in Adolescence," *American Political Science Review* 65 (1971), 1033–47. In another study, using a different methodology (measuring attitude crystallization by the use of factor analysis) Merelman concludes that little development of coherent, structured thinking occurs between sixth and twelfth grades. Richard M. Merelman, *Political Socialization and Education Climates,* pp. 71–74.

[23]As for the argument that as these adolescents enter adulthood they will be forced to confront political reality and thus develop a greater sophistication, this may be true for this generation in the future but comparable adult data suggest that no additional development occurs. The high school seniors of the 1965 Jennings study are not too dissimilar to adults in their ability to define liberalism and conservatism and correctly attach these labels to political parties. See Converse, "The Nature of Belief Systems in Mass Publics," *Ideology and Discontent,* pp. 219–27 and Campbell *et al., The American Voter,* Chap. 9 "Attitude Structure and the Problem of Ideology."

The Acquisition of Partisan Identification

One of the most politically important orientations acquired during childhood is a sense of partisan identification. Studies of adults demonstrate that party preference is much closer to a broad, pervasive political perspective coloring many specific dispositions than merely one of many preferences. Being a Democrat, for example, not only encourages more positive perception of the Democratic party but also distorts perceptions of candidate and issue to make them consistent with one's partisan identity. Perhaps most important, sense of party loyalty is a powerful force in people's voting decisions. Claims of impartial weighing of objective evidence aside, at least at the presidential level most citizens dutifully vote for the man of their party. Many citizens evaluate all arguments without bias, but more common are the party loyalists whose judgment of the evidence can only lead to one choice—a vote for the candidate of one's own party.[24]

The political importance of partisan identification is further emphasized by its pervasiveness among Americans. More than thirty years of polling have demonstrated that about three-quarters of the adult population in varying degrees support either the Democratic or Republican parties. Evidence also indicates that partisan loyalty is remarkably stable over time despite occasional wide variations in voting behavior. Democrats tend to remain Democrats and Republicans remain Republicans even though some cross-over voting occurs. Particularly when we view only those most likely to be politically active, the picture we see is one of two large groups of committed partisans who rarely, if ever, switch sides for more than a moment.[25]

It would be easy to dismiss this adherence to partisan loyalty as irrational or inefficient. Allowing one's party attachment to influence issue and candidate perceptions need not, however, be disfunctional. The very opposite may be true—relying on one's party as a general guide simplifies and rationalizes political behavior. That is, rather than tediously collecting and analyzing masses of relevant data, one could

[24]The classical analysis of the importance of partisan identification on both policy preferences and voting behavior is found in Campbell *et al.*, *The American Voter*, Chapter 6, "The Impact of Party Identification." There is not, however, universal agreement among researchers on this question. See, for example, Louis A. Froman, Jr. and James K. Skipper, "An Approach to the Learning of Party Identification," *Public Opinion Quarterly* 27 (1963), 473–80.

[25]The tenacity of partisan identity has been documented in numerous studies. Among others, see Campbell *et al.*, *The American Voter*, Chapter 7, "The Development of Party Identification"; Herbert McCloskey and Harold E. Dahlgren, "Primary Group Influence on Party Loyalty," *American Political Science Review* 53 (1959), 757–76; and Angus Campbell, Philip E. Converse, Warren E. Miller, and Donald E. Stokes, *Elections and the Political Order* (New York: John Wiley and Sons, Inc., 1966), Chapter 7.

decide which party generally best approximates one's preferences and then permanently take the party's position as one's own.[26] Partisan identity would thus be comparable to taking the advice of a movie critic whose tastes were similar to your own rather than collecting information about each movie.

What is important for informed participation is the basis for partisan identification, not the mere existence of party loyalty. We must therefore ask whether acquiring party loyalty is an informed or a poorly understood decision. Do Americans know to what they are committing themselves when they cast their lot with a political party or is this an act of blind faith? The attitudinal and behavioral results may be identical but in the former case citizens are rationally participating, while in the latter instance perceptions and actions may frequently run contrary to one's preferences and interests.

As with many broad adult political orientations, considerable evidence indicates that partisan identification emerges long before adulthood. In his New Haven study Greenstein found that by fourth grade (about age nine) more than 60 percent expressed a preference for either the Democrats or Republicans. Especially among middle-class children there is some development of an independent disposition with maturation, but even in this group the norm remains one of partisan loyalty.[27] A similar national pattern was reported by Hess and Torney when they asked children whom they would vote for if they could vote: from fourth grade onward a majority sided with one or the other party though again the proportion saying "sometimes one party and sometimes the other party" increased with age.[28] Evidence also shows the widespread development of a norm disparaging voting solely on partisan grounds, but it is clear that early in life most Americans are already committed to one of the two parties.[29]

On what basis is party preference determined? As we would expect considering the early age during which this preference emerges, it rarely (if ever) is based on a rational review of the evidence. First, Greenstein finds that in New Haven it is not until eighth grade that as many as half of the middle-class respondents—who are also the most

[26]This argument is further elaborated by Anthony Downs in *An Economic Theory of Democracy* (New York: Harper and Row, 1957), pp. 230–34.

[27]Fred I. Greenstein, *Children and Politics*, p. 73.

[28]Hess and Torney, *The Development of Political Attitudes in Children*, p. 103.

[29]It seems fair to say that children's rejection of blind party loyalty when boldy stated (e.g., would you always vote for the same party) probably reflects feelings about the absence of free choice rather than a lack of partisan loyalty. No doubt few of the most avid partisan supporters would admit that they would, regardless of candidates or issues, support their party. The *norm* of free choice is a powerful one despite behavioral evidence of its violation.

informed—can give any meaningful answer to a question on how the parties differ (among lower-class children the corresponding figure was about a third). Even then, these answers were typically simpleminded, e.g. "there are two sides," "the parties put up different candidates."[30] When children are asked about broad ideological party differences, the political sophistication demonstrated is only slightly better than miniscule. For example, when asked whether the parties differed on favoring the rich or helping the unemployed, the vast majority saw no difference between the parties.[31] This lack of an evaluative framework becomes more evident when children answer more open-ended questions merely asking them about *any* party differences.[32] Finally, the results are similar when we measure the information basis of partisanship. Again relying on Greenstein's analysis, among fourth-graders (over 60 percent of whom had a party preference) only about a third knew the names of a party leader and less than a fifth could name leaders of both parties.[33]

It could be argued, of course, that unsophisticated responses are normal for grade-school children and hence a more informed basis for partisan identification must wait at least until adolescence. This is obviously true, but we must also realize that once formed, partisan loyalty exerts a strong influence on subsequent political perception. A high school senior identifying with Democrats for eight years views political events differently than a nonpartisan high school senior. Once a partisan choice is made, it typically becomes rationalized not through continual reevaluation and possible change of the initial decision, but rather through selective perception and assimilation of new information. Thus, a nine-year-old Republican's faith in his party's virtues is strengthened as additional understanding and information are acquired. Whereas he previously supported the GOP because it was "the best party" or "my party," as an adolescent he will be aware of specific virtuous accomplishments to justify his position.

If partisan identity is not acquired through a rational process of information gathering and evaluation, how then is it acquired? Research clearly indicates that party identification, like religious and ethnic identification, is transmitted by the family. Exactly how this partisan identity is instilled remains an open question, but little doubt exists that Republican parents by and large have Republican off-

---

[30]Greenstein, *Children and Politics,* p. 67.
[31]Hess and Torney, *The Development of Political Attitudes in Children,* p. 92.
[32]Greenstein, *Children and Politics,* p. 68.
[33]Greenstein, *Children and Politics,* p. 73.

spring.[34] Even during late adolescence, when parent-child agreement on many political issues is very low, defection from one's family political party is relatively small.[35] Indeed, it is in the transmission of this identification that the family plays one of its most politically influential roles. So powerful is this early family impact on party loyalty that it frequently requires a major political or personal crisis to produce permanent switches.[36]

Does the family transmission of partisan loyalty necessarily mean that Americans usually acquire the wrong identification in terms of issue positions and voting behavior? It can be argued that since children share their parents' social and economic characteristics, and since many issue positions are closely related to those characteristics, it is therefore not irrational for children to adopt their parents' partisan loyalty.[37] For example, a lower-class, black Democrat would not be totally irrational if he socialized his children to be loyal Democrats. Nor would the sons of rich businessmen be politically irrational if they blindly followed their family's Republicanism. Moreover, where the discrepancy between early partisan socialization and one's adult position is extreme, changes are possible. Family influences are not absolutely determining: someone raised as a strict Republican might switch parties if he continually agreed with Democratic policies and candidates. In the 1930s, for example, many Negroes who had staunchly supported the party of Lincoln changed their minds and began with equal fervor to support the party of Roosevelt.

[34]The inter-generational agreement on partisan identification is further described in Herbert Hyman, *Political Socialization,* p. 56; Campbell *et al., The American Voter,* pp. 146–49; and M. Kent Jennings and Richard G. Niemi, "The Transmission of Political Values from Parent to Child," *American Political Science Review* 67 (1968), 169–84. Chapter 8 considers the transmission in greater detail.

[35]Jennings and Niemi in their 1965 national study found that only about 10 percent of their sample of high school seniors differed from their parents in party loyalty. In areas such as position on specific issues and evaluation of social groups, parent-child disagreement was considerably lower, frequently almost a zero relationship. See Jennings and Niemi, "The Transmission of Political Values from Parent to Child," p. 173.

[36]One event that does not encourage partisan switching is so-called adolescent rebellion. Such rebellion is rarely political even when it occurs (and it occurs relatively infrequently). On this subject see Russell Middleton and Snell Putney, "Political Expression of Adolescent Rebellion," *American Journal of Sociology* 68 (1963), 527–35 and Eleanor E. Maccoby, Richard E. Matthews, and Anton S. Morton, "Youth and Political Change," *Public Opinion Quarterly* 18 (1954), 23–29.

[37]This is argued by Arthur S. Goldberg who shows that as children diverge from their father's socio-economic group, their partisan identification shifts in the rational direction. This rational reconsideration of party loyalty was more pronounced, however, among the better educated. See Arthur S. Goldberg, "Social Determinism and Rationality Bases of Party Identification," *American Political Science Review* 68 (1969), 5–25. A different view is presented in Campbell *et al., The American Voter,* pp. 458–59.

There is much to be said for these arguments. Nevertheless, passively accepting one's father's or mother's partisan identification is clearly far from the most rational way of making this crucial decision. As rational as it may be in certain circumstances, e.g. a poor black with little information unquestioningly accepting his father's Democratic identification, politics is not so unchanging that what was good for one's parents is equally good twenty years hence. Particularly when this transmission pattern persists for many generations, the present day result might be quite ludicrous. Consider, for instance, the eastern Tennessee hillbillies who owe their Republicanism to ancestors who more than a hundred years ago supported the Whig party (the forerunner of the Republican) because of its pledge of building roads and canals. Although extreme, the example shows that a traditional family party identity may be a poor guide to current choices.

As for the argument that change is always possible, this is perhaps the most relevant in extreme cases. If, for example, a Republican manual worker continually finds himself at odds with Republican policy, he might reconsider his allegiance. Economic crises like the Great Depression can also force a rethinking of loyalty. Such extremes, though very important politically, are comparatively uncommon. Furthermore, political issues and events are typically complex and ambiguous and thus open to selective perception and distortion. For every Republican manual worker discomforted by his party's policies, many more probably find such a dilemma less disturbing or even nonexistent. The opportunity to change partisan loyalties, while undoubtedly important, does not guarantee automatically that people will support parties consistent with their own preferences. The fact that changes in identification are so rare underlines the limitations of partisan switching as a method of readjusting party choice with one's own position.[38]

PREADULT POLITICAL PARTICIPATION

The acquisition of future participatory options not only involves acquiring participation-related orientation and skills, but in addition also requires an opportunity to practice one's political skills. Since

[38]We are not, however, suggesting that Americans are socialized as robots to vote regularly for their parents' party. In the first place, many citizens are genuine independents and thus free to vote with no partisan disloyalty. Second, and more important, even the most partisan citizen occasionally crosses party lines for rational reasons. Though partisan identification as an influence in voting and issue perception is very strong, it should not be exaggerated to the point to where citizens are complete captives of their past. On this point of rational, issue-oriented voting, see V. O. Key, Jr., *The Responsible Electorate* (Cambridge, Mass.: The Belknap Press of Harvard University, 1966).

political activity is in part a learned habit, we cannot expect it to emerge spontaneously upon reaching adulthood. It seems unlikely that citizens with no political experience whatsoever, regardless of their attitudes, could overcome years of childhood passivity. Such preadult political activity can be, however, far more than practice for future activism. As the youthful character of inner-city riots and antiwar demonstrations illustrates, one need not be old enough to vote to have a political impact. Indeed, except for voting and holding office there is no reason why even grade-school children cannot be genuine political activists. Let us consider some of the political possibilities open to children and the extent to which these opportunities for practice are utilized.

Paying attention to politics and discussing events with others, are among the most simple forms of participation open to preadults. Such activity, despite its undemanding character, is hardly unimportant. Consider what political life would be like if citizens were ignorant of the behavior of leaders, oblivious to events beyond their personal experience, and had little desire to share their opinions with others? Such citizen ignorance and uncommunicativeness would hardly encourage a government responsive to citizen demands and interests. Paying attention to politics and communicating one's thoughts are no guarantees of influencing policy, but without such participation, more demanding behaviors are probably either impossible or ineffective.

In Table 4.3 we see the proportion of children in grades three through eight taking part in political discussion or reading about political events. Even in the earliest grades these political activities are quite common among American children. We do not know whether political discussions among third-graders were anything more than a very unsophisticated exchange of political cliches or oversimplifications, but the habit of political discourse is being learned. By eighth grade the overwhelming majority are actively engaged in these activities. Whether these children eventually become politically interested adults cannot be answered here, but we can say that almost all of these future adults will at least have had some practice at this type of participation.[39]

Moreover, this involvement is not without emotional meaning for many children. Hess and Torney found that most children chose sides

[39]In view of the cultural value of being an informed, involved citizen these high levels of claimed participation should be treated cautiously. Many children probably confuse what they *ought* to do with what they have actually done when asked questions like whether they follow events. This response to values is beautifully illustrated by an experiment at a Midwestern University where a voting stand suddenly emerged on campus. About 50 percent of the students voted for one of three fictitious candidates, and *many of the voters claimed to have worked for one of the candidates.*

TABLE 4.3   Participation in Political Discussions and Reading about Candidates, by Grade

Grade	ACTIVITY			
	Talked with parents about country's problems	Talked with parents about candidate	Talked with friends about candidate	Read about candidate
3	57	52	49	60
4	59	62	57	75
5	66	77	76	88
6	71	80	81	92
7	73	84	87	95
8	72	85	89	95

Source: Adapted from Hess and Torney, The Development of Political Attitudes in Children, *pp. 81, 100.*

in the 1960 presidential elections and only about one in seven were unconcerned about the outcome.[40]   Even in the third grade the vast majority was not indifferent to the Kennedy-Nixon contest. Though divisive conflict situations were strongly avoided, electoral contests were able to generate considerable emotional enthusiasm and interest.

Early participation also includes activities involving more commitment and effort than merely discussing politics and following the issues. As the data in Table 4.4 show, significant numbers of children

TABLE 4.4   Participation in Campaign Activities, by Grade

Grade	ACTIVITY	
	Wore a campaign button	Handed out buttons and handbills
3	44	22
4	46	21
5	57	22
6	62	26
7	65	29
8	63	27

Source: Adapted from Hess and Torney, The Development of Political Attitudes in Children, *p. 100.*

[40]Hess and Torney, *The Development of Political Attitudes in Children*, p. 101.

from third grade onward wore a campaign button, and by eighth grade, more than a quarter were behaviorally participating in electoral conflict.

Though these figures, especially when compared to those in Table 4.3 may not suggest great activism, they indicate considerably greater activism than among adults. Survey Research Center data collected during the 1960 election (the election closest to Hess and Torney's study) show that only 21 percent of the adult population wore a campaign button or put a campaign sticker on their car, while only 12 percent participated in some campaign activity.[41] Assuming for the moment that these children are not dishonest or merely responding to the socially desirable alternative of political activity, these discrepancies are suggestive. One possibility is that since children in the early 1960's were more disposed to activism than adults, subsequent adult participation rates will thus change as these children mature. Another possibility, however, is that many adults are resocialized away from the participatory habits acquired earlier in life. Perhaps due to more pressing demands of job and family, or maybe to increased cynicism resulting from exposure to political reality, the adult is more passive than the child. Other explanations are also possible, but the limitations of our data preclude anything more than this brief mention of various possibilities.

Our analysis thus far has focused largely on election-related participation. Politics is, however, much broader than voting and paying attention. Politics, broadly defined, occurs everywhere—in schools, on the job, in private clubs, and wherever decisions are made. Hence, our analysis of preadult political participation must be extended to include areas of experience not directly related to formal government. We must ask whether Americans gain experience early in life in making decisions directly affecting them in areas outside of electoral politics. Such experience is important not only for the particular social sphere in which it occurs, but also to the extent that it spills over into other areas of life. That is, a general predisposition to participate may be fostered by home, school, and job experiences. Moreover, skills and habits acquired influencing school or family decisions can be applied to influencing government decisions. Early political experience can be acquired in many areas of social life but we shall consider the two that are undoubtedly the most important—the family and the school.

[41]For a fuller description of adult political activity see Robert Weissberg, "The Political Activity of American and Democratic Citizenship," in *American Democracy: Theory and Reality,* eds. Robert Weissberg and Mark V. Nadel (New York: John Wiley & Sons, Inc., 1972).

Family Participation

The idea that early experience with family authority is ultimately generalized to behavior with political authority is not new. Many a theorist has argued that individuals seek congruence between parental and political interactions.[42] This reasoning easily leads to assertions that democratic government ultimately begins in democratically structured families or, alternatively, that autocratic government is rooted in authoritarian family structures. Our goal here is not to analyze the family's impact on the political system, but to ask whether Americans frequently participate in their early family decisions, and thus gain participatory experiences and habits. Table 4.5 presents data on the degree of family participation among a national sample of high school seniors.

Analyses of family authority patterns are frequently formulated in terms of either a democratic model where the child is actively and meaningfully involved in decision-making and an autocratic model characterized by passive obedience to authority. Judged by these hypothetical standards it seems that most of these adolescents live in family environments falling somewhere between these two extremes. It certainly is not true that most children are socialized into a seen but not heard role. Nor are these adolescents, despite some popular imagery of all young adults running wild, continually engaged in resisting and questioning parental authority.[43] It is significant that the vast majority of respondents have, at least on occasion, asserted themselves in family decision-making. It is a long way from complaining to Pop about one's allowance to influencing governmental tax policy, but such family involvement is undoubtedly a necessary beginning in acquiring the skills and confidence needed for adult behavior.[44]

School Participation

Another important area replete with participatory opportunities is the school. Like the family, the school environment can be viewed as a miniature political system in which learned relationship to authority

[42]See, for example, Harry Eckstein, *A Theory of Stable Democracy*, Research Monograph No. 10, Princeton University, Woodrow Wilson School of Public and International Affairs, Center for International Studies, 1961.

[43]See note 37 above on the question of adolescent rebellion.

[44]The participatory habits from one's family to the larger political system is much more complex than indicated in our analysis. Though complex, evidence does suggest that there is some transfer from one environment to the other. This question is further developed in Almond and Verba, *The Civic Culture*, particularly pp. 346–68.

may eventually be generalized to the larger political system. Also like the family, the school environment is a complex web of formal and informal relationships providing ample opportunities for student involvement in political decision-making. As in our analysis of family environments, we must be selective in analyzing school participation since everything from kindergarten rhythm band leader elections to collective decision-making on the high school football team cannot possibly be examined. Instead, our focus limits itself to participation in high school elections and interaction with teachers.

School elections are a ubiquitous phenomenon in American schools. Particularly at the high school level where student body president, student council members, and club and organization leaders are selected, school elections can closely approximate adult politics. To be sure, many of these elections are meaningless charades contested between officially sanctioned goodie-goodie candidates, but even these provide rich opportunities for practical political experience. The extent

TABLE 4.5   Adolescent Involvement in Family Authority Patterns

How much influence do you feel you have in family decisions affecting yourself?	
Much influence	48
Some influence	48
None	4
	100%
If a decision is made that you don't like, do you feel free to complain?	
Feel free to complain	71
Feel uneasy about complaining	15
Better not complain	14
	100%
If you do complain, does it help?	
A lot	17
Some	69
None	14
	100%
Do you ever actually complain?	
Often	14
Once in a while	82
Never	4
	100%

Source: M. Kent Jennings, The Student-Parent Socialization Study, *ICPR edition code book (1971), variables 184–87. Data made available through the Inter-University Consortium for Political Research.*

of student involvement in these school related elections is shown by the data in Table 4.6.

As we might expect given our earlier discussion of voting norms, turnout is remarkably high. Indeed, the figures in Table 4.6a compare extremely well to the usual 60 percent presidential voting turnout among adults. Perhaps even more striking is the number of students who have run for political office (Table 4.6b). Over 40 percent of these respondents had run for some school office, which contrasts with an almost miniscule proportion of the adult population who ever runs for political office. Even among those who had not run (Table 4.6c) a substantial number had at least been active in a political campaign. Put another way, only about 29 percent of these respondents resisted the urge either to run for office or campaign for someone else.

In the same way that adult political participation is not restricted to voting and elections, school political activity need not be limited to elections. School politics could certainly include curriculum decisions, the hiring and firing of teachers, the administration of sports teams, and the collective settlement of grievances as well as electing the prom

TABLE 4.6   Participation in High School Electoral Activity

(a) Have you ever voted in school elections (asked only of those in schools where elections held)?

Voted in most elections	93%
Voted in some elections	4%
Voted rarely	2%
Voted, don't know how often	.05%
Did not vote	.05%
	100%

(b) Have you ever run for elected office in school or out of school in the last three years?

YES, school	28%
YES, outside of school	13%
YES, both	14%
NO	45%
	100%

(c) Have you ever helped anyone running for office in the last three years (asked of those who did not run for office)?

YES	35%
NO	65%
	100%

Source: M. Kent Jennings, The Student-Parent Socialization Study, *variables 38, 40, 42. Data made available through the Inter-University Consortium for Political Research.*

TABLE 4.7   Remembered Involvement in School Decisions*

NATURE OF INVOLVEMENT

Felt free to protest unfair treatment from teachers	Actually discussed unfair treatment with teacher	Participated in classroom discussion
45	46	40

* Note — unlike our previous data, these figures are based on recollection of adults, not respondents currently in school. Given all the problems of recalling past experiences accurately, these data should be treated cautiously.
Source: The Civic Culture: Political Attitudes and Democracy in Five Nations by *Gabriel A. Almond and Sidney Verba (copyright © 1963 by Princeton University Press), published for the Center of International Studies, 332-33. Reprinted by permission of Princeton University Press.*

king. Such activities are nonpolitical only if we narrowly limit politics to selecting formal positions of elected authority. We must also realize that participation in such decisions (e.g., the choice of curriculum) is obviously of greater consequence than electing the class president. Do adolescents acquire participatory habits and competence in decision-making areas much closer to their daily lives in addition to electoral experience? Table 4.7 presents data on student involvement in school decision-making.

If one of the goals of American education is to give students democratic experience in decision-making, these data indicate only limited, though far from minimal, success in achieving this goal. Perhaps most surprising is that only 45 percent actually *felt* free to object to their treatment from teachers.[45] More recent high school data confirm the inaccuracy of the image of contemporary students actively expressing

[45]Nevertheless, though the figures for the United States may appear to be low, they are much higher than in other nations studied by Almond and Verba. The comparable figures in four other nations are:

Nature of Involvement

Nation	Felt free to protest unfair treatment from teacher	Actually discussed unfair treatment with teacher	Participated in classroom discussion
Great Britian	35	36	16
Germany	34	30	12
Italy	29	32	11
Mexico	40	38	15

Source: *The Civic Culture: Political Attitudes and Democracy in Five Nations* by Gabriel A. Almond and Sidney Verba (copyright © 1963 by Princeton University Press), published for the Center of International Studies, 332–33. Reprinted by permission of Princeton University Press.

their dissatisfaction with their school experience. Jennings in 1965 found that among high school seniors only about a third thought teachers treated them unfairly. Within this minority claiming unfair treatment, 44 percent never voiced a complaint (and about half of those who did complain said it didn't do any good).[46] American schools deviously do not straightjacket their students, but it is also clear that neither are they hotbeds of dissatisfaction inculcating the habits of political activism. Schools provide important participatory experiences, but these become more infrequent as we move from electioneering toward more important areas.

CONCLUSIONS

We begin our analysis with the question: what participatory options are available to Americans as a consequence of their early political socialization? Of the full range of possibilities, our concern was for the likely choices.

A detailed review of our numerous findings is not necessary to make it clear that American political activism is strongly biased in the direction of electoral participation. It is not so much that other forms of participation are unknown or prohibited, but rather they are viewed as less natural and less necessary. Whether we examine expectations of ideal citizen behavior, preadult political involvement, or school politics, it becomes perfectly obvious that once we move beyond voting and elections we enter a behavioral void. It thus should come as no surprise that efforts to motivate citizens away from voting and into additional forms of activism are largely unsuccessful.[47] Compared to other countries where the appropriate behavior is apathetic acceptance of the futility of any political action, this support for elections is hardly insig-

[46]Jennings, *The Student-Parent Socialization Study*, variables 31 and 32. It should be noted that 56 percent of these respondents claimed to be an officer or committee chairman of a school organization. Though such activism has obvious political potential, it is unclear whether such experiences do effect participatory orientations.

[47]The unwillingness of adults to tolerate or engage in "deviant" forms of political activity even when such activities are perfectly legal has been well documented. For example, Verba and Brody's spring 1967 study indicated that only about one half of one percent of the population took part in a demonstration. Recall that this was during the height of anti-Vietnam War activity. See Sidney Verba and Richard Brody, "Participation, Policy Preferences, and the War in Vietnam." *Public Opinion Quarterly* 34 (1970), 330. Moreover, according to polls taken by the Survey Research Center in 1968 only about 15 percent of the population would approve of someone who went to jail rather than obey an unjust law. Finally, the difficulty of going beyond voting is evident on something as simple as trying to influence local government—Almond and Verba's 1959 study shows that the vast majority of citizens have never even attempted this task. Almond and Verba, *The Civic Culture*, p. 188.

nificant. Nevertheless, we should remember that election-related participation is only one of a large number of possibilities for affecting government policy.

The political socialization process also limits the quality of election-related activity. Our evidence suggests that few Americans are prepared for a vigorously fought campaign between sharply differing candidates, each basing his appeals on complex, detailed issue positions. Given their inability to face divisive political conflict and problems in analyzing all but the simplest of messages, most citizens would find such a situation both psychologically intolerable and intellectually bewildering. Despite the existence of major social problems requiring complex solutions, most citizens are trained to prefer exciting, but not too meaningful, contests among alternatives that demand little serious analytical effort to comprehend. Participation, to a significant extent, becomes more symbolic than instrumental.

Our analysis so far may give the impression that in some form or fashion existing socialization for participation is defective. Nothing of the sort is intended. If one's objective is total citizen involvement in every public decision, then current socialization practices are defective since they are obviously not meeting this stringent requirement. These same practices are also defective if one's goal is complete apathy, for it is equally clear that most Americans are socialized in the direction of some participation. What we have argued is simply that of all the possible ways of participating in political decisions, Americans by virtue of their socialization gravitate to only a handful of possibilities.[48] Whether these available opinions are good or bad, desirable or undesirable, is a question that we shall defer for the time being.

---

[48]A related issue that should be noted concerns the options thus available to political authorities. Early learning not only foreclosed certain individual choices, but as a consequence opens and closes possibilities to the government. For example, given the focus on electoral participation rather than bureaucratic involvement, public officials probably have many more policy options available to them in the area of administrative decision making. Also consider the range of alternatives open to corporate managers so long as the public views these areas as effectively beyond direct public participation.

5

Group Differences in Participatory Socialization

So far we have shown that by the time Americans are old enough to vote, most participation options are effectively closed. From a wide range of behavioral possibilities only a relatively few survive as reasonable. It is also clear that not all citizens are socialized the same way. Regardless of our measures, whether the attitude or behavior is simple or complex, a range of learning exists. Most future citizens are socialized to accept a comparatively moderate level of participation (especially electoral involvement), but this general description does not apply equally well to all citizens. The nature and social distribution of differences in these participatory options will be our focus in this chapter.

Understanding the significance of variations in participatory options first requires that we recognize the importance of political activity in the attainment of individual and group goals. The essence of politics is conflict over goals, and while active engagement in this

conflict does not by itself guarantee success, it is undoubtedly a necessary condition for success. Unless one lives in a totally unselfish and
altruistic society, the wages of apathy are political defeat. Indeed, one
of the most potent weapons in political struggle is denying one's opponents entrance into the struggle. The historical repression of the Southern Negro is perhaps the best known, but far from the only, example
of disastrous political defeats suffered by a group who did not engage
in politics and lost, but never even took part in the game.

Our approach to variations in participatory socialization focuses
on the training received by children within different social groups. The
chances of specific individuals winning and losing in politics are
affected by their socialization, but it is clearly impossible to consider
the fate of millions of separate *individuals.* We ask instead whether
distinctive *groups* are educated to strive actively to achieve valued
ends. The political system is viewed as continual conflicts between
interests, some of which are embodied in social groups. Among the
relevant resources are the willingness and capacity to fight for one's
goals. Numerous social divisions exist in American society, but we
shall consider only three: social class, race, and sex.[1] We want to know
whether working-class and middle-class citizens, blacks and whites,
men and women, are socialized to be unequal contestants in the political struggle. Let us begin with one of the social divisions that has
received perhaps the greatest scholarly attention: social class.

SOCIAL CLASS

That rich people and poor people have fundamentally different
interests, and that political conflict thus revolves around class conflict,
is an ancient idea. The best known proponent of this view of political
conflict was Karl Marx. For Marx, all social life, from fine arts to
politics, was based on social class; and the history of society was the
history of one class struggling against the other. In modern industrial
society this conflict is expressed in the battle between the workers and
the bourgeoisie and thus on each and every issue there is a workers and
capitalist position.

[1]The number of possible relevant groups is infinite. One could perhaps even envi-
sion group conflict between fat and thin people, tall and short people, or even between
blond haired and brown haired people. Political conflict between smokers and non-
smokers has even occurred over airline seating arrangements. Some traditional social
(and sometimes political) distinctions we are not considering are: religion, ethnicity,
region, size of residence, and age. Our decision to exclude these groups reflects either a
general lack of data on these social groups, e.g., ethnicity, or a relatively limited political
impact of the social criteria, e.g., religion.

This picture of class polarization and hostility is obviously an exaggerated description of American society. We have seen already that in such fundamental issues as the persistence of the existing political community and political institutions social class differences are negligible. Studies of adults also suggest that the notion of class war, the rich against the poor, is summarily rejected by almost every citizen.[2] Unless one accepts the extreme Marxist position of social class determining each and every preference, a lack of consistently strong class related conflicts should not be surprising. After all, what is the objectively correct class position on issues such as water pollution, school decentralization, or legalization of marijuana?

The lack of all-pervasive class cleavages should not mislead us into assuming a total absence of class conflict. Perhaps compared with other countries, differences between working- and middle-class people are less extreme in the United States, but government policy for businessmen, doctors, and teachers would not necessarily be best for blue collar workers or migrant farmers. Particularly in the area of economic policy, class related differences are large and deeply rooted. Numerous pollings of adult opinion show that poorer, less educated Americans show greater support for such liberal economic policies as unemployment insurance, government subsidized medical insurance, old age pensions, and many other so-called pocketbook issues.[3] If working-class citizens alone decided public policy, the government's economic policy would probably be far more socialistic than if middle-class citizens alone made the choices. Class differences also manifest themselves in tolerance of political dissent and nonconformity. Despite their economic liberalism, many less well-off Americans would be much quicker to suppress Communists, Nazis, anti-Vietnam war protestors, and other unpopular groups than their middle-class compatriots.[4] In short, at least in the areas of economic policy and civil liberties, class differences are significant enough that one group cannot rely on the other to take care of its interests: to the extent that lower-class people are incapable of active political involvement, they will likely be defeated.

[2]Lane, *Political Ideology* Chapter 8. A more general treatment of social class cleavages is found in Angus Campbell, *et al, The American Voter,* Chapter 13, and Richard Centers, *The Psychology of Social Class* (Princeton, N.J.: Princeton University Press, 1949).

[3]See, for example, Lloyd A. Free and Hadley Cantril, *The Political Beliefs of Americans* (New York: Simon and Schuster, 1968), Chap. 2; Herbert McCloskey, "Consensus and Ideology in American Politics," *American Political Science Review* 58 (1964), 361–82.

[4]Among others see John P. Robinson, "Public Reaction to Political Protest: Chicago 1968," *Public Opinion Quarterly* 34 (1970), pp. 1–10; Herbert McCloskey, "Consensus and Ideology in American Politics," *American Political Science Review* 58 (1964), pp. 361–82; and Seymour Martin Lipset, "Democracy and Working Class Authoritarianism," *American Sociological Review* 24 (1959), pp. 482–501.

Let us now consider whether working-class and middle-class children receive essentially the same training for participation. Do middle-class children have an advantage from the very beginning? Or, on the other hand, are adult variations in participation a function of adult experiences and resources?

Relationship to the Political System

In our general analysis of orientations toward the political system we found that many young citizens held views basically consistent with a paternalistic political relationship. That is, the authorities were so wise, good, and responsive that there might be little motivation for citizen involvement. Though the pattern is a general one, it is particularly evident among lower-class children. At each age level lower-class children lag behind their middle-class age cohorts in reaching political maturity. Thus, as a middle-class child begins depersonalizing and de-idealizing political authority, the lower-class child persists in his more naive and benevolent imagery.[5] Though some evidence suggests that eventually the lower-class child catches up, the lower-class child nevertheless spends a few extra years accepting the highly positive political images. Assuming that the longer something is accepted early in life, the more likely its persistence, this continuation of paternalistic orientations may be significant despite subsequent contrary learning.

Significant social class differences also exist in perceptions of the legal system. Young children almost uniformly perceive the law as absolute, unchanging, and inherently just; a similar pattern occurs in the emphasis on legal compliance as the mark of good citizenship. However, with increasing age, children tend to lose this image of laws as immutable dictates. This new understanding is disproportionately found among middle-class children who realize that laws can be changed, are sometimes unjust, and that discrepancies can exist between legal ideals and reality. Middle-class children also become less impressed with the policeman. Though most children acknowledge the policeman's power to punish, higher status children are comparatively less enamored of him personally and less convinced of his wide knowledge.[6] In short, while both working- and middle-class children are socialized to accept the law and its enforcer (the policeman) as givens, it is also clear that these are more flexible constraints to the middle-

---

[5]Fred I. Greenstein, *Children and Politics* (New Haven: Yale University Press, 1965), pp. 101–2; Robert D. Hess and Judith V. Torney, *The Development of Political Attitudes in Children,* (Garden City; N.Y.: Doubleday, 1968), pp. 154–59; David Easton and Jack Dennis, *Children in the Political System,* (New York: McGraw-Hill, 1969), pp. 343–53.

[6]Hess and Torney, *The Development of Political Attitudes in Children,* pp. 159–65. Also see Judith V. Torney, "Socialization of Attitudes Toward the Legal System," *Journal of Social Issues,* 27 (1971), 147.

class person who realizes not only that change is quite possible, but that actual legal implementation may not be perfect.

Social class differences also manifest themselves in perceptions of the political process. Our previous chapters indicated an overall tendency for children to view government in formal, mechanistic terms. Political decisions tend to be viewed as outcomes of institutional mechanisms (e.g., Congress passes the laws and the president signs them) rather than as results of bargaining and the play of interests. However, not every child receives the same message. Litt's analysis of ninth-graders in three Boston suburbs indicates that only in upper status communities do children learn to view the political process in nonformal, nonmechanistic terms.[7] For these children, but not for their lower-class counterparts, what happens in government is not too far removed from everyday life—people with different interests fight to get ahead by whatever means available. On the other hand, for many a lower-class adolescent the processes in government are probably beyond the realm of everyday, comprehensible experience; to him the passage of a law may be viewed as a semimysterious process requiring all kinds of esoteric technical information.

Finally, different pieces of evidence suggest that the middle-class child is more politicized, more sensitive and involved with the surrounding political system. Such involvement is manifested when young children select people they would like to emulate, or when they indicate how they would change the world. In each instance lower-class children are less likely to offer a politically oriented response.[8] Moreover, even though no socioeconomic differences exist in support for elections, higher status children react more strongly to events following an election.[9] This greater middle-class politicization is also evident in their inclination to attribute to candidates the desire to improve society, while lower-class children are more likely to emphasize the preservation of the status quo as a motivating goal.[10] Though hardly an avid politico, it is clear that the middle-class child is more "with it" politically than his lower-class age mate.

Participation-Related Norms and Attitudes

We have suggested previously that beliefs in the legitimacy and appropriateness of political participation are an important prerequisite

[7]Edgar Litt, "Civic Education, Community Norms, and Political Indoctrination," *American Sociological Review* 28 (1963), 69–75.

[8]Greenstein, *Children in Politics.* pp. 95–96, 99.

[9]Hess and Torney, *The Development of Political Attitudes in Children,* p. 193.

[10]Hess and Torney, *The Development of Political Attitudes in Children,* p. 183.

TABLE 5.1   High School Seniors' Conceptions of "Good Citizens" by Parental Social Class

Attribute	Social Class*	
	Working Class	Middle Class
Supports the political system	31.1%	30.1%
Politically active	35.8	40.4
Participation in community affairs	11.2	9.5
Interpersonal and social behavior (helps others, is considerate, neighborly)	9.5	8.5
Moral and ethical traits (honest, religious, fair)	7.4	7.4
Other personal attributes (concerned about family and job, works hard)	4.1	3.7
Miscellaneous, don't know	.9	.4
	100.0%	100.0%

* The dividing line between working- and middle-class students was their father's education. Those whose father had graduated from high school or better were defined as middle-class. *Source: Jennings,* The Student-Parent Socialization Study, *variable 119. Data made available through the Inter-University Consortium for Political Research.*

166915

for future activity. Considering our findings thus far, we unexpectedly find no social class differences in support for the norm of active involvement. During grade school years and by the end of high school, children from lower-class homes do not believe that political activism is more suited to their socioeconomic betters. Both Greenstein in his New Haven study and Jennings in his national study find no socioeconomic difference in willingness to participate in adult politics.[11]

The lack of class-related variations in acceptance of participatory norms is further evidenced in high school seniors' conceptions of what traits characterize a good citizen. In Table 5.1 we see that while a minority of both middle- or working-class children see political activism as the primary trait of a virtuous citizen, their perceptions are on the whole quite similar. The differences of less than 5 percent supporting political activism certainly do not suggest a picture of middle-class children being socialized to view politics as their prerogative, while lower-class children accept passive obedience as their appropriate role. This is not to say, of course, that middle- and working-class children will eventually play the same political roles (our previous discussion

[11]Greenstein, *Children and Politics*, p. 100; Jennings, *The Student-Parent Socialization Study*, variable 211.

has already suggested the contrary), but rather, whatever participation differences that do emerge are not reinforced by norms of appropriate behavior.

Political Awareness and Participatory Skills

The normative support for political activism, though important, is only one factor affecting future behavior. Without the necessary skills and dispositions the ideal of participation remains only an ideal. We must in addition ask whether working- and middle-class children are equally educated to be competent political activists. Let us first consider the acquisition of political information.

A crucial function of eary formal education is to convey basic facts about the political system. Since state law typically requires that such factual information be taught to all students in a particular grade, it is not surprising that social class differences in this learning are nonexistent.[12] However, higher status children acquire a better understanding of the *informal* aspects of politics. The higher status child, who likely comes from a more sophisticated and politicized family, surpasses the lower status child in his knowledge of the more controversial, but politically highly useful inside dope. For example, Sigel reports that higher status Detroit children were better able to recall numerous political rather than personal aspects of President Kennedy's administration. Middle-class children were also considerably more likely to suggest that Kennedy would be best remembered by adopting the policies he advocated.[13] As Greenstein suggests, the school's unwillingness to venture beyond uncontroversial description undoubtedly handicaps working-class children who, because of their family's lack of sophisticated knowledge, are more dependent on the classroom as a source of political information.[14]

With maturation, even the equality in formal knowledge seems to disappear. By age seventeen middle-class adolescents are significantly better informed than working-class preadults on many of the elementary facts of political life. For example, Jennings found that while the level of information on such questions as the length of a United States senator's term, the number of Supreme Court justices, and the partisan identity of Franklin Roosevelt is generally not high, middle-class high school seniors are better informed on these and similar areas.[15] Given

[12]Greenstein, *Children and Politics,* pp. 97–98.

[13]Sigel, "Image of a President: Some Insights into the Political Views of School Children," *American Political Science Review* 62 (1968), p. 222.

[14]Greenstein, *Children and Politics,* pp. 98–100.

[15]Jennings, *The Student-Parent Socialization Study,* variables 222–26.

the uncomplicated nature of such information, and the almost universal exposure to these facts, we can only surmise that middle-class children somehow acquire a greater motivation to learn these facts. That is, the higher status adolescent is more likely to find such items as the length of a senator's term relevant and worth knowing. This explanation receives support from Hess and Torney's finding of no social class-related differences in interest in current events, but significant differences in family reinforcement of this behavior.[16] Thus, without reinforcement for his political learning, the lower-class child soon loses interest in being well-informed.

When we examine more sophisticated political thinking, class related differences appear with regularity. Even among politically unsophisticated grade school children, middle-class children show a greater capacity for more complex reasoning and evaluation. In the acquisition of partisan identification, although no major class difference exists in the tendency to adopt a partisan loyalty, the middle-class child's party identification is better grounded in information and issue position.[17] No child, regardless of social class, makes his partisan choice perfectly rationally; but at least the middle-class child is able to offer more informed and realistic justifications for his decision. This greater sophistication is also reflected in differing abilities to use partisan identity as an evaluative criterion. When asked to evalute candidates and policies, the middle-class child is more likely to use his partisan affiliation as the basis for judgment, whereas the lower-class child has greater problems connecting his general loyalty to political specifics.[18]

Not surprisingly, we find strong social class-related differences in the capacity to associate abstract ideological labels with political parties. As the data in Table 5.2 indicate, the lower-class adolescent is less likely to be sophisticated enough to place the two parties in an ideological context. Only 17.1 percent of the working-class versus 29.1 percent of the middle-class adolescents correctly associate both parties with some broad ideological perspective. A relatively large number of working-class students (43.0 percent) cannot see any differences between the Democrats and Republicans. As was the case in political knowledge, while political sophistication is not extensive, whatever there is is disproportionately found among middle-class preadults. Hence, even if participation levels were identical, the middle class's greater knowledge and sophistication might still give it the advantage.

[16]Hess and Torney, *The Development of Political Attitudes in Children,* pp. 174–76.
[17]Greenstein, *Children and Politics,* pp. 95–96.
[18]Greenstein, *Children and Politics,* p. 96.

TABLE 5.2 Ideological Perceptions of Political Parties among High School Seniors, by Parental Social Class

	Social Class	
Perceptions of Party Differences:	Working Class	Middle Class
Accurate, broad definition (correctly matches ideological labels "liberal" and "conservative" to party and can provide broad, abstract meaning to ideological concept)	17.1	29.1
Accurate, narrow definition (correctly matches party and ideological label but can only offer narrow, e.g. spend more money, meaning to ideological concept)	9.7	10.7
Some Error (cannot match party and ideological concept)	13.5	12.8
No definition of ideological terms	15.4	14.6
No difference between parties	43.0	30.9
Don't know, no answer	1.3	1.8
	100.0%	99.9%

Source: Jennings, Student Parent Socialization Study, *variable 317. Data made available through the Inter-University Consortium for Political Research.*

The socialization process provides the middle-class child with other participation related advantages. The greater ability to perceive partisan ideological differences is only one aspect of a more general class-related difference in intellectual abilities. Considerable evidence indicates that middle-class parents provide home environments more conducive to intellectual development and this emphasis frequently results in higher school grades, higher test scores, and a greater desire to employ intellectual skills.[19] Given the complexity of contemporary political life, and the requisite analytical skills necessary to success, these general cognitive abilities are highly relevant to efficient political participation. Without such skills, regardless of the supporting norms and motivations, one's behavior will undoubtedly be less than successful.[20]

The middle-class family environment is also politically relevant in

[19]Much of this evidence is discussed in Greenstein, *Children and Politics,* pp. 90–91.

[20]A closely related question here is class difference in intelligence (at least as measured by standard I.Q. tests). It should be obvious that existing socialization practices that apparently provide an intelligence advantage to middle-class children also, though perhaps unintentionally, provide a political advantage as well.

encouraging a less fatalistic orientation toward events. The middle-class parent is more likely to treat the child's opinions seriously and to be more accommodating to the child's individuality, which in turn results in greater feelings of self-confidence and efficacy for the child.[21] Thus, compared to a working-class child, the middle-class youngster sees politics as more amenable to autonomous choice and change. Politics is not something like the weather that just seems to happen, but it can be manipulated to conform to one's desires. It is significant that these social class differences in feelings of political capacity are large even in early childhood, and that they increase with age.[22] The middle-class child also seems to acquire a greater confidence in his own judgment and standards. For example, Greenstein reports that when asked whose advice they would seek when voting, middle-class children volunteered that they would make their *own* choice. Lower-class children, on the other hand, lacking this political self-assurance, displayed greater deference to their teacher's advice.[23]

Finally, the middle-class family also encourages a capacity to delay immediate gratification for the sake of longer-range goals. This capacity for future-oriented behavior is not only highly relevant to economic planning, but insofar as most political action requires foresight and planning, it is also a helpful political orientation.[24] It is difficult to imagine effective political action in all but the most extreme circumstances if each action were taken on an immediate *ad hoc* basis without concern for future consequences. In short, the middle-class home environment with its fostering of cognitive skills, feelings of self-confidence and efficacy, and futuristic orientation produces a citizen better able to cope with political life.

Preadult Political Activity

As we suggested in the previous chapter, preadult political activeness not only can have direct political consequences, but even when it is mock participation, it provides valuable experience for future behavior. Given our findings thus far on social class differences, we expect that the lower participation rates characteristic of working-class adults

[21]On the consequences of working- and middle-class family practices, see Melvin L. Kohn, "Social Class and Parent-Child Relationships: An Interpretation," *American Journal of Sociology,* 68 (1963), pp. 471–80; George Psathas, "Ethnicity Social Class, and Adolescent Independence from Parental Control," *American Sociological Review* 22 (1957), pp. 415–23.

[22]Hess and Torney, *The Development of Political Attitudes in Children,* p. 177: David Easton and Jack Dennis, "The Child's Acquisition of Regime Norms: Political Efficacy," *American Political Science Review* 61 (1967), pp. 25–38.

[23]Greenstein, *Children and Politics,* p. 103.

[24]Greenstein, *Children and Politics,* p. 93.

emerge relatively early among children. On the whole, this pattern of differential activity does exist, though stronger in some activities than others.

Hess and Torney find that higher status children are significantly more likely to engage in political discussions with their parents and friends. Moreover, this social class difference emerges as early as grades three and four, suggesting that these tendencies may be deeply rooted in early socialization practices.[25] Data on the propensity of high school seniors to engage in political conversations with their family and friends confirm the tenacity of this class difference.[26] Similarly, lower status children are also less likely to engage in campaign activities such as wearing campaign buttons or working for a candidate. Here again these class-related differences exist in early grades, though the gap does not increase with maturity.[27] Greater middle-class political activism is further indicated in consumption of political messages in the mass media. Except in their use of television, lower-class adolescents are not as likely as middle-class adolescents to seek out political information in newspapers, the radio, and magazines.[28]

When we extend political activism to include high school activities, the social class differences generally conform to the previous pattern. In Table 5.3 we see that only in voting in school elections are there no social class differences. When we examine more demanding activities such as running for office or campaigning, once again students from less well-off homes are less active.[29] Many lower-class students do, of course, have these political experiences, and in absolute numbers they may outnumber their middle-class schoolmates, but the middle-class head start on political success remains undeniable.

Finally, we also find middle-class preadults exercising greater political power within their families. To be sure, the data do not reveal the lower-class adolescent to be completely stifled in a hierarchical, authoritarian home atmosphere, while his middle-class counterpart runs family life; differences are a matter of degree rather than extremes. Middle-class adolescents are more likely to consider themselves influential in family decisions, to feel free to complain about

[25]Hess and Torney, *The Development of Political Attitudes in Children*, p. 178.

[26]Jennings, *The Student-Parent Socialization Study*, variables 141–42.

[27]Hess and Torney, *The Development of Political Attitudes in Children*, p. 189.

[28]Jennings, *The Parent-Student Socialization Study*, variables 128, 130, 134, 138.

[29]This pattern of greater middle-class involvement in school decision-making is not limited to the United States. In their study of Great Britain, Germany, Italy, and Mexico (in addition to the United States) Almond and Verba find a consistent tendency for better educated citizens to be more likely to discuss unfair treatment with their teachers and to participate in school discussions and debates. See Almond and Verba, *The Civic Culture*, p. 336.

TABLE 5.3 Participation in School Politics among High School Seniors, by Social Class

Voted in School Elections

	Working Class	Middle Class
Yes, most of time	93.3%	94.3%
Yes, some of time	3.2	2.7
Yes, but not much	2.4	1.9
Yes, don't recall how frequently	.5	.7
No	.5	.1
Don't know, not available	0.0	.1
	99.9%	99.8%

Ran for Office

	Working Class	Middle Class
Yes, school office	26.8%	29.7%
Yes, non-school office	10.0	15.3
Yes, both	11.4	15.9
No	51.7	39.0
Don't know, not available	0.0	.1
	99.9%	100.0%

Helped Others Run for Office (if they themselves had not run)

	Working Class	Middle Class
Yes	34.2%	37.1%
No	64.7	61.5
Don't know	2.1	2.4
	101.0%	101.0%

Source: Jennings, The Student-Parent Socialization Study, variables 38, 40, 42. Data made available through the Inter-University Consortium for Political Research.

their decisions, to feel that such complaints do help, and actually do complain more when necessary.[30]

RACE-RELATED DIFFERENCES

Compared with the long-standing concern by social scientists for class conflict, political conflicts among racial groups have received less attention. Nevertheless, at least in the United States, conflict between whites and blacks has been a continual, if sometimes subtle, phenomenon, though rarely have both racial groups been completely united. From the Civil War to the present, blacks have differed with many whites on such issues as voting rights, segregation in schools and public accommodations, representation in government, and economic equality, to mention only a few prominent issues.

Until relatively recently, blacks have fared unsuccessfully in these political goals. Excluding an occasional limited legal or symbolic victory, the majority of blacks have remained in an inferior political, social, and economic position in American society. The extensive violence and intimidation employed to insure the subservient position of blacks are well known (and as an occasional violent act still illustrates, the physical repression of black Americans is hardly a historical relic). Less obvious, but no less important, has been the long history of attempts to depoliticize black citizens and to socialize them to accept their inferior status as just and unchangeable. Critics of American society have frequently argued that the image of justifiable inferiority is conveyed to blacks almost daily from their earliest years. Together with overt physical coercion, the more subtle form of repression has historically barred blacks from competing politically on an equal basis with whites.

The question to be answered, then, is: Are black citizens still being socialized to be political losers? Is the participatory training received by young blacks similar to that received by whites, or, as in the past, is one group educated to rule, while the other is socialized to be ruled? We begin our analysis of racial differences with general orientations toward the political system.

Relationship to the Political System

One of the historical images of American blacks was the one of political powerlessness coupled with acquiescence and contentment. What made this combination possible was the black acceptance of paternalism—good treatment would flow from the benign and know-

---

[30]Jennings, *The Student-Parent Socialization Study*, variables 184–87. A similar, cross-national pattern is also reported in Almond and Verba, *The Civic Culture*, p. 335.

ledgeable white folk (provided, naturally, that blacks kept out of trouble and accepted their place). Government was akin to a big, benevolent father whose goodness and generosity were not subject to direct political pressure. Does this image have any contemporary validity? Do young blacks still look up to the government as the all-powerful, all-knowing provider?

Like lower-class white children, young blacks do display one aspect of a paternalistic mentality—a tendency to conceptualize the government in personal rather than institutional terms.[31] In each grade, young blacks are more likely to choose figures such as the president or the policeman rather than Congress as symbolic of the government. Even when we compare middle-class blacks with middle-class whites, we continue to find blacks more likely to personalize authority.[32] Eventually this tendency declines sharply among all groups, but vestiges of what was once typical of many blacks in the past linger on among young black children.

However, other indicators of paternalistic orientations fail to confirm this tendency. Though the pattern is not perfectly consistent, the evidence indicates that *both* blacks and whites responded similarly to questions on whether the government cares for us, is helpful, knows a lot, is powerful, and can be trusted.[33] Nor are young blacks very different from young whites when evaluating specific authority figures such as the president and the policeman. In both groups images are initially highly positive and then decline with age.[34] In short, if political apathy does exist among blacks, it cannot be attributed to a persistence of a paternalistic mentality that conceived of political goodies descending from the good, powerful (white) leaders.

Another important aspect of an individual's relationship to the political system involves an appreciation of the importance and consequences of politics. Certainly one of the surest methods of promoting apathy is to convince people that nothing in government really mat-

[31]Edward S. Greenberg, "Political Socialization to Support of the System" p. 121.

[32]Greenberg, "Political Socialization to Support of the System," p. 130.

[33]Greenberg, "Political Socialization to Support of the System," pp. 293–99.

[34]Greenberg, "Political Socialization to Support of the System," p. 315, 317. We are not, of course, suggesting that holding totally negative perceptions of the government and authority figures maximizes political participation. Involvement is probably the greatest where a balance exists between idealistic admiration and complete cynicism. In the former instance activism would be unnecessary; in the latter instance it would be useless. It also must be noted that adolescent data suggest that hostile attitudes toward the government and political leaders increase with age. However, this tendency is only moderate: adolescent blacks are not so overwhelmingly hostile that all activity, save perhaps revolutionary violence, would be perceived as pointless. See Schley R. Lyons, "The Political Socialization of Ghetto Children: Efficacy and Cynicism," *Journal of Politics* 32 (1970), 295, and Jennings, *The Student-Parent Socialization Study,* variables 156–60.

ters. Greenberg's study of children in Philadelphia indicates that, while white children are more likely to appreciate the importance of national, state, and local government, the majority of black children also acknowledge this relevance.[35]   Thus, we do not find, as we might among a sample of parochial peasants, a rejection of government as immaterial to one's life.

Participation Related Norms and Attitudes

It will be recalled that, while lower-class children are almost invariably socialized toward greater apathy than their middle-class counterparts, one of the few areas of equality is support for the norms of political involvement, particularly as expressed in voting and elections. A similar pattern also appears in comparisons across racial lines. Lyons, in his study of racial groups in Toledo schools, reports that both groups overwhelmingly express their intention to vote as adults.[36] Another study using high school students finds that blacks are even more likely than whites to assert their intention to play a highly active political role.[37]

We get a different picture, however, when we move away from reiteration of popular norms and probe deeper into the perception of blacks and whites of what constitutes good citizenship. In Table 5.4 we see the responses of blacks and whites when asked to describe a good American citizen. Compared to the social class differences on this question, these racial dissimilarities are substantial. It is particularly significant that twice as many whites as blacks (40.3 percent vs. 19.5 percent) define political activism as the trait of good citizenship. These 1965 data provide little conformation of an image of politically hyperconscious black youth. Nor do the data suggest that black activist tendencies are conceptualized in terms of community involvement—only 8.7 percent of these black students see the good citizen as one who is active in his community. If anything, Table 5.4 suggests that many of the civic virtues typically associated with "good" traditional blacks who knew their place—loyalty and good personal habits—still remain at least partially valid.[38]

---

[35]Greenberg, "Political Socialization to Support of the System," pp. 290–92.

[36]Lyons, "The Political Socialization of Ghetto Children," p. 292.

[37]Jennings, *The Student-Parent Socialization Study*, variable 211.

[38]This is not to argue that great changes in black political consciousness have not occurred. Data collected twenty years ago conceivably could have indicated that almost every black defined a good citizen as a loyal citizen. Thus, the data in Table 5.4 might depict a very dramatic change. Lacking such comparative data, we must limit our inferences to the present.

TABLE 5.4   High School Seniors' Conception of "Good Citizen," by Race

Attribute	Race White	Black
Supports the political system	29.0%	42.8%
Politically active	40.3	19.5
Participates in community affairs	10.6	8.7
Interpersonal and social behavior (helps others, is considerate, neighborly)	7.9	16.9
Moral and ethical traits (honest, religious, fair)	7.3	6.7
Other personal attributes (concerned about family and job, works hard)	4.1	5.4
Miscellaneous, don't know	.8	0.0
	100.0%	100.0%

Source: Jennings, The Student-Parent Socialization Study, *variable 119. Data made available through the Inter-University Consortium for Political Research.*

What might explain this greater emphasis on the less active aspects of citizenship? One possible explanation is that these blacks do not accept the more passive roles as legitimate for themselves, but are instead merely acknowledging the existence of certain political realities. That is, the average young black knows from his own experiences that the only real alternatives open to others are loyalty and nonpolitical behavior, so his response to the question is to describe reality, not state what ought to be the proper citizen role. The implicit assumption here is that the young black himself does not necessarily personally accept the passive role attributed to others. Unfortunately, the validity of these arguments cannot be directly tested with these particular data. What can be done is to explore further the young blacks' participatory socialization to see whether this explanation is corroborated by other data.

When we examine additional participation-related attitudes and beliefs, the evidence again tends to support the argument that blacks are socialized toward greater apathy. For example, numerous studies indicate that the sense of political efficacy—beliefs about one's impact on government—is stronger among young whites. Significantly, this social gap seems to increase with age, so that as more and more white children come to perceive the political system as amenable to their influence, fewer and fewer blacks share this view.[39] Moreover, these lower feelings of political efficacy seem to reflect a more general orientation to manipulating the government. Compared to whites, black children tend to be more fatalistic and more likely to see things happening to them than to see themselves affecting events. This fatalistic orientation, moreover, is not merely a consequence of economic deprivation, for even when compared with white lower-class children, young blacks see themselves as less in control of their lives.[40] Such attitudes are obviously inconsistent with an active citizen role.

Political Awareness and Participatory Skills

That black children do not progress as rapidly as whites in the acquisition of information and scholastic performance is well documented. Even by first grade the average black is at a disadvantage and by high school the black student is typically over three grades behind as measured by standard achievement tests.[41] This gradual falling behind whites in academic performance is not without its political corollaries. For example, Laurence in her study of Sacramento, California children found that while there was no racial difference in factual knowledge at age eleven, within only a few years whites surpassed blacks.[42] By the senior year of high school (when many of the less knowledgeable blacks have probably dropped out), these racial differences have become very substantial.[43] Thus, even if blacks were as

[39]See Lyons, "Political Socialization of Ghetto Children," p. 294; Joan E. Laurence, "White Socialization: Black Reality," *Psychiatry* 30 (1970), 179; Jennings, *The Student-Parent Socialization Study*, variable 308. Here again it is reasonable to argue that black children better understand political reality—the government *is* in fact less responsive to their demands. Although this greater sensitivity to reality may be valid, it is nevertheless true that blacks are less likely to acquire attitudes fostering participation among adults. This question of reality testing is considered in much greater detail in Paul R. Abramson, "Political Efficacy and Political Trust Among Black Schoolchildren," *Journal of Politics* 34 (1972), 1243–77.

[40]Esther S. Battle and Julian Rotter, "Children's Feelings of Personal Control as Related to Social Class and Ethnic Groups," *Journal of Personality* 31 (1963), 482–90. Jennings, in *The Student-Parent Socialization Study*, variable 310 also finds substantial racial differences in ego strength with blacks having less confidence in their ability to affect the world. Similar results among black adults are reported in H. M. Lefcourt and G. W. Lading, "The American Negro: A Problem in Expectancies," *Journal of Personality and Social Psychology* 1 (1965), 377–80.

[41]The most systematic presentation of these developments is found in U.S. Department of Health, Education, and Welfare, *Equality of Educational Opportunity*, 1966 (The Coleman Report).

[42]Laurence, "White Socialization: Black Reality," pp. 178–79.

[43]Jennings, *The Student-Parent Socialization Study*, variables 221–26. An alternative argument is that while blacks are less knowledgeable about formal government (much of which may be irrelevant to their daily lives), they are more savvy about how things really operate in their community. Thus, they may not know their senator's name, but

willing as whites to be active politically, their lack of knowledge about government would prevent equally effective action through normal channels of political communication and influence.

Blacks also fare less well than whites when evaluating the ideological character of the Republican and Democratic parties. Recall that previous discussion of this ability indicated that the overall sophistication of perceptions was not very high. Even so, only three-quarters as many black as white high school seniors have some broad conception of the terms liberal and conservative and are able to associate these labels with the appropriate political party. Young blacks were also at a significant disadvantage in supplying almost any kind of definition of liberal and conservative.[44] To be sure, many young blacks know the word *liberal* and may regard it positively, but it is perhaps more a symbol for them rather than a concept conveying specific information.

Preadult Political Activity

Actual preadult political participation data present yet additional confirmation of this differential socialization. In analyzing racial differences in participatory training an important question involves the stage of development when such differences emerge. If racial differences manifested themselves very early in life, the implication is that changes must be made during early childhood (assuming that such changes are desired). Given the great difficulty of influencing numerous individual family units (as opposed to schools), the early emergence of black disadvantage would thus pose formidable problems for change. On the other hand, if black-white gaps evolved later in childhood, then not only would such learning be less deeply rooted, but it would be more amenable to change through school experiences. Table 5.5 reports the political activities of preadult whites and blacks in Sacramento, California. These data are further divided by age so we can see how far back this differential socialization emerges.

The data in Table 5.5 do not present a clear pattern. Among the youngest children, reports on the first three activities show no major differences between blacks and whites. On the other items, however, differences of between ten and twenty percentage points exist, with the

they know who really counts in local affairs. This may be true, and no doubt many young blacks would claim such inside information. Unfortunately, data are nonexistent on this interesting question; but even if blacks were much more informed about local covert matters, e.g., why laws are differentially enforced, this does not make their relative ignorance about more general political matters less significant. Whether a person knows about the mechanism of the national government or not, it still affects him and any attempt at influence requires some specific knowledge.

[44]Jennings, *The Student-Parent Socialization Study*, variable 317.

TABLE 5.5   Preadult Political Activity, by Race and Age

Political activity	Young (8-11)		Old (12-15)	
	White	Black	White	Black
Written letter to president	6%	7%	6%	9%
Helped a candidate campaign	10	12	18	14
Worn a campaign button	22	23	40	29
Talked with parent about candidate	49	30	65	41
Talked with friend about candidate	51	31	64	46
Talked with parents about our country's problems	57	47	69	47
Read about candidate in newspaper or magazine	54	43	70	52
Talked with parents or friend about Vietnam War	73	55	77	59
Watched the president on TV	80	70	74	65
Number of Respondents	404	100	396	60

Source: Adapted from Laurence, "White Socialization: Black Reality," p. 180. By permission of the publisher.

whites being more active in each instance. Within a few years this white advantage has increased somewhat. Only in the first two items are racial differences minor, and differences on the other questions have either increased or stayed about the same. On the whole, these findings thus suggest that (a) participatory propensities to a degree have their origins in early childhood (before age eight); but also that (b) subsequent socialization in the direction of racial equalization would probably require a continuous effort rather than intervention at only one stage of development.

Our analysis becomes more complex when we consider racial differences in school political participation. Our discussion thus far leads us to predict greater apathy among blacks in school politics. In some activities this is true, but in other, and perhaps more significant behaviors, the reverse is the case. Black high school seniors are more passive than their white classmates in complaining to teachers about perceived unfair treatment. Nor are blacks as regular in their school voting habits as whites, though only a handful of blacks completely abstain. However, when it comes to the more demanding activities of running for office or helping others run for school office, black students are every bit as active (if not more so) than whites.[45]   Perhaps this equality merely reflects the fact that when these data were collected in

[45]Jennings, *The Student-Parent Socialization Study,* variables 38, 40, 42.

1965 many blacks attended virtually all black schools where every candidate for school office would be black. Or, alternatively, perhaps the very nature of high school politics—symbolic offices with little actual power, adult supervision to keep things under control, the lack of overt repression, and the general norm of taking part in one's own government—minimizes the factors hindering greater black participation in the larger political system. In any case, what is important here is that at least in one area—high school student politics—blacks obtain socializing experience equal to those of whites.

SEX-RELATED DIFFERENCES

Social class and racial conflict have been an integral part of American politics, but only recently has the idea of political division between males and females been seriously considered. Largely female political movements, e.g. the suffragettes and the temperance movement, are well known, but these groups never advanced a women versus men political program. Universal suffrage and abstinence from alcohol were for everyone, not merely females; these positions just happened to be largely advocated by women. Today, some militant feminists make a very different argument. For them, certain political conflicts are struggles between men and women, where one's victory is the other's defeat. Laws making women unequal marriage partners or prohibiting them from certain occupations, as well as many other limiting social structures, are now considered the battleground in which women pit their energies against men.

This vision of political war between the sexes is not universally accepted. It can be argued that political differences between males and females are secondary to more fundamental racial and economic divisions. Sexual differences are thus politically no different from distinctions in hair color or height. To these arguments the militant feminist response is that people are so brainwashed to ignore sexual domination and subservience that, unlike economic and racial domination, these relationships are seen as natural and nonpolitical. Hence, the first step in political change is making people aware of the significant political nature of male/female relationships.

Whether American society is oblivious to the political dimension of male/female conflict, or whether such conflict is politically real, are difficult questions requiring lengthy analysis. Our concern is the simpler, but still relevant question of whether females are socialized out of political activity and into a passive women's role. Are women trained to be inferior political competitors, and hence inevitable losers regardless of whether the cause is feminist or not? Must the female role be pretty much limited to baking brownies and brewing coffee while the men handle the serious business? Or are women as well suited and well motivated for politics as men, but held back by outright discrimination?

Relationship to the Political System

Both scholarly and popular observers of American life have noted that despite some talk of the aggressive American female, women are generally confined to dependent, passive social roles. While young boys aspire to be doctors or airplane pilots, young girls are encouraged to be nurses or stewardesses. Even in children's games girls tend to be directed away from activities stressing assertive leadership, independence, and aggressive behavior. Almost all school classrooms and families emphasize compliance to constituted authority, but this message seems to be particularly more appropriate for young females.[46] Additional illustrations from almost every aspect of childhood could be found, but the point should be obvious that girls do not receive the kind of general socialization preparing them to take an aggressive stance towards authority.[47]

Given these overall dispositions, it is not surprising that young females hold a similar view of their relationship to the political system. Compared to young boys, young girls are likely to see authority figures like the president and the policeman as more powerful and able to punish. Significantly, this male/female difference in perception becomes more pronounced in subsequent grades.[48] In a rough sense the female relationship to political authority is like a family pattern in which the young daughter must always exhibit the proper deference to male leadership. It is interesting to note that this attribution of greater power to authority does not spill over into a more positive

[46]For example, Rosenberg and Smith find that boys in grades four to six prefer games emphasizing physical contact, dramatization of conflict between males roles, and complex team games. Girls choose games stressing dramatization of static behavior, verbal games, and ritualistic noncompetitive games. G. G. Rosenberg and B. Sutton Smith, "The Measurement of Masculinity and Femininity in Children," *Child Development* 30 (1959) 373–80. The evidence on greater female deference to authority suggests that this trait may emerge at around age fifteen rather than in early childhood. Perhaps it is only when female sexual identity becomes manifest that pressure is exerted to be feminine, i.e., dependent. See Elias Tuma and Normal Livson, "Family Socio-economic Status and Adolescent Attitudes Towards Authority," *Child Development* 31 (1960), 387–99.

[47]Bardwick and Douvan in their survey of the literature on early sex differences report that girls are described by such traits as: dependence, passivity, fragility, nonaggression, noncompetitiveness, yieldingness, receptivity, and supportiveness. Boys, however, are characterized by: independence, aggression, competitiveness, assertiveness, courage, and confidence. Judith M. Bardwick and Elizabeth Douvan, "Ambivalence: The Socialization of Women," in *Women in a Sexist Society,* ed. Vivian Gornick and Barbara K. Moran (New York: New American Library, 1972), p. 225.

[48]Hess and Torney, *The Development of Political Attitudes in Children,* p. 208.

evaluation of government and its activities.[49] At least in this instance, a position of comparative weakness does not increase idolization of the strong.

The greater female acceptance of obedience and conformity to norms is also reflected in young girls' views of the legal system. Beginning in about sixth grade, girls are more likely to believe that all laws are fair and that the legal system is responsive to their needs. Moreover, girls view the policeman as more competent and would be less likely to complain to him if they received unfair treatment.[50] This political immaturity and greater dependence on big-father-like authority among young girls is also manifested in their greater emphasis on personal figures or protectors rather than impersonal and institutional structures.[51] While a young boy comes to realize that the laws governing his life are impersonal rules enforced by less than perfect authorities, girls are likelier to hold a more immature picture of presidents and policemen as closer to absolute monarchs than constitutional officers.

Another dimension of male/female relationship to the political system concerns the extent to which political roles are looked up to as worthy of emulation. Here again the evidence suggests that boys receive a greater push towards politics. For example, in his extensive review of studies in this area conducted as long ago as 1903, Hyman finds that boys consistently are more attuned to political figures and events.[52] This pattern was reconfirmed in 1958 by Greenstein who found that boys were more likely to mention political figures as people to be emulated. Similarly, Greenstein reports that when asked about a news story that interested them, boys were more likely than girls to recall a politically related experience. Boys were also more likely to respond politically when asked how they would change the world though this sex difference declines with age.[53] In other words, the perceptions of politics as a man's concern seem to emerge quite early in life.

Participation-Related Norms and Attitudes

When we examine attitudes surrounding voting and elections, our findings parallel those presented for socioeconomic and racial groups. Again we confirm the social pervasiveness of the American infatuation

---

[49]Hess and Torney, *The Development of Political Attitudes in Children*, p. 212.

[50]Hess and Torney, *The Development of Political Attitudes in Children*, pp. 207–8.

[51]Hess and Torney, *The Development of Political Attitudes in Children*, p. 205.

[52]Herbert H. Hyman, *Political Socialization*, pp. 22–24.

[53]Greenstein, *Children and Politics*, p. 117.

and respect for the electoral process. Young males and females are equally supportive of the legitimacy of voting and elections—virtually the identical proportions intend to vote when of age and believe elections are important.[54] Nevertheless, lying beneath this equality is another attitude that could conceivably undermine the achievement of equality of power or participation. The commonly noted phenomenon of wives voting their husband's choices does not appear to be a result of immediate adult circumstances; rather, it appears during childhood as another corollary of a "politics as men's business" mentality. Thus, Greenstein observes that while fourth-grade boys seek voting advice from fathers and girls tend to choose their mothers, with maturity girls become increasingly more likely to choose their fathers for political counsel.[55] Needless to say, such political deference is not calculated to bring success to women's political causes.

This greater dependency among young girls also emerges in conceptions of appropriate citizen roles. Among both sexes the emphasis on obedience to laws as the mark of the good citizen declines with age, but at every age level girls are more likely to stress this conception than boys.[56] While this gap remains constant during primary school, data from high school seniors suggests that this early training can be overcome. Specifically, Jennings found that girls are somewhat (40.9 percent versus 35.9 percent) more likely to define good citizenship in terms of political activism (no sex related differences existed in choosing loyalty as the defining trait).[57] This finding provides a vivid contrast to the responses of blacks (a group to which women are sometimes compared in terms of political power) who place much greater emphasis on loyalty. Why the earlier pattern seems to reverse itself is a question for which we have no answer. It does suggest, however, that early learning related to participation may change with maturity.

Another type of learning where female socialization is more conducive to apathy than activism is toleration of divisive conflict. Recall that acceptance of sharp opinion differences is an important prerequisite for meaningful, as opposed to purely perfunctory, participation. This tolerance, it will be remembered, was not widespread; but we now see that when it does exist, it is disproportionately found among males. When asked about partisan differences or political disagreements between people, boys are better able to recognize the necessity of such differences. Young girls also tend to place a greater emphasis on consensus rather than conflict as a goal of political parties.[58] Hence, while

[54]Greenstein, *Children and Politics,* p. 117. Also Hess and Torney, *The Development of Political Attitudes in Children,* p. 217.

[55]Greenstein, *Children and Politics,* p. 119.

[56]Hess and Torney, *The Development of Political Attitudes in Children,* p. 208.

[57]Jennings, *The Student-Parent Socialization Study,* variable 119.

[58]Hess and Torney, *The Development of Political Attitudes in Children,* pp. 217–18.

proportionately more boys accept the divisions and battles of politics, young females, consistent with their general socialization towards docility and niceness, are more likely to find such din and clamor upsetting and thus to be avoided.

Finally, when we analyze sex differences in sense of political efficacy we find a puzzling pattern. Contrary to our findings on social class and racial differences, at least from grades three through eight, political efficacy scores show no sex-related difference.[59] However, by the senior year of high school, and consistent with the adult pattern, males exhibit a greater sense of capacity to manipulate the political environment.[60] What makes this change interesting is that the nonpolitical corollary of political efficacy—ego-strength (self-confidence)—shows no sex-related differences among high school seniors. This is not the case among working-class and black adolescents, where efficacy and ego-strength differences parallel one another. It thus seems as if girls learn that their capacity to affect their environment, while no less than that of males, nevertheless does not extend equally to the political world. With increasing age girls come to realize that getting things done politically is more suited to men despite their own feelings of confidence and ability.

Political Knowledge and Skills

While blacks clearly lag behind whites, the lower-class children do substantially less well than middle-class children in intellectual and academic performance, sex-related differences are not nearly as sharp. Boys may excel in spatial and numerical abilities, but girls hold an edge in verbal ability and general academic achievement, and there seems to be no sex-related difference in intelligence.[61] Whatever advantages girls have in intellectual ability are not necessarily translated into political advantages.[62] Girls do not master the political world with the

[59]Easton and Dennis, "The Child's Acquisition of Regime Norms: Political Efficacy," p. 37.

[60]Jennings, *The Student-Parent Socialization Study,* variable 308. For comparative adult data, see Angus Campbell, Gerald Gurin, and Warren Miller, *The Voter Decides* (Evanston, Ill.: Row Peterson, 1954), p. 191.

[61]Eleanor E. Maccoby, "Sex Differences in Intellectual Functioning," in *The Development of Sex Differences* ed. Eleanor E. Maccoby (Stanford, Calif.: Stanford University Press, 1966), pp. 25–28.

[62]In fact, Bardwick and Douvan suggest that certain female cognitive advantages may be political liabilities rather than assets. Skills allowing girls to analyze and anticipate adult demands result in greater conformity to expectations of nonagression and obedience. Rather than being sensitive, sophisticated political analysts, girls instead show greater understanding of their appropriate subservient social position. See Bardwick and Douvan, "Ambivalence: The Socialization of Women," *Women in a Sexist Society,* p. 226.

same eagerness as they approach spelling, learning new words, and getting good grades. Thus, as early as fourth grade, boys are more informed about political matters.[63] Even by their senior year of high school, when virtually everyone has progressed through numerous required civics courses, boys continue to be more politically attuned.[64]

This greater male political competence also manifests itself in informal learning. For example, young boys claimed to know about the political parties at an earlier age and were better able to associate parties with issues. When asked whether one or the other party did a better job of keeping us out of war or helping the rich people, girls were more likely to answer that both parties were the same. This pattern was evident as early as fourth grade and remained constant until at least eighth grade.[65] Data from high school students further suggests that girls acquire a less sophisticated grasp of politics than do boys. While a quarter of the males (25.8 percent) in Jennings' sample could correctly associate the two parties with broad ideological positions, only a fifth (20.6 percent) of the females could perform this task. As in grade school, females were more likely to be unable to distinguish between the Democrats and Republicans.[66]

Though most of the differences in male/female political competence are not very large, their very existence is significant, since they indicate the possibility of socializing young citizens away from knowledgeable participation despite the lack of real differences of ability. One could argue that in the case of lower-class and black children comparative political incompetence is an inevitable corollary of their general socioeconomic position that also results in low academic motivation, poor grades, poorer verbal facility, and so on. Thus, if lower-class and black children were only made educational equals, equality in political socialization would soon follow. When we examine the education of American females, however, we see that comparable academic and intellectual ability does not necessarily lead to political equality. Obviously, it is one thing to possess the potential for sophisticated political activism and quite another to be motivated to employ these abilities.

Preadult Political Activity

Turning to actual political activity during childhood and adolescence, we find that in many areas sex-related differences are absent. When they do emerge, females are usually more apathetic than males.

[63]Greenstein, *Children and Politics*, p. 117.
[64]Jennings, *Student-Parent Socialization Study*, variables 221–26.
[65]Hess and Torney, *The Development of Political Attitudes in Children*, p. 218.
[66]Jennings, *Parent-Student Socialization Study*, variable 317.

For example, no sex-related differences are found in political discussions with friends and family, and girls are just as emotionally concerned about election outcomes. But, boys are more likely to take sides in these discussions and contests.[67] This pattern is consistent with our earlier observations that young girls avoid conflict situations.

Boys are also more active during grade school in various political campaign activities. Activities such as wearing election buttons, reading about candidates, and helping candidates, increased dramatically for both sexes between third and eighth grade; but at each age level boys were the more active. It may be significant that with increasing age reports of these behaviors converge so that by eighth grade sex-related differences are very small.[68]

The pattern of sex-related participation differences declining with age also receives further confirmation when we examine high school political activism. Jennings finds that girls are just as active as boys in school voting and running for office; and, in the case of helping the campaigns of others, they are more active than boys.[69] These findings recall parallel patterns among racial groups: despite numerous tendencies in the socialization process to discourage equal participation, the high school environment somehow managed to foster male-female equality. Furthermore, outside of school sex-related differences in the consumption of political messages in the mass media and political discussions with friends and family were either slight or nonexistent.[70]

Finally, and again contrary to the general pattern of differences, we find that adolescent boys enjoy no advantage in participation in family decision-making. Despite the tendency among females to show greater deference towards authority, female high school seniors are even more likely than males to claim considerable influence in family affairs. Nor are there any significant differences in willingness to complain about family decisions, the consequences of this complaining, or the frequency of these objections.[71] To be sure, inferences from these data must be treated cautiously since the methods employed by females may not be consistent by participation at the broader level (e.g. getting one's demands met by being very obedient to parental desires). Nevertheless, these and other data in this section should caution us from exaggerating the import of early socialization on limiting the political involvement of females.

[67]Hess and Torney, *The Development of Political Attitudes in Children,* pp. 215, 220.
[68]Hess and Torney, *The Development of Political Attitudes in Children,* p. 219.
[69]Jennings, *The Student-Parent Socialization Study,* variables 38, 40, 42.
[70]Jennings, *The Student-Parent Socialization Study,* variables 128, 130, 134, 141.
[71]Jennings, *The Student-Parent Socialization Study,* variables 185–87.

CONCLUSION

To anyone familiar with adult patterns of political participation, the overall results of our analysis should come as no surprise. Though the particular details vary from group to group, and in some instances the data are limited, it is nevertheless clear that lower-class children, black children, and young females are socialized to be handicapped in the political struggle. In many instances we can expect these groups not to lose by participating and being defeated, but rather by not participating in the conflict. Even when participation would be equal or nearly equal, differences in knowledge and sophistication provide an advantage to middle-class individuals, whites, and males.

At the same time, these group differences should not be exaggerated. Working-class individuals, blacks, and females are not permanently confined to political inertia while politics is run by the middle class, whites, and males. In the first place, the norm of political activism is virtually universal and shared by all the social groups we have examined. Regardless of what actually occurs in adult politics, no group rejects political activism as illegitimate or personally irrelevant. Second, many of the group differences are matters of degree, not polar opposites. For example, though whites are more likely than blacks to choose political activism as the trait of good citizenship, it is hardly the case that all whites select the trait and all blacks reject it. Rather, only a difference of about 20 percent exists between the two groups. Finally, exceptions do exist in many areas of participation related learning. Thus we find that both blacks and females were very active in high school politics and females equaled males in many important politically relevant intellectual abilities.

At a broader level our findings suggest that inequalities in existing patterns of political involvement must be considered more as a given than something that could be remedied by legalistic changes. To be sure, many formal barriers to equality of participation do exist, e.g., complicated registration systems, which may discourage working-class citizens, blacks, and females, but given inequalities in political socialization it is clear that removing these barriers will not produce instantaneous equality. Moreover, the extent to which differential participatory socialization occurs means that fundamental changes in this process must involve many diverse areas of learning. Put another way, the choices made on who to encourage and discourage politically are not readily changed. As much as one may find this biasing of participatory opportunities to be objectionable or a violation of the democratic spirit, this biasing is nevertheless an integral though frequently dimly perceived, part of the existing political system.

b

Support for
Democratic Values

Political systems vary not only in their basic institutions and levels of citizen participation, but also in their rules and customs governing decision-making. For example, in an absolute monarchy it is customary for a ruler to decide all political questions without popular consultation. On the other hand, an attempt at such behavior would be considered inappropriate under less authoritarian rules of governance. The range of acceptable decision-making rules, like institutional patterns and modes of participation, is virtually infinite. Of the hundreds of contemporary governments and the thousands existing in the past, probably no two shared the same rules guiding the business of politics. Even words such as theocracy, democracy, absolutism, oligarchy, and despotism typically employed to describe variations in decision-making processes cannot capture the full range of differences across systems.

Among all the alternative patterns of rules, one in particular is of special importance for us—democratic rules. We do not assume that merely because the present political system is usually characterized as democratic does it necessarily follow that most of its citizens are staunch democrats. Such might be the case, but it also could be that democratic institutions are foisted on an unwilling populace. Thus, our focus here will not be on how young Americans are socialized to be good citizens of a democracy, but rather on whether or not young children are educated to be future supporters of the democratic method. At the same time, we must realize that this approach studies dispositions of citizens, not the political system's actual operation. Just as we cannot assume that citizens of a functioning democracy are democratically oriented, so we must not conclude that a democratically oriented citizenry necessarily makes for a democratic system. A democratic system is probably much more likely where each and every citizen agrees with these principles, but the matter is much too complex to posit a one-to-one relationship between an overall quality of the political system and mass attitudes.

Our examination of the childhood development of democratic sentiments is divided into three sections. First, and most important, how extensive and deeply rooted is support for democratic principles among young Americans? Is it possible that despite the common assertion that we are a democratic nation, young children are socialized towards fascistic or antidemocratic values? The democratic faith includes many principles, but our analysis will focus on three major areas: (1) the right of free speech; (2) equality of political competition; and (3) freedom from government coercion without due process. The second section considers the social distribution of support for these democratic rules. For example, are children from well-off, high status families less committed to democratic values than those who perhaps have more to gain from these values? Are young blacks more sensitive to violations of political freedom than young whites? Our third question explores the emergence of a coherent, comprehensive democratic ideology among maturing children. Can children integrate the many principles of democracy into a general perspective, or do the many rules remain pretty much unrelated and applicable only to very specific situations if at all?

SUPPORT FOR DEMOCRATIC VALUES AND BELIEFS

The Right of Free Speech

The right to speak one's mind, regardless of the popularity of one's opinions, is perhaps the most fundamental of all democratic political rules. It is important not only for itself but also as a prerequisite for other democratic rights. We cannot imagine majority rule being anything more than a formal procedure unless all points of view can be presented freely. Nor would the right to participate in politics mean much if only a single, official version of the truth were allowable. Free speech can also be justified in more utilitarian terms. It can be argued that truth emerges in the marketplace of ideas and that the clamoring of ideas for attention necessarily involves noise and diversity of opinion. Attempts to stifle the babble of diverse opinion will thus not only mean political repression, but less-effective policy choices as well.

Despite these and other virtues, very few of even the most ardent democrats would advocate completely unrestricted freedom of speech. It is possible to *oppose* the right of someone to express himself and yet still remain a good democrat. Surely the screaming of fire in a crowded movie theatre or the publishing of national defense secrets would be hard to justify as within the bounds of free speech. The balance between such limitations and the right to express oneself has, of course, been actively debated both legally and informally for many years, but no single solution is universally accepted. Excluding perhaps the most restrictive interpreters of free speech, most analysts view such constraints as exceptions limited to specific situations. Unless it can be demonstrated clearly that the exercise of free speech is significantly injurious, free speech prevails. Hence, the good democrat only opposes the right of free speech when such injurious consequences are clearly beyond a reasonable doubt.

When we examine the development of children's support for this fundamental democratic value, the results are not completely encouraging. Even at the abstract general level, where we expect support to be virtually unanimous, the findings are mixed. Zellman and Sears, in their 1968 study of nine-through 14-year-old Sacramento, California children, report that while only 15 percent do not believe in free speech, only 60 percent fully support it.[1] This outright rejection, plus the quarter responding with "don't know," suggests that this right lacks the qualities of a self-evident, obviously true political value for many children. An even more dismal picture of democratic support is provided by Remmers's study of high school students in 1960—only 29 percent agree that "newspapers and magazines should be allowed to print anything they want except military secrets." Perhaps just as discouraging is that the same question asked in 1951 received greater

---

[1]Gail L. Zellman and David O. Sears, "Childhood Origins of Tolerance for Dissent," *Journal of Social Issues* 27 (1971), 117. The question was "I believe in free speech for all no matter what their views might be."

support (45 percent agreed).[2] If American youth is becoming progressively more enlightened, it is not evident in this question.

Turning the issue around to the toleration of censorship (rather than supporting free speech) produces an essentially similar pattern. Both in 1951 and 1960 Remmers finds that 60 percent of the interviewed high school students agreed that the police and other groups should have the right to censor books and movies. Likewise, 77 percent agreed that the Post Office should censor obscene materials.[3] This concern with obscenity, rather than political subversion, seems to be utmost in the minds of teenagers when they consider the free speech issue. The following are the reasons (and their popularity) given for censoring printed matter and movies (more than one choice was allowed so percentages sum to more than 100 percent):[4]

Sex-perversion, sexual promiscuity, pornography	63%
Irreligion, profanity, atheism	43
Political un-Americanism, radicalism	35
Violence—assault, sadism, gore	28
Should not be censored for any reason	15

This nonpolitical smut motivation in opposition to freedom of expression is perhaps ironic considering the clear political roots of constitutional guarantees of this right. Nevertheless, the relatively low degree of political motivation in desires for censorship may be of some consolation to those deploring these findings. Provided radical political books are not illustrated with naked bodies in sexually perverted poses, free political expression will probably not generate widespread calls for censorship. This conclusion may not be much of a consolation for those interpreting First Amendment guarantees as applicable to all areas of free speech.

Our discussion thus far has focused on general support for free speech without regard to what was advocated or by whom. A stronger test of this support comes when adherents of unpopular or immoral views avail themselves of this right. It requires little conviction to defend free expression of opinion when the speaker states agreeable or inoffensive opinions. Much more difficult, but also much more important, is the willingness to defend the rights of unpopular and offensive speakers to have their say. What happens when children are confronted by advocates of positions they oppose?

[2]H. H. Remmers and Richard D. Franklin, "Sweet Land of Liberty," in *Anti-Democratic Attitudes in the American Schools* (Evanston, Ill.: Northwestern University Press, 1963), p. 62.
[3]Remmers and Franklin, "Sweet Land of Liberty," *Anti-Democratic Attitudes in the American Schools*, p. 64.
[4]Remmers and Franklin, "Sweet Land of Liberty," p. 63.

TABLE 6.1 Support for Specific Applications of Free Speech Principle among Children 9-14 Years Old.

Question	Percent tolerant	Percent intolerant	Percent don't know	Total percent
"Should a Communist be allowed to make a speech in this city saying that Communism is good?"	21%	50%	29%	100%
"Should this man who wants to help the Vietcong be able to buy time on television to make a speech?"	28	54	18	100%
"Should the police give the head of the American Nazi Party permission to have a meeting on a street corner?"	13	65	22	100%

Source: Gail L. Zellman and David O. Sears, "Childhood Origins of Tolerance for Dissent," Journal of Social Issues, *27 (1971), p. 117. By permission of the publisher.*

At the most general level young children show a willingness to extend the right of free speech to supporters of unpopular causes. Seven of ten Sacramento, California, children agreed with the statement that "People who hate our way of life should still have a chance to talk and be heard." This enlightenment is not, however, extended to concrete situations.[5] As the data in Table 6.1 indicate, the principle of free speech seems only to be the right of free, acceptable speech.

One must wonder what unpopular groups these children have in mind when they agree with the general, abstract position on free expression for those hating our way of life. Moreover, these views do not appear to be immature opinions that will soon transform into more democratic sentiments, once the true nature of free speech is better understood. Though Zellman and Sears report some small increase in tolerance with age, the persistence of this intolerance is strongly suggested by other studies. For example, Remmers finds that only 18 percent of his 1960 sample of high school students would allow a Communist to speak on the radio even during peacetime.[6] Numerous adult studies conducted from the 1930s to the present tend to confirm further this unwillingness to allow Communists, Nazis, and other political

[5]Zellman and Sears, "Childhood Origins of Tolerance for Dissent," p. 118.
[6]Remmers and Franklin, "Sweet Land of Liberty," *Anti-Democratic Attitudes in the American Schools,* p. 66. On the other hand, Merelman reports a 16 percent increase in support for freedom of speech between sixth and twelfth grade in two California communities. However, Merelman's free speech questions all deal with free speech in the abstract, not specific applications. See Richard M. Merelman, *Political Socialization and Educational Climates,* (New York: Holt, Rinehart and Winston, 1971), p. 77.

radicals to express their views as openly as those glorifying the status quo.[7]

If there is one area in which considerable support for free expression does exist, it appears to be support for religious freedom. Perhaps due to our early civics courses that emphasize religious liberty as a basis for the founding of the American colonies, children develop a particular sensitivity to violations of religious expression. For example, 83 percent of the students in Remmers' study would not restrict by law religious beliefs and worship, and only 9 percent would favor such religious restrictions.[8] Jennings' study of high school seniors five years later finds that 86 percent of them would also not prohibit a speech against churches and religion.[9] These findings, which stand in sharp contrast to our free speech data, suggest that religious liberty occupies a unique place in children's thinking.

Political Equality and Free Political Competition

That all men are created politically equal is one of the most basic democratic tenets. The aristocratic notion that some men, whether by virtue of their wealth, family lineage or physical prowess, are inherently better suited to rule is incompatible with democracy. This does not imply that all people are biologically equal or that each citizen ought to possess exactly the same political influence as every other citizen. Democratic political equality refers to equality of rights, e.g. the right of free speech or the right of participation, not to the physical or social characteristics of individuals. Political rights given to some citizens must therefore be extended to all citizens; politically and legally, society must be classless.

The corollary of the principle of equality is the existence of a political process in which everyone can compete and in which decisions are made on the basis of majority rule. That is, regardless of one's social class, race, political persuasion, or any other trait, one cannot be excluded from trying to exert influences for given special advantages. Everyone can play the game of politics and the basic rule is one man, one vote.

As in the case of support for free speech, we find that most young children are democratically oriented at the abstract, general level. According to Laurence's study, about two-thirds of children aged eight to

[7]See, for example, the data collected by Hazel Erskine in *Public Opinion Quarterly* 34 (1970), 483–96.

[8]Remmers and Franklin, "Sweet Land of Liberty," *Anti-Democratic Attitudes in the American Schools,* p. 66.

[9]Jennings, *The Student-Parent Socialization Study,* variable 121.

eleven and three-quarters of those twelve to fifteen agree that all adults should have the right to vote.[10] Similarly, Hess and Torney report that with increasing age the proportions defining democracy in terms of universal adult suffrage and political equality rises dramatically so that by eighth grade these responses are chosen by more than three-quarters of the students.[11] Obviously, then, the general ideal of political equality is attractive to most children.

When we provide a more difficult test for this support, democratic orientations decline substantially. When children are confronted with a statement such as "When you have elections, the votes of the important people should count more than the votes of the average man" or "In a city election, only people who know a lot about the problem being voted on should be allowed to vote," the principle of equality fares much more poorly than in the general abstract situation, though the democratic responses still hover around the 50 percent level.[12] These reactions are not limited to politically unenlightened youngsters lacking the proper civic training. In Table 6.2 we see the responses of high school students to very similar questions, and here again we see the willingness of many, though not a majority, to place the criteria of expertise and propriety ahead of the principle of political equality.

Perhaps the most difficult test of one's support for democratic equality arises when one confronts a completely fair, perfectly legal victory by one's enemies. As in the case of protecting the free speech

TABLE 6.2   Support for Political Equality among High School Students

Question: "People who have wild ideas and don't use good sense should not have the right to vote." (1960)		Question: "People should not be allowed to vote unless they are intelligent and educated." (1960)	
Agree	28%	Agree	18%
Undecided, probably agree	13	Undecided, probably agree	8
Undecided, probably disagree	15	Undecided, probably disagree	11
Disagree	43	Disagree	60
No response	1	No response	3
	100%		100%

Source: H.H. Remmers and Richard D. Franklin, "Sweet Land of Liberty," in Anti-Democratic Attitudes in American Schools *(Evanston: Northwestern University Press, 1963), pp. 69-70. By permission of the publisher.*

[10]Laurence, "White Socialization: Black Reality," *Psychiatry* 33, (1970), p. 182.
[11]Hess and Torney, *The Development of Political Attitudes in Children,* p. 75.
[12]Laurence, "White Socialization: Black Reality," p. 182.

rights of those one disagrees with, a temptation will undoubtedly occur to suspend the rules of equality of competition and majority vote. Resistance to such a temptation is perhaps the truest mark of a genuine supporter of democratic procedure. Without the willingness to lose to one's bitterest enemies, one's position is perhaps better described as "democracy when I win, enlightened minority rule when I lose."

Given our previous results when preadults faced difficult decisions involving specific unpopular groups, it comes as no surprise that support for this democratic principle is very low. Zellman and Sears' study of children indicates that only 26 percent agree that people should allow a communist mayor to take office even if he is legally elected.[13] Nor does greater maturity and additional schooling produce dramatic changes. Employing the identical question as did Zellman and Sears, Jennings finds that only a little more than a third of a sample of high school seniors would accept a communist mayor.[14] Studies of adults indicate further the pervasiveness of this unwillingness to let all competitors play politics. Both in Ann Arbor, Michigan and Tallahassee, Florida, two cities hardly in peril from a communist takeover, the majority would bar a communist from office.[15] In short, when most children learn that democracy means government by the people, it is clear that communists and other such groups are not included.

Freedom from Capricious Government Power

Our last aspect of support for democratic values concerns citizens' resistance to unrestrained political coercion. The notion that authorities cannot do whatever they desire or what is convenient without a legal mandate was, it will be remembered, one of the fundamental issues of the American revolt against the British. The tension between individual liberty and extensive use of government power did not end with our successful revolt. Such contemporary issues as the legal rights of accused criminals, government wiretapping and surveillance, and legislation of personal morality are only a few of many areas counterposing individual freedom to governmental power. As was true for other democratic values, there exists no universally agreed upon position on this issue. Especially in war time and during national emergencies, even the staunchest democrat would likely accept some government restriction on individual freedom. Others considering

---

[13]Gail L. Zellman and David O. Sears, "Childhood Origins of Tolerance for Dissent," *Journal of Social Issues* 27 (1971), 118.

[14]Jennings, *The Student-Parent Socialization Study*, variable 122.

[15]James W. Prothro and Charles W. Grigg, "Fundamental Principles of Democracy: Bases of Agreement and Disagreement," *Journal of Politics* 22 (1960) 276–94.

themselves good democrats might go even further and claim that a certain amount of unauthorized wiretapping, detention without trial, and similar practices however distasteful, are nevertheless necessary for the survival of any modern government including democratic ones.

In judging whether existing political socialization meets this particular democratic requirement we follow a similar strategy to the one adopted in examining support for free speech. Unless there are clearly stated special circumstances, e.g. war time, the pro-democratic response to a question favors individual freedom over government power. No doubt some respondents may impute such special circumstances to every question dealing with government coercion versus individual freedom and thus would be unfairly considered antidemocratic, but such occasional miscategorization is necessary if responses are to be analyzed at all.

Considering our previous findings showing the child's enormous admiration for the government and its leaders, it is not unsurprising that very few young children worry about the authorities overstepping their bounds. The very idea of a godlike benevolent president breaking the law is probably incomprehensible. This early lack of awareness that government action could unfairly impinge upon one's rights is clearly reflected in Gallatin and Adelson's study of childrens' attitudes toward government regulation of peoples' lives. Gallatin and Adelson ask children ranging in age from eleven to eighteen their opinions on laws that would require citizens to do such things as have annual health examinations or paint their houses every five years. Among the youngest children there is little concern that such laws may involve an infringement of personal freedom. On the mandatory health examination question the vast majority of the eleven-year-olds simply go along with the government decree. Even where most children oppose a government regulation (as in the case of the required house painting) the opposition is essentially utilitarian, e.g. some houses would not need to be painted, rather than based on the principles of freedom from government coercion.[16]

With increasing age, however, more children express reservations about these government decrees on the basis of infringement of personal freedom. Thus, the proportion of those objecting to required medical exams because they violate individual freedom goes from 4 percent at age eleven to 30 percent at age eighteen. Even so, a greater proportion (41 percent) of eighteen-year-olds uncritically accept the government's position. Similarly, the proportion of eighteen-year-olds perceiving

[16]Judith Gallatin and Joseph Adelson, "Legal Guarantees of Individual Freedom: A Cross National Study of the Development of Political Thought," *Journal of Social Issues,* 27 (1971), p. 97.

mandatory house painting as government coercion, though substantial (41 percent), remains less than a majority.[17] A parallel pattern is displayed in the related area of willingness to suspend individual freedoms during national emergencies: older respondents show greater caution in abandoning their rights to the government, but a significant number (43 percent) would readily surrender to the government regardless of the specific situation.[18]

Though these figures may be discouraging to a Jeffersonian democrat viewing an enlightened citizenry as a bulwark against government coercion, American children appear to do as well if not better than their British and German counterparts. On the whole, American children are as sensitive to government infringements of freedom as British and German children on the compulsory medical exam and considerably more sensitive to this problem on the issue of house painting. British and German children are considerably more willing to suspend personal freedom during national emergencies. Respondents were also asked what kinds of laws should be permanent and here again Americans show themselves to be more libertarian than their British or German counterparts: 71 percent of the Americans favor placing laws guaranteeing individual freedom compared to 34 percent of the British and 50 percent of the Germans.[19]

When we examine the attitudes of high school seniors on a different set of government coercion questions, we find stronger support for the right of the individual against constituted authority. Data from Remmers' 1960 poll of seniors, presented in Table 6.3, indicate the extent of this resistance. Compared to Gallatin and Adelson's findings, these data provide a more pleasant picture to supporters of democracy. What might explain these partially conflicting results? One simple explanation would be differences in samples and time period—the two studies describe separate groups of adolescents at two different points in time. A more likely explanation, however, concerns the type of questions asked. Given the nature of social welfare legislation in the United States (e.g., mandatory social security), questions on required medical examinations or house painting are perhaps less clearly perceived as violations of freedom than unauthorized search by police. The laws used by Gallatin and Adelson are viewed as being closer to such things as consumer protection legislation or other protective acts than to illegal search and seizure. What is important is that when it comes to very clear governmental excesses of power a majority of adolescents object.

[17]Gallatin and Adelson, "Legal Guarantees of Individual Freedom," p. 97.
[18]Gallatin and Adelson, "Legal Guarantees of Individual Freedom," p. 101.
[19]Gallatin and Adelson, "Legal Guarantees of Individual Freedom," pp. 100–101.

TABLE 6.3   Toleration of Government Coercion

Questions	Percent Agreeing
"In some cases the police should be allowed to search a person or his home even though they do not have a warrant."	33%
"In some cases the government should have the right to take over a person's land or property without bothering to go to court."	6%
"Local police may sometimes be right in holding persons in jail without telling them of any formal charges against them."	13%
"The police or F.B.I. may sometimes be right in giving a man the 'third degree' to make him talk."	42%

Source: Remmers and Franklin, "Sweet Land of Liberty," Anti-Democratic Attitudes in the American Schools, pp. 67-68. By permission of the publisher.

GROUP DIFFERENCES IN SUPPORT FOR DEMOCRACY

To understand the political significance of group differences in adherence to democratic values we must first make clear some things about the nature of political power and the role of democratic values in the exercise of this power. It is a truism that political power or the potential for power is always distributed unevenly: a very few have enormous power while most citizens have either little or no influence. In some situations discrepancies in political status lead to the blatant subjugation of the weaker by the stronger. In an oligarchic form of government an economic elite dominates those who are less well-off. Though democratic values, no matter how vigorously supported, cannot by themselves bring about political equality, these values may help reduce the blatant political subjugation of the weak by the strong. Practices such as universal suffrage, the right to organize opposition to government policy, and freedom to state unorthodox views all help redress the balance between the powerful and the less powerful.

It should be obvious that willingness of the powerful to go along with such democratic practices is crucial. The right of peaceful opposition and individual freedom from government coercion would hardly mean much if political elites rejected them. When we consider that democracy may run counter to the economic and political interests of the powerful, it is worth examining the possibility that support for democracy may only be strong among those it benefits the most, i.e., the poor masses. In undertaking this examination we shall focus on social class and racial differences in democratic support. We want to know whether those who are politically advantaged—in this case, middle-class and white children—are less committed to democratic practices. We are not suggesting that the middle class and the Caucasian race constitute a powerful political elite. The vast majority of whites, for instance, will never advance beyond voting as their most influential political behavior. Nevertheless, it is true that important decision-makers are overwhelmingly recruited among the middle-class and white segments of the population. Hence, comparisons across class and racial groups, while hardly a comparison of rulers and ruled, still manage to reflect a distinction between those who will be politically privileged and those less influential.

Social Class Differences

Though one might surmise that those with fewer economic resources might be the staunchest advocates of democratic liberties, numerous adult studies disprove this supposition. Most citizens regardless of economic status endorse democracy in the abstract, but far less support exists for specific applications of democratic principles, with working-class citizens almost always the least supportive. For example, Prothro and Grigg found that while 36.7 percent of low income citizens of Tallahassee, Florida and Ann Arbor, Michigan would not prohibit a Communist from speaking, 52.2 percent of the high income group would be similarly inclined. Parallel differences were found on issues such as allowing only the informed to vote and barring Communists from office.[20] Are such class-related differences strictly an adult phenomena or do they go back to earlier learning?

On the whole, numerous pieces of data confirm the early origins of these class-related differences. Unfortunately we lack relevant data from very young children, so we cannot say precisely how early these differences originate, but Zellman and Sears find strong association between attitudes toward free speech and parental income among their sample of nine- to fourteen-year-olds.[21] Likewise, Litt's study of ninth graders in three communities in the Boston metropolitan area shows a clear correlation between social status and preferences for democratic values. Students in "Alpha," an upper middle-class, politically active

[20]Prothro and Grigg, "Fundamental Principles of Democracy," pp. 276–94. Similar social class related data are reported in Samuel A. Stouffer, *Communism, Conformity, and Civil Liberties* (New York: Doubleday, 1955) and Herbert McCloskey, "Consensus and Ideology in American Politics," *American Political Science Review* 58 (1964), pp. 276–94.

[21]Zellman and Sears, "Childhood Origins of Tolerance for Dissent," p. 126. However, the authors find that parental education is virtually unrelated to tolerance.

suburb, were more supportive of political equality and freedom to criticize government than their agemates in "Beta," a lower-middle-class community. In turn, these "Beta" students were more likely to endorse the democratic creed than students in the working-class town of "Gamma."[22] Working-class children are also less supportive of an alleged criminal's civil rights. When a sample of Detroit school children were asked about President Kennedy's assassination, children from less well-educated families were more likely to be glad that Jack Ruby killed Oswald and more desirous of having Oswald beat up or shot.[23]

Perhaps the strongest evidence indicating that a background of economic privilege makes one more disposed to democracy rather than favoring more elitist philosophy comes from Laurence and Scoble's analysis of grade-school children from exceptionally high status families. The parents of these children were not only distinguished by their educational and occupational levels (e.g., 79 percent of the fathers were college graduates and over 60 percent were either professionals or business executives), but their level of political activity was well above the national norm. When asked many of the same questions asked of adults, these children in most instances not only were more democratic than the general population, but were also more democratic than samples of well educated and high income adults as well as a national group of political influentials.[24] These results become even more impressive when we recall our previous discussion of the cognitive difficulties experienced by most young children in grasping democratic principles. If these data are typical of other groups of potential elite decision-makers, a fear that the well-born and powerful will reject those values favoring the many over the few will prove groundless.

Racial Differences

The same argument made in the case of social class differences in democratic values can also be made for racial differences. Even more than members of the working class, black Americans have lacked almost every resource necessary for political influence. Given such pow-

---

[22]Litt, "Civic Education, Community Norms, and Political Indoctrination," p. 73.

[23]Kenneth P. Langton, "Peer Group and School and the Political Socialization Process," *American Political Science Review* 61 (1967), p. 758.

[24]Joan E. Laurence and Harry M. Scoble, "Ideology and Consensus Among Children of the Metropolitan Socioeconomic Elite," *Western Political Quarterly* 22 (1969), 151–62. It should be pointed out, however, that while Laurence and Scoble's sample is very privileged economically, these are hardly the children of America's most powerful and influential families. It would be fascinating and highly relevant to examine the degree of democratic support among very young Rockefellers, Mellons, and Fords, but such data are unavailable.

erlessness, we would hardly expect blacks to reject the principles of equality and individual rights. Indeed, considering the historical pattern of systematic and blatant violations of black citizens' rights, we would expect this social group to be especially sensitive to such violations.

Compared to research of socioeconomic class differences in adherence to the democratic creed, analyses of racial differences have been far fewer. There is a particular paucity of studies on early learning, so our conclusions must be limited. Fortunately for our analysis, the few existent studies are in general agreement with each other so our inferences can be made with some degree of confidence.

The most comprehensive analysis of white/black differences in support for democratic values was conducted by Laurence in her study of grade-school children in Sacramento, California.[25] Laurence employed questions on a variety of democratic values (e.g., due process of law and majority rule) and divided children into "young" (aged eight to eleven) and "old" (aged twelve to fifteen). Among the young children, race related differences tend to be very small and statistically insignificant. Among the older children these differences become larger, but the pattern is not consistent. Table 6.4 presents some representative questions from Laurence's survey.

These data confirm among both whites and blacks the pattern described in our first section: support for democratic values declines sharply when we move from the abstract to specific applications. For example, children of both races overwhelmingly endorse the principle that everyone, regardless of belief, should be equal (first question) yet also deny the rights of Vietcong supporters and Nazis. Moreover, despite an objective reason for being more sensitive to violations of political freedoms, blacks do not demonstrate a consistently higher level of support than do whites. Like their white counterparts, blacks of both age groups tend to be antidemocratic on many issues. The possibility that the same kinds of arguments for denying television time to a Vietcong (e.g., they "stir things up") may someday be applied to unpopular black speakers apparently does not occur to many black children. To be sure, on some issues blacks may be more democratic than whites, but such differences are usually quite small and certainly do not alter the overall pattern of racial similarity.[26]

[25]Laurence, "White Socialization: Black Reality," pp. 180–84.
[26]The one question in which blacks score considerably more democratic than whites concerns allowing only people paying taxes to vote on issues involving taxation. This sentiment does not square, however, with allowing important people to have a greater say in elections. Why black children show greater sensitivity on the taxation issue is unknown.

TABLE 6.4 White and Black Support for Democratic Values, by Age (percentages indicate the proportions giving the democratic response)

Questions	Young (8-11) White	Young (8-11) Black	Old (12-15) White	Old (12-15) Black
No matter what a person's political beliefs, he should have the same rights and protections as anyone else	69%	64%	83%	76%
If a communist won an election for mayor, the people should not let him become mayor	25	30	25	29
When you have elections, the vote of the important person should count for more than the vote of the average man	39	31	60	33
People who hate our way of life should still have a chance to talk and be heard	68	65	74	78
A person who wants to help the Vietcong should be able to buy time on television to make a speech	26	30	29	32
The head of the Nazi party should be able to buy newspaper space for an advertisement attacking the president	10	10	17	11

Source: Adapted from Joan Laurence, Psychiatry *33, pp. 182-83. By permission of the publisher.*

What happens to these racial differences as children mature and presumably develop a greater capacity to see the implication of denying democratic freedoms? Do adolescent blacks perceive that their freedoms may be linked to the rights of Communists or Nazis? Data from Jennings' national study suggest that age brings no increase in black sensitivity to democratic values. For example, on the question of allowing an elected Communist to hold office, 67 percent of the black high school seniors, compared to 63 percent of the whites, would not allow it to happen. A similar pattern occurred when respondents were asked about allowing a speech against religion—while adolescents of both races overwhelmingly support this particular right, blacks are again slightly less in favor.[27] In sum, as was true in our analysis of socioeconomic differences, we find that those having the most to gain from democratic values are not the greatest supporters of these values.

[27]Jennings, *The Student-Parent Socialization Study,* variables 121–22.

THE EXISTENCE OF DEMOCRATIC IDEOLOGY

Our analysis of democratic values has thus far focused on responses to specific questions. We examined, for example, approval of free speech for communists or the right of government to confiscate property without due process; the possible relationship between two such separate, but supposedly interrelated values, was not of concern. It is possible, however, to treat such specific questions not as isolated policy preferences but as integral parts of a broad, logically coherent democratic (or antidemocratic) ideology. Unlike a position on a single issue, an ideology provides a general framework for evaluating a wide variety of political phenomena. Thus, someone with a democratic ideology would be able to place in a single context such seemingly different events as depriving a duly elected communist from office, police use of the third degree, and allowing only informed people the voting right. A person without such an ideology might miss the democratic implications of these diverse events.

It is obvious that if the creation of a democratically oriented citizenry is our goal, the existence of a democratic ideology is preferred over an unintegrated set of policy positions. Once a broad, comprehensive ideology is created, new phenomena touching on democratic principles can be interpreted in the light of this comprehensive belief system. It would thus be unnecessary to teach people the appropriate democratic response for each and every new situation. On the other hand, a lack of this ideological capacity would mean an *ad hoc* type of policy choice that would undoubtedly heighten the probability of a wrong (i.e., antidemocratic) choice by someone who thinks of himself as a good democrat but is unfamiliar with the general principles guiding democratic behavior or beliefs. Do young Americans learn to grasp a democratic ideology or are responses to questions a hodge podge of answers more reflective of situational factors than of a broad framework?

Given the primitive nature of much political thinking among young children we obviously cannot expect them to articulate a complex, closely reasoned democratic philosophy. A more modest, but still relevant, test of the emergence of a democratic ideology would be to look for a consistency between an abstract principle and its specific application. This is a simple but nevertheless quite clear test, for it is difficult to imagine a democratic ideologue contradicting himself on such a basic level. We must also bear in mind that consistency can also be achieved by being an antidemocrat. In Table 6.5 we see the proportions of grade school children who are consistent in their general support of free speech and their toleration of free speech for unpopular speakers such as communists and Nazis.

TABLE 6.5   Consistency Between Abstract Principle of Free Speech and Applications in Concrete Situations

	CONCRETE SITUATIONS		
	Allow Communist to speak	Allow Vietcong supporter to buy TV time	Allow Nazi to have street-corner meeting
Consistently tolerant	15 (+7)*	18 (+3)	9 (+2)
Consistently intolerant	9 (+1)	10 (+1)	10 (−1)

* Each figure indicates the percent agreeing with both abstract free speech and free speech in the particular situation.
The number in parentheses indicates the change in consistency between the younger respondents aged nine to eleven and older respondents aged twelve to fourteen.
Source: Adapted from Zellman and Sears, "Childhood Origins of Tolerance for Dissent," p. 119. By permission of the publisher.

It is obvious that even on this simple test, most young Americans do not meet the requirements of a democratic ideology. Even when we include those consistently opposing democracy among an ideologue group, the proportion remains small (and note that in the case of allowing a Nazi to hold a street-corner meeting, there are about as many consistent antidemocratic responses as consistent pro-democratic responses). Perhaps even more surprising than the degree of inconsistency is the lack of major changes as children mature and (supposedly) become more sophisticated. Even the largest increase—7 percent increase in the case of favoring free speech abstractly and also allowing a communist to speak—hardly represents a sudden blooming of democratic ideology. The magnitudes of the other age-related shifts all suggest that however important these age periods are in more general intellectual development, a capacity for policy consistency, if it indeed ever emerges, shows almost no development here.

Another dimension of democratic ideological consistency concerns the capacity of individuals to adhere to the same general principles regardless of the details of a specific situation. That is, if one believes in free speech, this belief should not only extend to all groups, but to all *types* of free speech, e.g. staging rallies, TV appearances, etc. Zellman and Sears in their analysis of grade-school children's support of free speech explored this type of attitudinal consistency when they measured tolerance for Vietcong supporters and Nazis engaging in the identical activities. Thus, we can not only measure the toleration of free speech for Nazis to organize corner meetings, buy newspaper space, etc., but also see whether the right to organize a street-corner meeting, for example, is equally extended to both groups.

Given the lack of policy consistency noted earlier between general, abstract principles and specific applications of these principles, it comes as no surprise that most children are not consistently democratic in their preferences. Indeed, in five tests of consistency (two groups and three concrete situations) the proportion giving consistent democratic responses ranges between 2 and 7 percent! The proportion able to give consistent *anti*democratic responses is substantially higher. For example 45 percent would deny free speech to Nazis in all three situations (street-corner meeting, newspaper ad, auditorium speech); similarly, 41 percent would deny a TV speech and newspaper advertisements to both Vietcong supporters and a Nazi. In no instance is the proportion of consistent pro-democratic responses higher than the proportion of consistent antidemocratic responses.[28] Thus, if there is evidence for the emergence of any ideological propensity, it is a propensity for intolerance—though much more has to be known before we can label young Americans as ideological antidemocrats.

This question of the development of a coherent democratic ideology has also been explored by Richard Merelman in his study of children in two California communities. Merelman's analysis is of particular relevance for us since he traces the formation of democratic ideology from sixth through twelfth grade, a period during which intellectual development is virtually completed. Merelman's mode of analysis differs sharply from that of Zellman and Sears, but his general conclusion remains the same despite the inclusion of more sophisticated adolescents: very little evidence exists that these future citizens have a coherent, comprehensive democratic perspective. Older children may have a better understanding of freedom of speech, but this one aspect of democracy remains unconnected with other democratic freedoms and rights.[29] Having failed to develop a democratic ideology during high school with its required citizenship training, it seems unlikely that most young citizens will do much better as adults.

CONCLUSIONS

The existing political process in the United States may or may not be characterized as democratic, but one thing is clear: Americans early

---

[28]Zellman and Sears, "Childhood Origins of Tolerance for Dissent," p. 121.

[29]Merelman, *Political Socialization and Educational Climates*, pp. 66–74. Whereas Zellman and Sears use consistency as a measure of ideological thinking, Merelman employs the complex statistical technique of factor analysis to uncover underlying dimensions of democratic thinking. The dimensions found by Merelman are composed of a variety of questions rather than similar questions that should have been interrelated.

in life are not being socialized to be staunch supporters of the democratic creed. We cannot deny the possibility that with greater maturity
these children will display heightened appreciation of democratic values. In view of our evidence on age related changes, the more general
importance of early learning, and data showing strong antidemocratic
tendencies among adults, this possibility must be considered remote.

To be sure, the picture we have drawn is not completely dismal.
In the areas of abstract support for free speech and the rejection of
blatant government coercion without due process, majorities are supportive of democratic values. The social distribution of this support is
also somewhat encouraging. Contrary to what we might expect solely
on the basis of self-interest, groups with greater political power, i.e., the
middle class and whites, are not less favorably disposed toward rules
of the political game that help redress the balance between weak and
strong. The democratic impetus at least does not have to depend on the
relatively powerless members of society.

However, as soon as we move into more difficult (and probably
more important) democratic requirements, the performance of young
Americans is deplorable from the perspective of a fervent democrat.
This is particularly true in the case of extending free speech and the
equal opportunity to participate (and win) to unpopular groups such as
Communists or Nazis. Young citizens also fare poorly in the development of an integrated democratic ideology. Even among adolescents
(who are supposedly virtually mature intellectually) little evidence
exists of a capacity to see the connection between diverse, but nevertheless inter-related, elements of democracy.

Our analysis suggests that if the existing political system is to be
democratic, this state of affairs cannot depend on a staunchly democratically oriented citizenry. Most Americans enter adulthood with
many antidemocratic policy preferences. Perhaps these citizen preferences do not preclude the possibility of a democratic political system,
but if these values do have behavioral correlates, they place major
constraints on the opportunities for a free and open political process.
Political leaders may choose democratic policies, but such choices are
not the alternatives children are trained to support.

7

Manipulating
Political Socialization:
A Framework for Analysis

This book began by suggesting that the elimination of some political choices from serious consideration was not a neutral act. Thus, that virtually all of us decide that our first political loyalty is owed to America rather than our social class is a victory for some interests and a loss for others (even though most people may be completely unaware of having made any decision, let alone who the victors and the vanquished are). Moreover, as we have seen in the last few chapters, the elimination of alternatives is a pervasive phenomenon that extends not only to basic loyalties and identities, but to more specific issue positions and activities.

In any situation where important decisions are made, be they overt or covert, it does not seem likely that all potential winners and losers would sit idly by hoping for the best. This would seem especially true in the case of what is learned by young children. Not only is much of this learning difficult to change once established, but the very nature of the socialization process invites attempts at manipulation. After all, convincing a four-year-old of the merits of a particular proposal does not seem very difficult, and a multitude of avenues of influence are available. Only the politically naive or the altruistic would reject the idea that the socialization process attracts systematic manipulation.

When we consider the possibility of conscious, systematic manipulation, we should not let our use of the term manipulation convey a pejorative connotation. It should be obvious that what one person considers blatant manipulation may be viewed as enlightened education by another. When American educators and reformers speak of restructuring the school curriculum to produce more humanitarian, less prejudiced, more democratic citizens, such people are hardly viewed as manipulators. On the other hand, let Soviet educators talk about collective responsibility and proletarian brotherhood, and most Americans will think of brainwashing, not education.

APPROACHES TO THE ANALYSIS OF MANIPULATION

That the existing political socialization process is biased toward some interests is beyond contention. However, it is one thing to acknowledge this bias, quite another to demonstrate the existence of systematic, purposeful manipulation. If such manipulation does exist —and it is entirely possible that there is *no* such effort to bias systematically the socialization process—this manipulation is probably far from obvious. No doubt clever manipulators prefer to keep their successful efforts as obscure as possible. One could even go further and claim that we cannot perceive this manipulation since we have all been socialized to be oblivious to it.

Given these complexities, we must first ask how we can best determine and measure this supposed manipulation before plunging into the actual question. A number of reasonable approaches is feasible. First, we could argue that the very importance of the socialization process precludes its being left to accident and that those interests benefiting the most from existing practices must therefore be the manipulators. Hence, one only has to ask who wins in order to learn "who manipulates." This reasoning is not unlike that employed in determining the existence of a "power elite" in national politics. Since political decisions typically favor the values of the entrenched economic elite, it is therefore concluded that the economic elite determines these decisions.

A second alternative is to examine *attempts* to influence the socialization process. Here we would concern ourselves with such things as the messages conveyed by children's TV programs, school textbook content, comic book themes, and other such attempts to mould opinion. This strategy, particularly in comparison with the first alternative, has the considerable advantage of dealing with relatively visible and mea-sureable phenomena. Instead of having to ask the difficult question of whose interests benefit from the socialization process, we could ask the simpler question of who tries to influence young children and for what purpose.

Both these approaches have their advantages, but neither is with-out considerable difficulty. The first may sound convincing initially, but as formulated it is impossible to disprove the existence of system-atic conscious manipulation. That situations benefit some more than others is not conclusive proof that the benefiting interests *caused* that state of affairs.[1] People can, in fact, knowingly or unknowingly, prefer policies that disadvantage themselves. Take, for example, the support given to socialistic economic policies by men whose large fortunes would be affected adversely by such policies. Moreover, how do we determine who benefits from existing arrangements? Do we measure benefits objectively (e.g., income, social status, political power) or do we employ more subjective indicators of benefits such as satisfaction with the status quo? If the latter type of measure is used, how do we know that those who think they are benefiting (or seem to be benefiting) have not in fact been brainwashed into a false sense of satisfaction? Consider the fact that many economically and politically disadvantaged Ameri-cans consider themselves to be benefiting from the existing system. Does it then follow that such economically disadvantaged citizens are manipulating the socialization process?

The second approach, which is widely used by journalists and in educational research, also has problems in its assumptions.[2] Basically, we cannot equate attempts at manipulation, no matter how overpower-ing they appear to be, with successful manipulation. As anyone who has attempted to manipulate (or educate) young children can attest, it is one thing to convey information, quite another for this information

[1] The argument that those who benefit are those who rule and the counter-argument that this reasoning is unwarranted have been considered at greath length in other contexts, particularly in city politics. See, for example, Nelson W. Polsby, *Community Power and Political Theory* (New Haven, Conn.: Yale University Press, 1963), pp. 98–104.

[2] This approach has long been a favorite among liberal (and some conservative) reformers who regularly review textbooks to find instances of bigotry, intolerance, chauvinism, and other evils. It should be acknowledged that more sophisticated attempts to examine the influencing of school course content and structure are extremely valuable in understanding the broad political environment in which schools function. Among others, see Jack Nelson and Gene Roberts, Jr., *The Censors and the Schools* (Boston: Little, Brown and Company, 1963); and Neal Gross, *Who Runs Our Schools* (New York: John Wiley and Sons, Inc., 1958).

to be absorbed. Even very young children lacking critical ability can ignore the content of textbooks, selectively interpret television programs, and rebel against family influence. If the argument that manipulative attempts equalled manipulative success were perfectly true, no doubt grade-school teachers would be among the most powerful political groups in the United States.

Given the inadequacy of these two analytical strategies, what is a better alternative? How can we determine the existence of systematic manipulation without asserting what is to be proven or making unrealistic assumptions? Our approach is an indirect one and is divided into two parts. Our analysis first considers what methods of transmitting political orientations are most amenable to systematic manipulation. This analysis, while not telling us whether manipulation actually occurs, nevertheless points to areas where manipulation (if it exists) is likely. Having identified certain portions of the socialization process susceptible to manipulation, we then examine the success of actual attempts to mould political orientations. Hence, rather than ask "Who are the manipulators?" we instead ask the prior question "Where is systematic manipulation likely to occur?" We then ask how successful people have been in influencing the processes open to manipulation.

SOCIALIZATION AGENCIES
AND THEIR SUSCEPTIBILITY TO MANIPULATION

As Chapter 2 demonstrated, there exists great variety in the way political orientations can be acquired. Moreover, not every political attitude or behavior need be acquired from some particular source: children are hardly living sponges who passively absorb messages. Even at a relatively early age some children can draw independent conclusions about politics. Nevertheless, in the study of the acquisition of political orientations a number of agencies of learning seem particularly relevant. Our analysis considers three such agencies: the family, the school, and the mass media. Though not an exhaustive selection, it would be hard to imagine manipulation taking place without its being found in one or more of these agencies. Let us begin by considering the family's susceptibility to systematic manipulation.

The Family

If the vast literature on the role of the family in children's learning is correct, the early family environment should be the primary target of any systematic attempt to control political learning. It is sometimes almost automatically assumed that the family predominates in shaping an individual's basic character and hence his future behavior.[3]   As crucial as the family's role may be in learning, what is more relevant from our perspective is that of all the socializing agents, the family is probably the most difficult to manipulate systematically and directly. This insulation from direct pressure is a consequence of a number of conditions. First, the sheer number of family units presents a communication problem of enormous magnitude. Not only would communicating with millions of separate families be quite formidable, but the message must be made both crystal clear and convincing to parents with a wide variety of existing perspectives on child rearing. In recent American history there is perhaps only one illustration of a single source significantly influencing child rearing practices—Dr. Spock, through his widely read *Baby and Child Care.* Even in this instance, the process has been very slow and remains incomplete.[4]

Even if it were possible to have access to a significant number of families, a successful program of influence would require either extensive monitoring of these many families or separating children from their parents for lengthy periods. As was true for school textbook content and actual learning, we cannot automatically assume that because a message is communicated to parents it is absorbed. There would have to be some means of supervising this influencing process and both monitoring individual families and separating family units have their respective difficulties. As Russian leaders during the first decades of the Soviet Union found out, a major commitment of resources is no guarantee that attempts to penetrate families and instill new values will be successful. The manpower demands of keeping track of activities within separate family units are staggering. As for the second possibility, state-controlled child care centers that would serve as artificial families, these have the advantage of being much easier to monitor, but at least in the United States these are a long way from rivaling the family's importance. No doubt that some future attempt to manipulate early family related learning may try to operate through such centers, but we can probably say for sure that no *existing*

[3]Such claims are made in James C. Davies, "The Family's Role in Political Socialization," *The Annals* 361 (1965), p. 11 and Herbert H. Hyman, *Political Socialization,* p. 51.

[4]Urie Bronfenbrenner, "Socialization and Social Class through Time and Space," in *Basic Studies in Social Psychology,* eds. Harold Proshansky and Bernard Seidenberg (New York: Holt, Rinehart and Winston, Inc., 1965), pp. 349–65. Another possibility is that parents without explicit pressure will resocialize their children away from their own values so these children can better survive in a new environment. The possibility of fundamental social and political change occurring through the family is analyzed in Alex Inkeles, "Social Change and Social Character: The Role of Parental Mediation," *The Journal of Social Issues* 11 (1955), 12–22.

(or previous) manipulative attempt in the United States has made use of such surrogate families.

A third and final factor insulating the family from systematic manipulation is that in the United States (and other countries as well) most parents would reject explicit political propaganda as inappropriate to matters of child rearing. This is not to say that parents attempt to make their children apolitical; rather, unlike matters of feeding, health care, etc., offering advice about the proper political perspectives is usually considered illegitimate. Imagine what might happen if governmental authorities who regularly provide advice on children's diets, dental care, and similar matters, would suddenly offer comparable advice on political matters. No doubt such action would be viewed as a clear violation of some norm of appropriate behavior. Such would also be the case if other sources of family advice (e.g., doctors, television personalities, ministers) began to offer explicit directives on how to raise children politically.

We can thus surmise that where political orientations are largely transmitted through the family, the probability of widespread, systematic manipulation is small. We say probability rather than certainty since those factors insulating the family from manipulative influence are matters of mobilizing sufficient resources, not inherent properties of family life. No doubt a government with enough resources, patience, and insensitivity to cultural norms regulating appropriate child rearing messages *could* manipulate family political socialization, but there are more efficient methods of manipulation available.

The School

Usually considered second only to the family in transmitting political orientations is the school. As in the case of the family, it is almost impossible to avoid spending enormous periods of time with this agency of learning. Moreover, while the school does not have access to very young children, it is during school years that children are able to learn more important political attitudes and behaviors. Although the family and school are both of considerable importance, unlike the family the schools provide many more opportunities for systematic manipulation.

First, unlike the family, a would-be manipulator does not face the problem of dealing with millions of separate units to be influenced. Even though there are hundreds of thousands of schools in the United States, the accessibility problem is greatly simplified by the existence of school boards and state commissions of education wielding considerable influence over local units. In many areas local interests have considerable control over school affairs, but even in these instances, powerful mechanisms of centralized control exist that are without parallel in family matters. Compare, for example, the likely difficulties to be experienced in attempting to make home life more democratic versus trying to make school life more democratic. One might not be successful in either instance, but at least in the case of schools one would have a more accessible place to start.

Moreover, partly as a consequence of having fewer points of access, any manipulative effort via the schools is much easier to monitor. Not only would fewer situations have to be observed, but the very character of schools provides opportunities for evaluating how well messages have been communicated and absorbed. Such things as curriculum content, textbook content, subject time allocations, classroom and school authority patterns, the existence of extracurricular activities, and other politically relevant features of school life are either part of the written public record or readily discernible. American schools also provide numerous opportunities for actually testing students so that the impact of a manipulative effort can be determined relatively quickly. Indeed, in most schools one could even observe the process of political socialization as it takes place, an advantage rarely afforded by the nature of family life.

Finally, unlike the case of the family, conscious and conspicuous attempts to meddle in political learning are not widely regarded as inappropriate or morally unethical. In fact, particularly in the United States, the opposite is true: the school system has long been viewed as a means to shape social and political attitudes. Such time honored cliches as educating citizens for democracy are clear acknowledgements of the legitimacy of tampering with the education process for political ends. While city councils, state legislatures, and other governing bodies would have serious reservations about regulating the political content of parent-child relationships, this is clearly not the case when it comes to prescribing school political content.

The Mass Media

At the other end of the continuum of potential for systematic political manipulation from the family is the mass media. In recent years in particular, the mass media (including TV, magazines, the movies, comic books, and newspapers) have become as ubiquitous among young children as school or even family communications. No doubt some young children spend as much time glued to the TV or reading comic books as they do with their fathers or in school. Though the mass media hardly provide direct access to every child at the touch of a button, the commercial character of American mass media and their pervasiveness clearly provide enormous opportunities for access for those with sufficient resources. Of course, the resources necessary to produce television shows, publish children's books, and otherwise influence the content of the mass media are possessed only by a small handful of citizens, but certainly enough of these resources exist to make the possibility of systematic manipulation a real one. The financial structure of American mass media limits the number of potential manipulators, but at the same time, the media's availability for conveying political messages to large segments of the population is significantly greater than the family or the school.

Given the varying openness of these three socialization agencies to systematic manipulation, and given the nature of the research on the differential impacts on political learning of these agencies, our analysis will proceed as follows. First, we shall examine the kinds of political orientations acquired within the family. Consistent with our previous discussion of the family's insulation from manipulation, we shall assume that such learning is not the consequence of conscious, systematic manipulation. To the extent that family related learning is extensive and of fundamental political importance, this would cast serious doubts on the argument that Americans early in life are systematically brainwashed by those who have something to gain from this process. Our second question focuses on the successes (and failures) of manipulation attempts in the schools and the mass media. Though the educational system and the mass media exhibit the greatest potential for manipulation, the existence of such manipulation must nevertheless be demonstrated, not assumed. To the extent that we can show that attempts to influence schools and the media have actually resulted in attitudinal or behavioral changes among children, we shall have gone a long way toward determining whether what is learned is acquired haphazardly or through purposeful design.

LIMITATIONS ON OUR ANALYTICAL STRATEGY

The particular way we have chosen to examine the possibility of manipulation is not without its faults. So that any conclusion we draw will be viewed in the proper perspective, we shall briefly consider some of the possibilities lying outside the scope of our analysis. These are not meant to detract from our analysis, but rather indicate that whatever our findings are, the issue of systematic manipulation is not completely closed by our analysis.

First, as we saw in Chapter 2 when we considered the various ways political orientations are acquired, the socialization process is a very complex, ongoing one, in which learning takes place over a period of time, not in isolated learning experiences. The opportunities and possibilities for socialization are thus enormous, and by no means has existing political socialization research provided a clear understanding of the entire political learning process. Even if our review of the existing research demonstrated a lack of manipulation, the vast gaps in our knowledge would nevertheless make such a conclusion highly tentative. Moreover, even the research findings that do exist are very limited both in time and by the nature of their samples. A single study at one point in time of a hundred children is better than no study at all, but inferences from such limited and specific data must be treated cautiously when searching for the existence of widespread biasing of socialization outcomes. We should also remember that none of the studies we review had the issue of manipulation as their primary research focus.

Second, it can be argued that existing socialization practices result from conscious manipulation, but such manipulation does not *presently* occur. This argument claims that once a generation was inculcated with the proper values, these values would persist with little, if any, need for continual reindoctrination. Because this manipulation occurred in the unmeasurable past, contemporary research would be unable to locate it and would falsely conclude that it does not exist. Even if those forces successful in their manipulative attempts in the past found it necessary to intervene occasionally to reinforce the old pattern, such efforts would be much less conspicuous than attempts to create new attitudes and values. Advocates of this position would probably point to the role of the business community in the creation of free public schools, the suppression of radical ideas among certain groups of European immigrants and other events as crucial past actions that helped shape existing socialization patterns.

A third argument, and one that is very difficult to test empirically, is that the manipulators are so successful in shaping the socialization environment that any empirical research is unable to uncover this biasing of choices. What appear to be free choices among parents, educators, television program producers, etc., are really decisions greatly influenced by a wide variety of subtle but purposeful behavior cues. Thus, if school teachers were asked to justify teaching children that America is the world's best country, they would not indicate any pressure, but would instead say that this item of information is indeed true. If pushed further, the probable response would be "Everyone knows it's true." According to proponents of this third argument, the acquisition of this diffuse knowledge is a direct result of the manipulating elite's more general control over society. In terms of our analytical strategy, this reasoning suggests that it will be impossible to find *ex-*

plicit manipulation since everything is so structured that only rarely need anybody tell anybody else what children should learn.

Having considered some of the various ways of answering our basic question, let us now consider the data on the importance of the family, school, and mass media on the political socialization process.

8

Manipulating Political Socialization: The Family, Schools, and the Mass Media

THE FAMILY'S ROLE IN POLITICAL SOCIALIZATION

The very nature of childhood makes the early family environment of paramount importance. Even until the age of three or four, children have few, if any, sources of learning comparable to parents. Moreover, as Davies suggests, the child's almost complete dependence on his parents for basic needs provides little opportunity for resistance to parental pressures to conform. It is only a small step from acknowledging this enormous formative influence to suggesting that the family virtually determines an individual's postchildhood thoughts and actions. As Davies put it:

> The family provides the major means for transforming the mentally naked infant organism into the adult, fully clothed in its own personality. And most of the individual's political personality—his tendency to think and act politically in particular ways—have been determined at home,

several years before he can take part in politics as an ordinary adult citizen or as a political prominent.[1]

Despite such assertions, we cannot automatically assume that everything political that matters is acquired from parents during childhood. As any comparison between one's own parents and one's self should clearly indicate, few fathers and mothers, even despite heroic efforts, can completely determine the political character of their offspring.[2] Enormous influence is not identical with complete control; the family may be only one of many important determinants. What must be done, therefore, is to consider the extent of this influence empirically rather than assume its pervasiveness and power.

The Extent of Family Influence: Broad Attitudes and Behaviors

One of the major socializing functions of early family life is to provide children with a basic set of identities. For example, a young child soon learns that he belongs to a particular family and shares sexual characteristics with some, but not all, other children. In the United States (but not necessarily in all other countries) a similar process exists in the early family environment that moulds basic political identities. As Hess and Torney indicate, a general scholarly consensus exists that American families are the primary agencies for transmitting this nationalistic sentiment.[3] To be sure, the precise process by which young children learn to be Americans (and believe that this is the best of all possible choices) remains unknown, but it is clear that such patriotic orientations are well established before the child even enters grade school.

A similar consensus exists on the family's importance in the development of positive evaluations of political institutions and authority figures. Though evaluations of the government, the president, and the

---

[1]James C. Davies, "The Family's Role in Political Socialization," *The Annals* 361 (1965), 11.

[2]Like other researchers we are assuming that the degree of correspondence between parent and child indicates the efficiency of transmission across generations. The reader should realize that an identity of beliefs between parent and child is not sufficient in itself to prove scientifically that parents caused the child's beliefs. Nor do differences of opinion indicate a breakdown of perfect transmission. Regarding the latter point, it is possible that some parents successfully socialize their children toward positions different from their own. In the extreme case, parents might determine precisely their offspring's opinions by forcing a political rebellion resulting in complete rejection of parent values. Thus, such parents would have total control, but this would not take the form of correspondence of opinion. Nevertheless, despite these complications, we follow the custom of others and use the degree of correspondence as an indicator of strength of influence.

[3]Hess and Torney, *The Development of Political Attitudes in Children*, p. 110.

policeman undergo continuous change throughout childhood, it appears that the initial highly positive images emerge prior to entering school. As in the case of learning national loyalty, the precise nature of this type of learning remains largely unknown.[4] Such explanations of these positive evaluations as a generalization of high regard for the child's father to political father figures and personalized institutions, though plausible, nevertheless receives only very moderate confirmation by research.[5]

A third area of political learning in which the family probably plays a significant role is instilling respect for constituted authority.[6] A young child does not automatically obey rules and regulations. Not only must the meaning of these strictures be acquired, but a more general habit of following rules and regulations must also be established. Without this acceptance, each contact with authority becomes a contest of wills rather than unhesitating compliance. No doubt one's initial experiences with the exercise of family authority provide the basis for subsequent going along with laws without questioning their validity. Put another way, it is through the family that the young child learns that authority must be obeyed *merely because it is authority* (e.g., "Do it because I say so and I am your father").

Finally, and perhaps most speculatively, family environment probably plays an important role in the transmission and reinforcement of those widely shared and highly simplistic beliefs comprising much of what might be called the American political culture.[7] The intellectual capacity of the young child does not permit the understanding of complex political realities, so learning tends to involve such beliefs as "Americans have the most freedom," "democracy is the best form of government," and "the president would help me if I needed

[4]Our lack of knowledge about the family's role in developing national loyalty and positive evaluations of authority is a consequence of the difficulty of studying transmission processes within the family and the lack of extensive variations in these orientations. Consider the problems of trying to observe a lengthy (and sometimes unconscious) learning process within a single home. Also, since most children acquire roughly the same attitudes, it is methodologically impossible to relate family variations to this learning.

[5]Among others see Easton and Dennis, *Children in the Political System,* pp. 371–79; Hess and Torney, *The Development of Political Attitudes in Children,* p. 116. The generalization from one's father to more distant political objects is not found, among Appalachian children. See Dean Jaros, Herbert Hirsch, and Frederic J. Fleron, Jr., "The Malevolent Leader: Political Socialization in an American Subculture," *American Political Science Review* 62 (1968), 572–75. Nor are nonpolitical evaluations patterned after evaluations of one's father. See Leroy S. Burwen and Donald T. Campbell, "The Generality of Attitudes Towards Authority and Non-Authority Figures," *Journal of Abnormal and Social Psychology,* 54 (1957), 24–31. The most systematic discussion of the extrapolation of family relationships to political evaluations is found in Greenstein, *Children and Politics,* pp. 46–52.

[6]Hess and Torney, *The Development of Political Attitudes in Children,* p. 108.

[7]Hess and Torney, *The Development of Political Attitudes in Children,* p. 113.

it." Whether the initial source of this type of information is the school, the mass media, or the family itself, the family probably plays a significant role in perpetuating such beliefs. Imagine, for example, what an American family's reaction might be if its children suddenly announced that Russians had the most freedom and that communism was better than democracy. Even if such parents did not themselves convey the consensual wisdom, they would certainly very quickly resocialize this errant child toward the more socially accepted position. This correcting of deviant views can perhaps be seen as part of a more general tendency of parents to make their offspring into normal citizens.

The Extent of Family Influence: Specific Attitudes and Behaviors

It has frequently been observed that many political figures come from families with long traditions of political involvement. Families such as the Roosevelts, the La Follettes, the Byrds, the Longs and the Kennedys are perhaps the most conspicuous of such political families, but this transmission of political activism across generations is by no means limited to these famous examples.[8] Not every activist comes from a politically involved environment, but the data do suggest that having a participation oriented family does provide a boost toward future activity. In their study of four state legislatures, Wahlke and others found that legislators were significantly more likely than the population at large to come from politicized families.[9] Similarly, Hess and Torney, using children's perceptions of family interest in politics, find a small (but statistically significant) relationship between family and offspring political involvement.[10] Studies by Meine and Stark provide additional evidence of the transmission of participatory habits by parents.[11]

[8]The inheritance of political activism is considered in detail in Kenneth Prewitt, "Political Socialization and Leadership Selection," *The Annals* 361 (1965), 96–111.

[9]John C. Wahlke, Heinz Eulau, William Buchanan, and LeRoy C. Ferguson, *The Legislative System* (New York: John Wiley and Sons, Inc., 1962), pp. 82–84. Similar data confirming the importance of growing up in a politicized environment are reported by Marvick and Nixon. These authors found that almost 40 percent of a sample of Los Angeles campaign workers had at least one politically active parent; only 20 percent came from totally apathetic families. Dwaine Marvick and Charles Nixon, "Recruitment Contrasts in Rival Campaign Groups," *Political Decision-Makers*, ed. Dwaine Marvick (New York: The Free Press, 1961), p. 210.

[10]Hess and Torney, *The Development of Political Attitudes in Children*, p. 122. However, Freeman reports that parental political interest and the interest of offspring are associated, but only among males. J. Leiper Freeman, "Parents, It's Not Your Fault, But . . . ," *Journal of Politics*, 31 (1969), 812–17.

[11]These and a number of similar studies are briefly summarized in Herbert Hyman, *Political Socialization*, pp. 64–66.

One's family can also affect participatory dispositions through the family authority structure. Hess and Torney, for example, report that children with relatively ineffectual fathers are lower in their sense of political efficacy, political interest, participation in political discussions and activities, and concern for political issues. Hess and Torney also find that these same participatory dispositions among boys are negatively affected by the presence of a strong mother.[12] Further confirmation of the impact of family authority structure on political activism is reported in Flacks's study of University of Chicago students who seized the university's administration building. When compared to the family backgrounds of nonactivists, both male and female activists tended to come from families where parents were permissive and less severe in applying discipline.[13] The relationship between less authoritarian (or more democratic) family structure and participatory dispositions is also displayed in Almond and Verba's analysis of participation in family decision-making. Though the relationships are not large, citizens remembering taking part in family decisions are more likely to be politically active than those exhibiting more passive family behavior.[14]

Surely the most convincing data on the importance of the family in the political socialization process is found in the transmission of partisan identification. The overwhelming consensus of numerous studies, employing a variety of methods, is that most offspring acquire the party loyalty of their parents. In the most comprehensive and sophisticated of these studies, Jennings and Niemi report that about two-thirds of their sample of high school seniors basically share their parents' partisan preference. Equally impressive is the fact that less than ten percent of the students actually switch party loyalties.[15] Roughly comparable results are reported by McCloskey and Dahlgren, who note that three-quarters of their adult sample support the party of their parents.[16] Essentially the same pattern is also described by

[12]Hess and Torney, *The Development of Political Attitudes in Children,* p. 120.

[13]Richard Flacks, "The Revolt of the Advantaged: An Exploration of the Roots of Student Protest," *Journal of Social Issues* 23 (1967), 52–75. Other data on student demonstrators suggest that "permissiveness" is unrelated to activism. See Jeanne H. Block, Norma Haan, and M. Brewster Smith, "Socialization Correlates of Student Activism," *Journal of Social Issues* 25 (1969), 163-64.

[14]An 11 percent difference in actual attempts at influence existed between those with family influence versus those claiming no such influence. This finding was derived by a secondary analysis of the Almond and Verba data.

[15]M. Kent Jennings and Richard G. Niemi, "The Transmission of Political Values from Parent to Child," *American Political Science Review* 62 (1968), 172–74.

[16]Herbert McCloskey and Harold E. Dahlgren, "Primary Group Influence on Party Loyalty," *American Political Science Review* 53 (1959), 757–76.

Campbell, Gurin and Miller, Dodge and Uyeki, and many others investigating the congruence of partisan identification across generations.[17]

When we analyze the transmission of specific political attitudes, the evidence of the family's impact on the socialization process is less compelling. On the one hand, considerable research shows that at least on *some* issues a modest relationship exists between parental attitudes and those of their children. For example, studying middle-class seventh- and eighth-graders and their parents, Wrightsman found that parents who frequently discussed the possibility of war, expected war, and worried a great deal about the possibility of war were likely to have children with similar concerns and expectations.[18] Dodge and Uyeki report that not only is there substantial agreement across generations on evaluations of Democrats and Republicans, but that substantial agreement also exists on evaluations of a variety of policy judgments.[19] The family's capacity to influence policy preferences is given further credence by Flacks's study of University of Chicago student activists. Flacks found that while demonstrators were decidedly more liberal than their fathers, the demonstrators' fathers were in turn more liberal than the fathers of non-demonstrators. We can thus infer that while fathers did not produce carbon copies of themselves, they influenced significantly the direction of their offsprings' political attitudes.[20]

A fourth piece of evidence showing the positive impact of family beliefs comes from the Friedman, Gold, and Christie study of Columbia College freshmen. Unlike most other studies of this subject, Gold *et al.* focused on politically related attitudes not involving current controversial topics. On one of the five scales used in the study, a moderately strong correlation existed between the son's attitude and the attitude of his parents (the scale reflecting authoritarian moral values). In a few other instances significant correlations were found between parental and offspring values, but the relationship between the son and either one of the parents on any of the five measures was weaker than the

[17]Angus Campbell, Gerald Gurin, and Warren E. Miller, *The Voter Decides* (Evanston: Row, Peterson, 1954), p. 99; Richard W. Dodge and Eugene S. Uyeki, "Political Affiliation and Imagery Across Two Related Generations," *Midwest Journal of Political Science* 6 (1962), pp. 266–76.

[18]Lawrence S. Wrightsman, "Parental Attitudes and Behavior as Determinants of Children's Responses to the Threat of Nuclear War," *Vita Humana* 7 (1964), pp. 178–85. On the other hand, Helfant reports weaker child-parent agreement on issues of war and international relations. Kenneth Helfant, "Parents' Attitude vs. Adolescent Hostility in the Determination of Adolescent Socio-Political Attitudes," *Psychological Monographs* 66 (1952).

[19]Dodge and Uyeki, "Political Affiliation and Imagery," p. 274.

[20]Flacks, "The Revolt of the Advantaged," pp. 70–75.

correlation between father and mother's attitude.[21] In sum, as these studies and the many similar ones summarized by Hyman suggest, parents can have some, albeit limited and selective, effect on their children's more specific political orientations.[22]

At the same time, other data suggest that even this moderate claim for the family's influence may be overstated and unfounded. For example, Hess and Torney compared the agreement between siblings on over one hundred political attitudes with the agreement between randomly matched pairs of children and concluded that except for attitudes toward parties, the extent of intrafamily agreement was very small though some existed. This lack of correlation was true even when the age differences between siblings were small.[23] The Jennings and Niemi research cited earlier further brings into question the family's capacity to transmit successfully large numbers of relatively specific attitudes. To be sure, on such global issues as evaluations of social groups (e.g., Catholics, Jews, Southerners) moderate levels of agreement exist between parents and offspring, but in other areas—attitudes toward civil liberties and political cynicism—the degree of congruence between parent and child was minimal. Moreover, the low correlations on these issues are not improved even when we take into account the degree of family politicization or the extent of parent-child political discussion.[24]

More generally, Connell in his methodologically oriented review of the literature on family transmission of political values, suggests that many of the positive findings are a consequence of technical errors or faulty inference. Connell points out that many early studies relied on students to take home questionnaires to their parents. This method undoubtedly biased the sample toward parents and children who shared close relationships. When parents who did not initially respond to the questionnaire did respond after pressure was exerted, the agreement between parent and child substantially declined. Lower levels of agreement were also more common when parents were approached directly rather than through the child. More important, many of the claims of parent-child agreement have not been made on the basis of

[21]Lucy N. Friedman, Alice R. Gold, and Richard Christie, "Dissecting the Generation Gap: Intergenerational and Intrafamilial Similarities and Differences," *Public Opinion Quarterly* 36 (1972), 334–46. The five measures were: (1) traditional moralism; (2) Machiavellian tactics (endorsement of interpersonal manipulative techniques; (3) Machiavellian cynicism (belief in people's weakness and gullibility); (4) New Left Philosophy (belief in idealistic social actions); and (5) revolutionary tactics (endorsement of revolutionary violence).

[22]Hyman, *Political Socialization,* pp. 52–56.

[23]Hess and Torney, *The Development of Political Attitudes in Children,* p. 113.

[24]Jennings and Niemi, "The Transmission of Political Values from Parent to Child," passim.

direct comparisons of each parent with his children, but rather on the basis of overall agreement or disagreement between generational groups. Such analysis is faulty, for even if the level of support for a particular policy is identical across two generations, this does not prove that each child is in perfect agreement with his own parents.[25] This point is well demonstrated by the Jennings and Niemi data showing that while the average ratings of various social groups differ only slightly among parents and children, the degree of correspondence among pairs of parents and children is moderate at best and frequently minimal.[26]

The Family's Influence: A Concluding Note

It should be clear that despite some rather powerful claims, the early family environment does not completely insulate an individual from outside, systematic manipulative influence. The strongest argument for such insulation from manipulation can be made in the case of broad, consensual beliefs, particularly those regarding basic political loyalties and respect for constituted authority. As we have suggested in earlier chapters, these orientations are of fundamental importance despite the common tendency to take them for granted. In this respect, then, the family operates to provide much of the basic continuity of the broad outline of American politics. The family also seems to exert considerable influence in partisan identification, though the transmission process remains far from perfect. However, when we move toward political participation and more specific political orientations we can readily see that while the family usually has some influence, it is far from completely determining. In many important areas of learning the American citizen is thus available for systematic manipulation. Whether or not this availability to influence actually means that the individual can be manipulated is our next question as we consider the impact of the schools.

THE IMPACT OF THE SCHOOLS

As we have already mentioned, the school provides an enormous opportunity to influence the minds of young children. Because education involves far more than formal classroom instruction, we must

[25]R. W. Connell, "Political Socialization in the American Family: The Evidence Re-examined," *Public Opinion Quarterly* 36 (1972), pp. 323–33.
[26]Jennings and Niemi, "The Transmission of Political Values from Parent to Child," p. 176.

consider the educational process in broad perspective. Our analysis of the educational process will thus consider four distinct aspects of the total school experience. First, there are the explicit (and sometimes not so explicit) messages directly conveyed to students. The civics course is the most prominent example of this mode of attempted influence, but it can just as well occur in ostensibly nonpolitical courses such as art and music. Second, the nature of authority relationships within the classroom and school can also influence political orientations and hence must be considered separately from course content. By authority structure we denote such things as degree of student involvement in discussions, the existence of opportunities to criticize teachers, and similar factors defining a school's authority atmosphere. Third, though perhaps not as obvious as the first two, the social mixture of the school environment is also a potential means of influence. As is frequently advanced in discussions of racial integration, informal contact among students can be an important part of the educational process. Similarly, as we shall see, the mixing of different social groups within the same environment is yet another way of influencing the development of political attitudes and behaviors. Finally, systematic manipulation is also possible through the network of extracurricular clubs and activities that form an integral part of American school life. Indeed, such activities are usually justified in terms of their manipulative potential, although they are given such positive labels as "character-building" or training for democracy through participation in club elections and decisions.

Explicit Transmission of Political Orientations

Because formal civics courses typically do not begin until about sixth or seventh grade, the earlier period may appear to be apolitical. This impression is misleading, however, and some scholars even claim that American schools expend more time and effort on political indoctrination during these years than schools in the Soviet Union.[27] The inconspicuous nature of this political indoctrination is probably a consequence of most of its being directed toward reinforcing existing tendencies rather than developing new orientations. This characteristic of solidifying existing tendencies is particularly marked in the area of national loyalty. As Hess and Torney point out, and as all of us can recall, schools daily engage in a wide variety of patriotic behavior. By

[27]George Z. F. Bereday and Bonnie B. Stretch, "Political Education in the U.S.A. and U.S.S.R.," pp. 9–16.

the sixth grade the average student has probably solemnly pledged allegiance to the flag thousands of times, regularly celebrated the births and heroic exploits of national heroes such as Washington and Lincoln, and learned to venerate such symbols as the flag, the Constitution, and the Declaration of Independence.[28]

Equally important, the school continues the process begun in the family of strengthening respect for constituted authority. In part, this is a consequence of the very nature of the classroom—the presence of a single teacher with thirty or more students and the need to accomplish required tasks obviously demands emphasis on order and discipline. This law and order mentality not only spills over into more general orientations toward authority roles, but also has an explicit corollary in what teachers communicate as the norms of good citizenship. As indicated earlier, until the fifth or sixth grade, teachers overwhelmingly emphasize such characteristics as obeying the law as the appropriate role of the good citizen. It is only much later that the more active aspects of citizenship are given attention (if they are given any attention at all).

Despite the occurrence of considerable learning during grade-school years, the school's responsibility for much of this learning is indirect. By teaching children how to read, a whole world of political stimuli opens, but political learning is not the major goal of this instruction. Moreover, the child's mental capacity increases dramatically during school years and much of what is acquired during these years might even be acquired without the existence of grade schools. This is not to say that the grade school is inconsequential in the political socialization process; rather, despite some of the rhetoric on the grade school's importance, the bulk of its direct political influence is solidifying nationality and compliance attitudes initially acquired within the home.

Does this process of driving home love of country and obedience to its laws constitute systematic manipulation? If, for the moment, we define manipulation as a successful transmission of political orientations, it would appear that the grade schools are manipulating their pupils. If, on the other hand, we conceive of manipulation as the altering of orientations against the wishes or interests of those involved, our conclusion must be the opposite. Insofar as almost all American parents want their children to be loyal Americans obedient to authority, the schools are merely doing what parents want them to accomplish. Whether or not the parents have been brainwashed to want these

[28]Hess and Torney, *The Development of Political Attitudes in Children*, pp. 121–23.

particular dispositions instilled in their children is another question, but it is certainly not true that grade schools redirect children toward new values on the model of Soviet and Red Chinese schools.

A better test of the school's manipulative capacity is provided by considering the successes and failures of various civics courses. These courses, which commence in about sixth or seventh grade and continue until college, typically deal with topics less consensual than national loyalty or compliance. In many instances classroom messages do not reinforce family-acquired values and may even contradict them. Moreover, since these courses are specific events, rather than the more gradual process of grade-school political education, their effects on students are relatively easier to measure. To the extent that students' attitudes can be redirected by exposure to such courses, we shall have a good indication of the susceptibility of young Americans to systematic manipulative efforts. We shall review three studies of civics courses' effect on political attitudes and behaviors.

The first is Edgar Litt's analysis, using before-and-after questionnaires, of the effect of civics instruction in three communities in the Boston metropolitan area (referred to as Alpha, Beta, and Gamma).[29] In the first place, as measured by textbook material, the three communities are not equally committed to instilling the same political orientations. In the upper-middle-class Alpha, for example, textbooks make a relatively serious effort to inculcate politically realistic and activity-oriented values. At the other extreme is the working class community of Gamma whose texts heavily emphasize mere descriptions of political events and procedures. On the whole, the results of the before-after questionnaires do indicate some, though far from spectacular, impact of the civics curriculum on those topics where the textbooks made an effort at influence. For example, in Alpha, where textbooks devote a fair degree of attention to politics as a conflict-resolving process, perceptions of politics as a conflict-resolving process increased by 27 percent; in Gamma, where references to this view were minimal, almost no difference existed between students at the beginning of the course and when the course was completed. However, when the Gamma textbooks did attempt to convey messages other than sheer description, as in the case of support for democratic norms, the civics course did have an observable effect. It should be noted, however, that in no instance did the presence or absence of textbook material sway the opinions of more than a quarter of the students (and frequently fewer).

A more pessimistic picture of the capacity of civics courses to change attitudes is reported in Langton and Jennings' national study of

[29]Litt, "Civic Education, Community Norms, and Political Indoctrination," pp. 69–75.

high school seniors.[30] Despite the extended debate over the virtues of the traditional American history course versus the more politically oriented "Problems of American Democracy" course, the authors find that taking one as opposed to the other makes no difference in eight different areas of political learning.[31] If the more up-to-date "Problems" course is supposed to make students more knowledgeable, politically interested, and politically active than the more descriptive American history course, this is not confirmed by these data. Moreover, whether or not the students had taken *any* civics course appeared to be irrelevant to the development of their apolitical attitudes. Unfortunately, the authors do not provide data on exactly what the multitude of courses sought to accomplish, but we certainly can assume that all such courses in American schools make some effort at tasks such as increasing information and getting students to talk more about politics. The impact of such efforts, however, is minimal. Equally surprising, the lack of impact was found even when student evaluations of the course and teacher were taken into account, i.e., even highly regarded, well-taught courses generally made little difference on attitudes and behaviors.[32]

An important insight into the nature of this instruction is gained when the authors separately examine course impact on black students. Specifically, blacks taking these courses tended to increase their political knowledge (including ability to perceive partisan ideological distinctions), their sense of political efficacy, and support for civic tolerance. Similar effects were not, however, found in other areas of political learning. Blacks' political cynicism remained unchanged regardless of the number of courses taken, and among children from well-educated families, taking these courses had a *negative* impact on

[30]Kenneth P. Langton and M. Kent Jennings, "Political Socialization and the High School Civics Curriculum in the United States," *American Political Science Review* 62 (1968), 852–67.

[31]The eight areas are: political knowledge and sophistication; political interest; consumption of political messages in mass media; political discourse; political efficacy; political cynicism; civic tolerance; and participative orientations. It should be noted that the authors hold constant school quality, grade point average, sex, student's political interest, the number of history courses taken, parental education, and parental politicization in examining curriculum impact. On the other hand, a less complex analysis of the relationship between taking civics courses and political orientations by Almond and Verba indicates that such exposure does have a positive effect. Adults who recall being taught about government were considerably more likely to feel influential in political matters than those without this experience. Almond and Verba, *The Civic Culture,* p. 362.

[32]However, Ehrman in his study of a Detroit high school using many of the indicators used by Langton and Jennings reports that teacher willingness to discuss controversial issues, together with the openness of the classroom discussion, did have a sizeable though varied impact on political learning. Lee. H. Ehrman, "An Analysis of the Relationship of Selected Educational Variables with the Political Socialization of High School Students," *American Educational Research Journal* 6 (1969), 559–80.

political interest and talking politics (but the opposite was true for children from less well-educated families). Finally, black students' perception of what constitutes good citizenship is affected by their civics experience, but the direction of this impact runs contrary to expectations—rather than encouraging a participatory conception of good citizenship, the civics course instead results in a greater emphasis on loyalty as the mark of the good citizen.

Langton and Jennings' black subsample data are relevant for our purposes insofar as they indicate that the civics courses given in American high schools can have a significant, though unspectacular, political impact. However, as Langton and Jennings suggest, this occurs only where the information conveyed is not redundant. Because the civics curriculum provides lower-class blacks with their first contact with many political norms and bodies of information, learning takes place. On the other hand, by the time most white students reach eleventh- or twelfth-grade civics, thay have had sufficient contact with the materials to make a second version ineffectual in producing change. In sum, the Langton and Jennings' research suggests that while the current civics curriculum is generally without impact, this does not preclude success if nonredundant material is conveyed to students.

The last attempt at systematic political change we should consider concerns the college-level introductory political science course. The college experience has, of course, long been recognized as a catalyst of political change.[33] However, as striking as this change may be, this is not clear-cut evidence of the effectiveness of explicit college instruction in transforming students. It is entirely possible that the resultant change is more a consequence of nonclassroom events and the more general atmosphere on the campus. This possibility is clearly dramatized by Somit and others in their New York University study conducted during the mid 1950s.[34] Somit divided students enrolled in the introductory political science course into two types of classes: traditional courses stressing passive learning of facts about American political institutions and processes and participation-oriented courses exposing students to practicing politicians and providing ample oppor-

[33]Among others, see Charles H. McClintock and Henry A. Turner, "The Impact of College upon Political Knowledge, Participation, and Values," *Human Relations* 15 (1962), 163–76; Reo M. Christenson and Patrick J. Capretta, "The Impact of College on Political Attitudes: A Research Note," *Social Science Quarterly* 51 (1970), 315–20; Theodore M. Newcomb, *Personality and Social Change: Attitude Formation in a Student Community* (New York: Dryden Press, 1943); and Philip E. Jacob, *Changing Values in College* (New York: Harper and Row, 1957).

[34]Albert Somit, Joseph Tanenhaus, Walter H. Wilke, and Rita W. Cooley, "The Effect of the Introductory Political Science Course on Student Attitudes Toward Personal Political Participation," *American Political Science Review* 52 (1958), 1129–32.

tunity to join political organizations. Both before and after these courses students' attitudes toward personal political participation were measured.

The results generally indicate the more participation-directed course to be ineffectual. During a three year period during which three slightly different versions of the participation-oriented course were offered, only in one case was the difference between the first participation attitude measure and the second statistically significant (and in one of the activist-oriented classes a slight decrease occurred in interest in participation). For the most part students remained neutral about their role in political life, and even in the one instance where a change occurred, there was clearly not a dramatic movement toward increased activism.[35]

Classroom and School Authority Structure

That there are important political repercussions from variations in the structure of school authority relationships is frequently taken for granted by school reformers. The oft-repeated notion that democratically disposed citizens can only develop in democratically-oriented schools is perhaps the most familiar example of this thinking. Though attractive, this line of reasoning unfortunately lacks extensive empirical verification. In fact, only two major studies—Almond and Verba's five nation study and Ehrman's research on a single Detroit high school —significantly deal with this issue, and even here, the findings concern only a limited number of political orientations.

On the whole, Almond and Verba find that engaging in such democratic school practices as complaining about unfair treatment from teachers and taking part in classroom discussions have only a moderate impact on citizens' beliefs about their capacity to influence government.[36] Thus, while three quarters of the respondents who were active in school feel they can affect government policy, only slightly more than half who have not had such school experience feel the same way.

---

[35]Other findings on this subject are reported by Garrison in his study of students enrolled in a traditional American government course, an introduction to political science course, and a nonpolitical social science survey course. All three courses were associated with an increase in political apathy, but this trend was not most pronounced in the nonpolitical course and least evident in the traditional American government course. Unfortunately, Garrison does not connect these changes to specific course content. Charles L. Garrison, "Political Involvement and Political Science: A Note on the Basic Course as an Agent of Political Socialization," *Social Science Quarterly* 51 (1970), 305–14. Also see Dean Jaros and R. Dacy, "The Elusive Impact of Political Science: More Negative Findings," *Experimental Study of Politics* 2 (1972), 14–54.

[36]Almond and Verba, *The Civic Culture*, pp. 352–60.

Consistent with our previous discussion of the redundancy of learning experiences, we again find that among those having alternative opportunities to learn this lesson (in this instance, the highly educated), the school experience has almost no impact. In other words, to a child from a poorly educated family where there is probably little stimulus to feel politically confident, being able to take part in school dicussions, argue with the teacher, and so forth, does make a small difference. Where such dispositions are already present, however, these school experiences make no difference.

Unlike Almond and Verba who measure the impact of school structure directly, Ehrman hypothesizes that classroom freedom or intellectual openness plays an intervening role in political learning.[37] That is, the opportunity to freely discuss controversial issues with a nonauthoritarian give-and-take between student and teacher mediates the impact of curriculum content on political attitudes. Ehrman does find that classroom structure affects the outcome of civics courses, but this impact is ambiguous. It certainly is not true that classroom openness makes civics courses more effective in dramatically encourgaing political participation, political efficacy, sense of citizen duty, or lowering political cynicism. In some instances opportunities for open controversial discussions do have an influence in the expected direction, but the overall pattern is a mixed one.

The Social Mixture of the School Environment

That students may learn politically as much from one another as from teachers or textbooks provides yet another, though usually less obvious, method of manipulation. As mentioned earlier, this mode of learning is implicit in some of the arguments favoring the integration of lower-class blacks into middle-class white schools, i.e., it is assumed that the middle-class whites' academic motivation and values will somehow rub off on the lower-class blacks via the friendships that will develop in an integrated school. While political scientists have not examined the daily political interchanges among friends in the same school, they have examined two characteristics that are closely related to interpersonal contact among students: the political atmosphere in the school and the social heterogeneity of the student body and peer groups within the school.

The effect of the school's diffuse political atmosphere is well illustrated by Levin's analysis of the relationship between student changes

---

[37]Ehrman, "An Analysis of the Relationship of Selected Educational Variables with the Political Socialization of High School Students," pp. 576–79.

in partisan attachment and the overall partisan composition of different high schools.[38] Specifically, where Republicanism is the overwhelming choice, a greater proportion of students from Democratic homes convert to Republicanism than where the proportion of Republican students is smaller. On the other hand, where the Democratic party is stronger, it is the Democratic party that disproportionately benefits from partisan conversions. This tendency of the dominant political position to exert pressure for conformity on deviants is confirmed by Johnson's study of high schools in six Kentucky counties.[39] Johnson's data suggest that a very small party would be successful in retaining only about half its followers across generations, a fact that may help explain the general pattern of local one-party dominance in American politics. Hence, if one wanted to make Republicans out of young Democrats, one would merely insure that in as many schools as possible the Democratic party was the minority choice.

The importance of the student body's social composition on political resocialization is given further support by Langton's study of high school students in Jamaica, West Indies.[40] Consistent with the findings of Levin and Johnson, Langton finds a shift toward the values of the majority. Working-class students in working-class dominated schools maintained their working-class attitudes, but their social brethren in middle-class schools were closer to their middle-class schoolmates on many (but not all) political issues. For example, the working-class children in the minority situation were more supportive of personal liberty, more favorable toward voting and civic tolerance, as well as more politicized than similar students attending largely working-class schools. This persuasive influence did not, however, extend to all attitudes; in the area of economic attitudes, which Langton calls more basic, there was no shift in the middle-class direction.

Langton also reports a parallel process of political conversion within peer groups. Specifically, working-class students with middle-class friends are apparently resocialized away from their initial working-class values and toward middle-class positions. This resocialization pressure was found even in the area of economic attitudes, which, it will be recalled, resisted the influence of the more general school environment. Moreover, the impact of inter-class friendships and the social

[38]Martin Levin, "Social Climates and Political Socialization," *Public Opinion Quarterly* 25 (1961), 596–606.

[39]Norris R. Johnson, "Political Climates and Party Choice of High School Youth," *Public Opinion Quarterly* 36 (1972), 48–55.

[40]Kenneth P. Langton, "Peer Group and School and the Political Socialization Process," *American Political Science Review* 61 (1967), 751–58.

composition of the school is cumulative: working-class students in middle-class schools with middle-class friends receive the greatest impetus toward acquiring middle-class political values.

This process of dominant values affecting minority positions also appears to occur in the United States, though the evidence is very limited. Data collected in Detroit during 1964 on schoolchildren's reactions to the assassination of President Kennedy indicated that lower-class children were more likely to approve of Oswald's being deprived of his civil liberties than were middle-class children.[41] However, as was the case in Jamaica, West Indies, lower-class children in more heterogeneous social environments are resocialized toward the middle-class values; i.e., they were less happy about Oswald's being killed by Jack Ruby than were lower-class children who had not been resocialized. These lower-class children were also more similar to middle-class children in their evaluation of the president.

The Impact of Extracurricular Activities

Extracurricular activities are an integral part of American school life, and even if one does not participate in them directly, their considerable role in the school status hierarchy makes them a pervasive factor in the school environment. The range of activities encompassed by school-sponsored clubs is enormous—everything from chess clubs to football exists to serve the student body. Besides their obvious social value to participants, these activities can be politically justified in a number of ways. It could be argued that insofar as clubs usually have elected officers, decision-making functions, bargaining and compromise, and rules of fair play, they thus provide a realistic introduction to democratic politics. Moreover, they are usually small enough so that numerous students can acquire organizational skills and knowledge as well as increase their sense of competence, all politically useful attributes. At the broader level, it has been argued that by encouraging the joining habit early, such organizations help provide a strong network of secondary groups that not only multiply the individual's political influence, but prevent society from drifting toward an atomized mass society.[42]

Whether or not extracurricular activities do in fact perform all these functions has not, unfortunately, been the subject of extensive research. One study that did consider some of these questions was

---

[41]These data are cited in Langton, "Peer Group and School and the Political Socialization Process," pp. 757–58.

[42]This function is discussed in great detail by William Kornhauser, *The Politics of Mass Society* (New York: The Free Press, 1959).

Lewis's survey of students in one small Michigan community.[43] Lewis found that those taking part in high school extracurricular activities were more politically efficacious, more supportive of the role of political parties, showed less cynicism, and expected to be more active politically in the future. However, despite these positive relationships, Lewis did not conclude that the extracurricular activities were in fact responsible for these characteristics.

Ziblatt's study of high school students in a medium-sized Oregon community also suggests that extracurricular activities may have no direct influence on political attitudes. Using attitude toward politics as his basic measure, Ziblatt reports no relationship between this orientation and the extent of extracurricular participation.[44] This is even true when age, sex, and partisan identification are held constant. A second aspect of extracurricular activities considered by Ziblatt is the relationship between one's position in the informal status system and attitude toward politics. As Coleman has indicated, outside activities such as athletics constitute a powerful status system that clearly makes some students into winners and others into losers.[45] The question can thus be asked whether being an outsider in the school status system discourages a positive evaluation of politics. Once again we find no relationship—students rating themselves as insiders are no more positive toward politics than those rating themselves outsiders in the status hierarchy. This analysis is far from conclusive in measuring the political impact of extracurricular activities, but Lewis and Ziblatt's data should caution those perceiving the network of school-sponsored clubs and activities as an important means of moulding future citizens.

A Concluding Note on the School's Influence

Though our data are not conclusive, it is nevertheless quite clear that the schools do not provide a highly efficient tool for manipulating the political orientations of preadults. Whether the attempt at influence is through direct transmission of information, the nature of au-

[43]Helen Sonnenburg Lewis, "The Teenage Joiner and His Orientation Towards Public Affairs," unpublished Ph.D. dissertation, Department of Political Science, Michigan State University, 1962. Cited in David Ziblatt, "High School Extra-Curricular Activities and Political Socialization," *The Annals* 361 (1965), 24.

[44]Ziblatt, "High School Extra-Curricular Activities and Political Socialization," p. 25. However, despite this initial lack of association, Ziblatt ultimately concludes that a relationship does exist between extracurricular activities and attitude toward politics. This assertion is based on a complex linkage between father's education, integration into the school status system, social trust, and attitude toward politics. What is important for us, however, is that participating in school activities by itself does not result in attitude change.

[45]James S. Coleman, *The Adolescent Society* (Glencoe, Ill.: The Free Press, 1961), especially Chap. 8.

thority relationships, the political and social mixture of the student body, or the network of extracurricular activities, the successes are far from dramatic even when they do exist. Various features of school life may have an influence on certain political orientations, but no single factor can produce sizeable resocialization. In a rough sense our conclusions parallel those in current educational research suggesting that the school's direct impact in economic and social life may be far less than previously assumed.[46]   Nevertheless, we are not asserting that the schools are inherently incapable of being vehicles of systematic political manipulation. We certainly have yet to exhaust all the pedagogical alternatives, and the conditions that made influence difficult in the past may well change in the future. Nor, as our analysis of grade school socialization indicated, have we pushed existing methods and opportunities to accomplish dramatic redirections in political learning. Our initial statement on the school's limited capacity to manipulate stands, but we must also acknowledge that our analysis has not permanently answered the question of manipulation via the educational system.

THE IMPACT OF THE MASS MEDIA

In terms of sheer pervasiveness, the mass media, which include everything from comic books to television, are an equal to the school. Among families where TV is employed as a babysitter, the number of hours of television exposure may in fact far exceed time spent in school. As we have already mentioned, both the extent of the media's penetration into the daily life of children and its relatively accessible nature provide considerable potential for systematic manipulation. Indeed, this manipulative potential is so high that some have sought to regulate carefully children's program content lest young Americans become permanently brainwashed. The controversies over the extensive portrayal of TV violence, the implicit glorification of criminality and the emphasis on ghoulishness in some comic books are illustrative of the many debates involving the mass media's effect on childhood attitudes.

Although research abounds on the impact of mass communications in general, and a number of studies have analyzed the effects of media on children, studies concerned with explicitly political messages are surprisingly few in number. One major study analyzing the media's role in socialization is Chaffee's survey of junior and senior

[46]Christopher Jencks, *Inequality* (New York: Basic Books, 1972) among others.

high school students in five Wisconsin cities.[47] Chaffee reported that during the 1968 primary election students' political knowledge was significantly increased by their viewing of television public affairs programs and their exposure to newspaper political coverage. A relationship between public affairs media consumption and political participation was also found, but the association was weak. Perhaps equally significant, when students were asked to compare parents, friends, and teachers as sources of information and influence on their own opinions, the mass media were rated the most important. Unfortunately, however, these evaluations are based only on perceptions; the media's influence was not independently determined.[48]

The importance of the media in attitude formation has also been documented by Lovibond's study of grade school children in Adelaide, Australia.[49] Lovibond developed an attitudinal scale measuring fascistic attitudes among children, i.e., use of violence in personal relations, cynical view of human nature, sadism, idealization of war, faith in strong leaders rather than democratic methods, and the complete subordination of women. When this fascistic attitude was correlated with the consumption of mass media, Lovibond found that children who regularly attended movies or regularly read comic books were more fascistic than those not engaging in these activities. Moreover, the introduction of television into the region contributed significantly to an increase in fascistic attitudes (however, the effects of television and comics and movies are not cumulative since, as TV viewing increased, comic book and movie consumption declined).

The last analysis we shall consider is Tolley's survey of children's attitudes towards war.[50] When grade-school children were asked whether television had taught them a lot about the war in Vietnam, the vast majority responded affirmatively (and 80 percent had seen pictures of combat on TV). Moreover, regular television watchers and those who read newspapers a great deal were much more knowledgeable about the war. However, attitude differences about the war were unaffected by media consumption. The media were also found to be ineffectual in

[47]Steven H. Chaffee, L. Scott Ward and Leonard P. Tipton, "Mass Communication and Political Socialization," *Journalism Quarterly* 47 (1970), 647–59.

[48]Similar findings on the perceived importance of the mass media are reported by Hirsch in his study of Appalachian children. Herbert Hirsch, *Poverty and Politicization* (New York: The Free Press, 1971), pp. 34–39.

[49]S. H. Lovibond, "The Effects of Media Stressing Crime and Violence upon Children's Attitudes," *Social Problems* 15 (1967), 91–100.

[50]Howard B. Tolley, Jr., "Socialization to War: A Questionnaire Study of Children's Attitudes and Knowledge," paper presented at the American Political Science Association convention, 1972. Respondents were children in grades three to eight in a variety of schools in New York, New Jersey, and Maryland.

effecting more general orientations towards war. Even viewing television shows implicitly glorifying war and espionage (e.g., "Hogan's Heroes," "McHale's Navy," "Mission Impossible") did not encourage an acceptance of war. Nor did watching television news coverage increase children's tolerations of international conflict.

What about the possibility of the mass media as a manipulator of more basic political attitudes? Are some of the critics of the media correct when they argue that the mass media possess the power to shape basic patterns of American political life? Though research has not been directly addressed to this broad question, the more general research on mass communications does suggest the following limitations on the media's potential for producing fundamental political change.

First, it is well documented that the media's greatest persuasive influence occurs where attitudes are not deeply rooted.[51] Attitudes forming the basic core of one's identity, or ones held for long periods of time, are particularly resistant to media-induced change. As our previous discussions of early political learning clearly indicate, many fundamental political attitudes, e.g., national loyalty, positive evaluations of authorities and institutions, and partisan attachment, are acquired early in life and are deeply imbedded. The belief that America is the greatest country in the world and similar products of early learning differ fundamentally from more malleable preferences for a particular toothpaste. While the media's success in influencing the latter may be considerable, the same could not be said for any attempt to resocialize Americans away from their national identity via TV programs or newspaper stories.

Moreover, the commercial nature of American mass media requires that messages remain within the broad consensus of acceptability. To offend large numbers, whether politically, sexually, or artistically, is to go broke and most of those controlling the media do not desire bankruptcy. Hence, a strong pressure exists to avoid controversial areas.[52] As much as a TV or radio station owner or program sponsor may want to transform American youth politically, and regardless of the Constitutional guarantee of free speech, his livelihood nevertheless dictates staying within the limits of political conventionality. In Soviet and Red Chinese society where media are state-owned and profit is irrelevant, such constraints obviously do not exist.

---

[51]Joseph T. Klapper, *The Effects of Mass Communication* (New York: The Free Press, 1960), pp. 15–26, 45–59.

[52]Klapper, *The Effects of Mass Communication,* pp. 38–43.

A third restraint on the media's capacity to promote significant resocialization is the sheer multiplicity of viewpoints. It is well documented in communications research that people choose sources that are consistent with their own opinions, and even if the messages are contrary to what they believe, their content is usually selectively perceived and retained.[53] Thus, even if certain television programs, comic books, radio shows, etc. did convey radical messages to young children, the net impact on the audience is probably going to be considerably less than intended. Consider, for example, the typical child's reaction to a program arguing that the president was an evil, incompetent man. If this were the only message continuously conveyed by numerous sources, it might be effective in producing change, but excluding such a continuous bombardment, this description of the president would probably be ignored or distorted beyond recognition. Eventually, a more congenial source of information would be found.

This listing of the media's limitations is not intended to suggest that the mass media are without influence on the political socialization process. Our previously cited studies clearly show this not to be the case. Rather, our point is that contrary to some of the more spectacular claims for the media as a manipulator of the basic patterns of political life, the media's influence is limited to less fundamental areas. The United States has not yet experienced an extensive media campaign to alter fundamental orientations among children, so our analysis is only inferential. Nevertheless, since the very nature of the mass media in the United States makes it dependent on public approval, it is hard to see how the media would survive by purveying political opinions not shared by most people. If manipulation does take place, it is much more likely to occur in areas where new opinions are being formed or where preferences are only lightly held. Though hardly unimportant, these latter areas clearly do not constitute the basic aspects of American political life.

Conclusion: Does Systematic Manipulation Exist?

It will be recalled that our analytical strategy was (1) examine where political orientations were acquired and (2) review various attempts to change these orientations. Our basic argument is that manipulation is very unlikely (though not impossible) where either all important attitudes and behavior originated in the family or where conscious attempts at resocializing children (e.g. high school civics

[53]Klapper, *The Effects of Mass Communication,* pp. 19–26.

courses) were unsuccessful. In the first instance any would-be manipulator would experience enormous problems of access; in the second instance the techniques of manipulation would be insufficient.

Our review, on the whole, suggests that manipulation of the socialization process is a realistic possibility, but only on relatively nonfundamental areas and even then only in special circumstances. Supporting the possibility of systematic manipulation are:

Many political attitudes and behaviors are not totally family determined. Hence, citizens are "available" for persuasion toward new positions and actions in a number of areas.

High school civics courses may have an impact on students where a relatively large effort is made to convey a message. Success is particularly likely where the message is not redundant.

The political and social environment of the high school affects political attitude change. To a lesser extent, the school's authority structure also affects political orientations.

The mass media can influence a number of political orientations. This influence is underlined by the media's persuasiveness and the importance attributed to it by preadults.

At the same time, however, other data suggest that severe restrictions exist for those seeking to manipulate the basic outlines of American political life. Specifically:

Important political loyalties and authority dispositions originate within the family. Such orientations, though diffuse and initially held with little real understanding, are nevertheless tenacious and provide the support for fundamental features of American politics, e.g., the existing political community.

Schools, particularly elementary schools, focus the bulk of their socialization effort on reinforcing the lessons acquired within the family. The opportunity for resocialization away from parental values is not exploited.

Moreover, despite occasional successes, the preponderance of evidence indicates that the school civics curriculum, as well as other features of the school experience, usually has only a marginal impact on a wide variety of orientations for most students. This is not to say that the school cannot be an effective instrument of manipulation; but rather, schools usually are ineffective in producing desired results.

Finally, while the mass media may possess a demonstrated ability to affect, say, political knowledge, the very nature of American mass media places major constraints on the range of permissible manipulative efforts. That is, the need to stay in business channels political messages within a limited range of acceptable political positions.

What we thus appear to have is the persistence of broad, funda- mental patterns of political orientations without systematic manipula- tion to guarantee (or challenge) their persistence. Though some interests benefit considerably from the persistence, we find no evi- dence that these interests are able to intervene in the socialization process to enforce their values on unwilling or indifferent parents and children. If there is manipulation in these broad areas of learning, it is manipulation in the sense of one generation passing on to its offspring a certain acceptance of the status quo, not one interest defeating another via resocialization. Outside these broad areas, our analysis suggests that influence (but not control) in the socialization process by certain interests is likely. For example, more democratically-oriented educa- tors can increase support for democratic values among some adoles- cents. Likewise, mass media under certain conditions can encourage a greater appreciation for violence and toughness among young children. While even this type of influence may be disturbing to those desiring a society where everything is decided by free choice, we are neverthe- less a long way from a society in which political socialization is a crucial means by which one interest systematically and consciously dominates others.

9

Political Socialization
and Democratic Citizenship

Our analysis of the political socialization process suggests that by adulthood there are strong constraints limiting the acceptable range of reasonable political alternatives. Though existent political socialization does not determine the actions of each individual, or commit the existing system to an unchanging perpetuation of the *status quo*, it should be clear that many types of loyalties, beliefs, and behaviors are made highly unlikely by early learning. Important choices remain to be made, but even the most important of these decisions will probably be made within a framework defined by political socialization.

The question we shall now consider is the desirability of this particular range of reasonable alternatives. Specifically, we want to know whether the range of alternatives provided by existing political socialization is consistent with the demands of democratic citizenship.

Our basic question is: Are young Americans being socialized to be democratic citizens? To answer this question we shall evaluate the findings presented in previous chapters in the light of the demands of democratic citizenship. While the preceding chapters described what existed empirically, here we evaluate these empirical data against what ought to exist, i.e., normative democratic theory. Our analysis begins by setting forth the types of attitudes and behaviors required of good democratic citizens. Once these standards are established we shall determine whether or not these standards are satisfied by existing political socialization.

THE REQUIREMENTS OF DEMOCRATIC CITIZENSHIP

If there were a single, universally accepted version of what democracy was, our task would be simplified enormously. Unfortunately, this is not the case. Though virtually everyone agrees that democracy has something to do with people ruling, this basic notion by itself provides little guide for analysis. Beyond this idea of popular rule there are probably as many meanings of democracy as people who have attempted to define it. Nor can we unambiguously infer the meaning of democracy from its application in political life—nations as disparate as Great Britain and the People's Republic of China both would claim to be democracies.

Despite all the diversity in definitions and uses, it is possible to propose conceptions of democracy that capture many, if not most, of the features usually associated with democracy. However, rather than employ a single version of democracy as a guide to evaluate the socialization process, we shall instead formulate three distinct conceptions of democracy. By using more than one definition we cannot only include more of what different people mean by democracy, but also provide a more comprehensive set of standards to evaluate our data in political socialization. Thus, our analysis tells us both whether Americans are being socialized in accordance with the demands of a particular type of democratic citizenship, and what versions of democracy are not being promoted by the socialization process. The three versions of democracy we shall consider are: electoral competition democracy, representative democracy, and participatory democracy. Let us briefly describe the nature of each type of democracy and its respective socialization demands.

Electoral Competition Democracy

The basic idea of electoral competition democracy is that citizens have the right to choose their leaders.[1] Democracy thus exists when citizens choose among two or more candidates at election time. Why people choose particular leaders, the characteristics of these leaders, or the policies promoted by leaders are essentially irrelevant. Similarly, the vast array of freedoms and rights (e.g., freedom of speech) frequently associated with democracy need not exist for a political system to be democratic according to this conception of democracy. Advocates of electoral competition democracy claim that many of these so-called democratic rights will in fact exist whenever open competition for office occurs, but such rights and freedoms are not *definitionally* part of this form of democracy. As long as a voting choice exists and citizens avail themselves of this opportunity, the political system is no less democratic because leaders are irresponsive or laws infringe on political liberty.

A conception of democracy demanding no more than competition for citizen votes may not initially appear to warrant the label democracy. This conception is certainly a long way from the image of a New England town meeting in which citizens ruled political affairs directly. Nevertheless, electoral competition democracy has much to recommend it. In the first place, its relatively undemanding citizen requirements are very appropriate for large modern industrial societies. Direct control of political affairs by all citizens may have been feasible in small communities, but in nations of millions where people have other things to do besides being full-time politicos it is unreasonable to conceive of democracy in terms of large town meetings and direct policymaking. Second, by emphasizing popular choice of leaders rather than citizen control of policy, electoral competition democracy recognizes the complexity of modern government and the specialized expertise needed to make effective policy. Though citizens in an ideal democracy might decide important issues themselves, it is obvious that many, if not most, crucial contemporary political decisions are beyond the knowledge of the masses. Finally, the right to select one's leaders is an important and powerful political right. To appreciate how crucial this opportunity is, one must imagine situations in which citizens have no

---

[1]The conception of democracy we label electoral competition democracy is drawn almost entirely from the writings of Joseph A. Schumpeter. See Joseph A. Schumpeter, *Capitalism, Socialism and Democracy,* third edition (New York: Harper and Row, 1950), especially pp. 240–96. For a criticism of Schumpeter's approach, see Peter Bachrach, *The Theory of Democratic Elitism* (Boston: Little, Brown and Company, 1967), pp. 17–21.

voice in leadership selection. It is perhaps only when one cannot "turn the rascals out" that this prerogative is fully appreciated.

For electoral competition democracy to work effectively citizens must possess the following characteristics:[2]

(1) Because elections are a crucial mechanism of popular control, citizens must be supportive of electoral institutions and processes.

(2) Citizens believe that it is through the electoral process that they exercise their political power. Other forms of political influence, such as demonstrations, are not rejected as wrong; rather, as mechanisms of political control they are viewed as unnecessary.

(3) For elections to be competitive citizens must be willing to allow a variety of positions to be advocated. This is not an absolute requirement since electoral competition democracy does not require freedom for every point of view. Nevertheless, citizens must show toleration for some opposing positions if electoral choice is to be meaningful.

(4) Because duly elected governments have a free hand in order to best manage public affairs, citizens must respect the competence and intention of authorities. Leaders are not the servants of public opinion; they are experts chosen to perform a function and government cannot operate effectively where leaders are second guessed, mistrusted, disregarded, and held in low esteem.

Representative Democracy

What we shall refer to as representative democracy perhaps comes closer to what many people would label democracy. Representative democracy includes most of electoral competition democracy, but goes beyond it in many significant ways.[3] Specifically, in addition to the right of people to choose their leaders, representative democracy includes two additional requirements, that leaders are broadly respon-

---

[2]We should reemphasize that these requirements, and the requirements of the other democratic theories, are only the citizen portion of a larger set of demands, e.g., proper training of leaders.

[3]Unlike electoral competition democracy that has clear theoretical roots in the writings of Joseph A. Schumpeter, representative democracy is an amalgam of ideas drawn from writers associated with the idea of liberal democracy. Some of the origins of this conception are to be found in J. Roland Pennock, *Liberal Democracy, Its Merits and Prospects* (New York: Rinehart and Company, 1950), Chapter 6; Henry B. Mayo, *An Introduction to Democratic Theory* (New York: Oxford University Press, 1960), Chapter 4; and Austin Ranney and Willmoor Kendall, "Basic Principles for a Model Democracy," in *Empirical Democratic Theory*, ed. by Charles Cnudde and Deane Neubauer (Chicago: Markham Publishing Company, 1970).

sive to public opinion, and guarantees of certain key freedoms. Compared to their duties in electoral competition democracy, citizens in a representative democracy play a much more active and demanding role. The public not only choose their leaders, but they can engage also in the policy-making process via techniques such as joining interest groups, and can monitor leadership behavior to insure that it is consistent with public opinion. Similarly, representative democracy is much more stringent in the requirement of individual rights and political liberties. Whereas rights such as freedom of speech were likely, but not definitionally required, in electoral competition democracy, such rights and liberties are an integral part of this second version of democracy.

We should note, however, that along with these additional requirements come certain problems in deciding whether these demands are realizable. For example, to what extent should government action be congruent with public opinion in order to satisfy this democratic requirement? Should the public hold leaders responsible for enacting every public whim? Or, should citizens be concerned only with broad issues and leave the details to experts? A related problem involves the question whether leaders should respond to stated public demands or to the interests that lie behind these demands. This is no easy question to answer, for people can frequently request laws that produce the opposite of what is desired.[4] Finally, the extent to which basic rights can remain irrevocably intact poses yet another problem. Is it possible that under very special circumstances such as wartime emergency, that certain democratic rights can be abridged without seriously violating the requirements of representative democracy? Moreover, are some rights more important than others or does a violation of one mean that democracy no longer exists?

These, and other similar problems are not trivial issues and in a complete discussion of democratic citizenship they would require lengthy analysis. Despite these lingering issues, the general intent of representative democracy is sufficiently clear to allow us to formulate the following citizen requirements:

(1) As in electoral competition democracy citizens should be highly supportive of electoral institutions and view this as a legitimate means of exercising popular control.

---

[4]For example, what if a majority demanded that poverty be reduced by guaranteeing a high minimum wage. Let us also suppose that leaders believed (but were not absolutely sure) that a high minimum wage was likely to *increase* poverty by creating unemployment among unskilled workers. Should leaders respond to the specific demand for a high minimum wage or the diffuse and implicit demand for a reduction in poverty?

(2) The public is also favorably disposed toward nonelectoral forms of political participation and has the necessary skills to use these forms effectively.

(3) Because government must be kept responsive to the popular will, citizens not only carefully follow politics, but also possess the knowledge to evaluate the government's actual performance. Moreover, to insure government responsiveness, citizens must choose their leaders on the basis of who best approximates their policy preferences (as opposed to personality attributes).

(4) Government cannot be too far removed psychologically from the governed, hence the average citizen must maintain a degree of skepticism about the virtues and capabilities of leadership and institutions. Though stopping short of rejecting authorities as incompetent and harmful, the good citizen in a representative democracy does not go nearly as far as a good citizen of an electoral competition democracy in imputing good intentions and effectiveness to political leaders.

(5) Various democratic freedoms and liberties are staunchly supported by citizens. Attempts to abridge freedom of speech, the right to free assembly, the right to try to influence government, and other rights are quickly perceived and resisted.

Participatory Democracy

While representative democracy may be viewed as a more demanding extension of electoral competition democracy, participatory democracy is a fundamentally different conception of democracy.[5] At the core of participatory democracy is the belief that politics includes all social life, and people ought to have a voice in all matters affecting their lives. Politics is thus not limited to government—it occurs in the home, in school, on the job, and wherever else decisions are made affecting people's lives—and democracy is realized when citizens effectively control their own lives. Equally important, the purpose of participation in a participatory democracy is not to control leaders, but rather to develop fully one's personality. Supporters of this democracy believe that human beings reach their full potential only by being participants,

[5]As in the case of representative democracy, there is no single conception of participatory democracy universally accepted. The version presented here was drawn from a number of sources. Among others, see Peter Bachrach, *The Theory of Democratic Elitism*, Chapter 7; Henry Kariel, *The Promise of Politics* (Englewood Cliffs, N.J.: Prentice-Hall Inc., 1966); and *Participatory Democracy*, edited by Terrence E. Cook and Patrick M. Morgan (San Francisco: Canfield Press, 1971), Chapter 1.

and while this participation may have additional benefits, the human development benefit is primary.[6]

Compared to the previous versions of democracy and the nature of contemporary political life, the requirements of participatory democracy obviously present a large order to fill. Not only would political life be enormously expanded to include vast areas now considered non-political, (e.g., job decision-making), but basic institutional structure would have to be either radically reorganized or abolished completely. Certainly the idea of a centralized government and citizen influence primarily via the ballot box are incompatible with the requirements of participatory democracy. In many ways participatory democracy is a return to the ideals of Athenian and New England town meeting democracy with a heavy emphasis on psychological self-actualization.

Not unexpectedly, participatory democracy has been severely criticized as unworkable and inappropriate for large industrial societies. Even supporters of the participatory democracy ideal sometimes acknowledge enormous practical difficulties in implementation. This form of democracy is not, however, lacking in counterarguments. As for the criticism that modern industrial society does not permit the average citizen to decide political policy, supporters of participatory democracy claim that this criticism ignores vast areas of daily life in which citizens can participate. Politics not only involves foreign policy and balancing the national budget, but decisions on the job, in one's neighborhood, and so forth are amenable to direct citizen participation as well. The criticism that the public lacks political interest or sufficient ability to decide important issues is answered by the assertion that this interest and competence develop after people are given participatory opportunities. Why should citizens be politically aware and competent if they lack the opportunities for involvement? Hence, a low level of citizen competence is not an argument against participatory democracy, but an argument for it.

While the details of participatory democracy have yet to be fully developed, the broad outlines of this form of democracy suggest that citizens should possess the following attributes:

(1) Because in a participatory democracy the benefits of civic life flow from citizen involvement, and not from wise leaders or efficient institutions, formal structures of power are not glorified lest they discourage citizen participation. Moreover, good government is not a result of efficient policy-making, but a consequence of total citizen

[6]See, for example, Arnold S. Kaufman, "Human Nature and Participatory Democracy," in *Responsibility,* Nomos III, Carl J. Fredrich, ed. (New York: The Liberal Arts Press, 1960).

involvement. To believe that one has power apart from actually exercising it not only violates the demand of actual involvement, but also denies the individual the benefit of participation.

(2) Political activism is highly valued and is broadly conceived to include a very wide range of activities. Politics is a pervasive phenomenon so electoral involvement is only a small aspect of political involvement. Moreover, all citizens, regardless of social distinction, are participation-oriented—no one class believes itself to be rulers while other citizens accept a more passive role.

(3) For politics to involve important issues citizens must be willing to accept high levels of divisive conflict. Conflict is not necessarily desirable, but it is not to be avoided in favor of forced consensus. In addition, to suppress conflict would be to suppress individualism and eccentricity, and hence to limit the full range of human development.

(4) Because citizens do not rely on formally designated leaders to represent their interests, citizens must have the capacity to analyze political life in terms other than crude slogans and clichés. The average person need not be an expert on all matters, but moderate levels of competence are necessary to avoid having political life dominated by a few experts.

(5) Politics is a ubiquitous phenomenon and if it is to be meaningful interaction among people, the political process must be free and open. Civic intolerance is incompatible with participatory democracy. Furthermore, because politics occurs among the people, not merely among government leaders, support for an open political process must exist among all segments of the population, not merely the political leadership.

This completes the first part of our analysis, setting forth democratic ideals against which to evaluate the range of reasonable alternatives provided by political socialization. It should be understood that the demands of the three forms of democracy are ideals useful for providing a standard of comparison; it is unreasonable to suppose that any political socialization process could produce citizens who meet these demands exactly. We are more interested in determining the approximate closeness of these ideals to reality than in describing minor deviations from sometimes stringent requirements. It should also be understood that these respective citizen demands represent only a part of the requirements for each democracy. All three versions obviously involve more than democratically oriented citizens; institutions must be created and numerous rules formulated before each of these democracies could function. Hence, we must remember that our analysis of whether existing socialization practices produce democratic citizens is only a partial answer to the broader question of whether all politics—citizens, leaders, and institutions—conform to the democratic ideal.

POLITICAL SOCIALIZATION AND DEMOCRATIC CITIZENSHIP

Our analysis begins by asking whether the political socialization process is consistent with the demands of participatory democracy. Given the fact that the existing political system can hardly be characterized as a participatory democracy, asking whether children's learning can be consistent with these demands may strike the reader as unnecessary. However, it would be a mistake to assume basic congruence between the functioning of the political system and what citizens would be willing and able to accept as legitimate. Recall, for example, that during the first half of the nineteenth-century France experienced a wide variety of governments with more or less the same citizen base. Even if Americans were not being socialized into orientations consistent with participatory democracy, our analysis can at least indicate the discrepancy between these democratic demands and current reality. Our question thus becomes: to what extent do Americans acquire political orientations that would allow them to be good citizens of a participatory democracy?

On the whole, the overwhelming evidence of the previous chapters indicates that the range of political alternatives reasonably open to citizens does not include the dispositions and skills demanded by participatory democracy.[7] Consider the first requirement; the system should not be venerated as a distant, godlike benevolent power dwarfing the average citizen's capacity. As we saw in Chapter Three young children are highly enamored of existing authority structures and leaders. Beliefs that authorities know what is best for us, and are virtually infallible, as well as inherently good, decline with age, but this decline is only relative and many of these attributes are transferred from particular leaders to institutions. Hence, the system can obviously take care of itself without constant citizen input. Also, rather than learn that participation is something to be continually striven for, children instead learn that citizens do in fact run their government.

---

[7]Moreover, one could even argue that not only does the socialization process foster the wrong citizen attributes, but the very process of foreclosing important political choices early in life without debate contradicts the spirit of participatory democracy. That is, important choices like the composition of the political community should be made consciously with due consideration to alternatives rather than unthinkingly accepted in childhood.

This almost definitional linkage between citizen involvement and government output is accomplished through a number of mechanisms. For example, the concepts democracy and America are virtually inseparable so America is where the people rule and vice versa. Children also acquire an exaggerated view of the average citizen's political power as well as beliefs about public officials actually obeying citizen opinion. It is thus not surprising that slogans such as "All power to the People" are not rejected, but are much more likely to be perceived as redundant —the people *already* have all power (and given the basic goodness and responsiveness of leaders, even this power may not be necessary).

The demands of participatory democracy fare only slightly better when we consider the second requirement—a broadly defined participation norm staunchly supported among all segments of the population. The norm of political activity is highly valued among all children, even those from politically disadvantaged groups, i.e., working-class children, blacks, and females. However, contrary to this second requirement, the norm of involvement is focused very narrowly. One's participation responsibility can be discharged by merely being informed and voting. Indeed, the electoral process appears to be the exclusive focal point of this participatory orientation. Other forms of political activities, e.g., demonstrations and boycotts, are not rejected as inappropriate; rather, they are largely ignored in the socialization process. Moreover, politics is conceptualized narrowly; politics means government and elections, not the pervasive clash of interests found in all aspects of social and economic life. These dispositions and conceptions are well reflected in the pattern of preadult political participation; the farther we move from activities involving electioneering and voting toward more personal activities, e.g., complaining to a teacher about unfair treatment, the greater the decline in participation though by no means is such activity nonexistent.

Similarly, evidence on children's support for divisive conflict also indicates that Americans are not trained to be good participatory democrats. Recall that while most children were emotionally involved in election campaigns, the conflictual nature of this participation was minimized. Typically, one candidate or party was seen as good as another though one might be preferred over the other. Many children even deny the existence of political differences. These orientations are obviously far more consistent with a ritualized, largely symbolic politics than a politics in which deeply felt issues are meaningfully confronted.

The fifth requirement, the possession of a moderate amount of political knowledge and sophistication, receives about the same level of confirmation as the previous four, namely, very little. Even in the area of elementary knowledge about political life most children and adolescents display vast amounts of ignorance. Informal, but politically very important, knowledge of how things really work is also lacking in any great degree, and much of what does exist is found among middle-class children. Even among this group, however, many naive and overly idealistic political beliefs persist unchallenged. Though some data indicate that adolescents are capable of complex, abstract political reasoning, other data on the actual application of these capacities indicate a lower degree of sophistication. Recall, for example, that the vast majority of high school seniors were unsuccessful at giving meaning to liberal and conservative and associating these concepts with political parties. We also saw that the process by which children acquire their partisan identification is hardly conducive to future rational decision-making. It may be argued that these defects will disappear once citizens start making important decisions, but equal if not more likely is the possibility that this low level of competence will mandate the continual dominance of politics by experts, not average citizens.

Widespread support for a free and open political process is the last demand of participatory democracy and it too is only weakly met by the existing political socialization process. We saw that it is only on the abstract level that most children supported such rights as freedom of speech and the right to hold unpopular opinions. When the issue becomes more concrete, e.g., the right of a Communist, support for a free and open political process all but vanishes. Data on the consistency of opinions toward unpopular groups and various freedoms also indicate that whatever support for democratic processes does exist is much more a grab bag collection of slogans than an understood, coherent position. Perhaps most surprisingly, groups that have the most to gain from these rights, i.e., the working class and blacks, are usually the least supportive of these rights. It appears, then, that without significant changes in this learning, attempts at providing citizens with a wide-open forum to consider all possibilities will face significant resistence.

That political socialization does not produce citizens willing and able to take their place in a participatory democracy may come as no surprise to those who would argue that this version of democracy is inherently unworkable. What about the requirements of the less demanding representative democracy? It will be remembered that unlike participatory democracy, representative democracy does not require the average citizen to carry the major burden of governance; elected leaders run daily affairs so citizens need only be attentive and occasionally active spectators. Indeed, the purpose of having representative leaders is to spare citizens the numerous and difficult burdens of continual involvement. Nevertheless, despite the less demanding nature of representative democracy, it is clear from our discussion of the requirements of participatory democracy that in many, though not all, areas of socialization the requirements of representative democracy are not fulfilled.

Recall our analysis of socialization for future political participation. Support for elections and electoral activity, an important feature of representative democracy, is very high and varies only slightly across a number of social groups. However, representative democracy, like participatory democracy, also demands the willingness and capacity to engage in nonelectoral political behavior and as we have already seen, it is not that such behavior is explicitly discouraged; rather, nonelectoral methods of influence are largely ignored. Also as we saw in our discussion of participatory democracy, citizens are not trained at a high level of civic competence. On almost every measure we employed, from knowing elementary factual knowledge to being able to make sophisticated distinctions, almost all preadults fared poorly. It is especially relevant that the acquisition of partisan identification, a disposition of considerable influence on voting, was typically based on almost no information. Leaders in a representative democracy are chosen strictly on their policy preferences and are duty bound to respond to citizen demands, but such a state of affairs appears to be very difficult to achieve.

Other citizen requirements of representative democracy are also largely unfulfilled. Governmental action is to be evaluated on its responsiveness to public opinion. Leaders are more or less public agents whose tenure in office is terminated by unresponsiveness. However, as we have already seen, not only are most citizens unprepared to evaluate complex political policies, but their opinions of leaders and the political process encourage considerable prejudging of the issue. That is, non-empirically based beliefs about the government being a democracy and inherent responsiveness of leaders and institutions all discourage rational evaluations. We are not suggesting that Americans are politically socialized to believe that any official action is automatically congruent with citizen preferences. A number of recent political issues indicate that this automatic supposition of responsiveness does not always occur. Rather, the socialization process provides leaders considerable benefit of doubt in their favor—unless clearly and frequently proven otherwise one is likely to believe that leaders behave responsively. While such beliefs may be a boon to officials, they nevertheless undermine the ideal of leaders being held accountable closely by those electing them.

Closely related to citizens' belief of responsiveness virtually by definition is the more general attitude toward political authority and authority structures. Recall that representative democracy requires that citizens neither totally reject authority as evil or overwhelmingly embrace it as godlike. In the former instance leaders will lack the popular support necessary to govern, while in the latter case the public will be manipulated easily. On the whole, the evidence suggests that the socialization process produces adults much closer to the benevolent end of the continuum than the rejection end. With maturity children do acquire a more realistic, less positive view of authority, but this change is largely one of degree—for example, even adolescents believe that the government rarely makes mistakes and generally knows what's best for the people. In short, as we saw in the requirement of citizen scrutinization of government responsiveness, the demands of representative democracy are undermined by excessive deference to leaders at the expense of citizen control.

The final requirement of representative democracy—staunch citizen support for an open political process and political liberty—is, as we have already discussed, not fulfilled except at the level of support for abstract slogans. Once we progress beyond this sloganistic support, we not only find considerable political intolerance, but minimal comprehension of the meaning of democratic principles as well. It is only in the area of religious freedom that preadults acquire the disposition necessary for a representative democracy; even the granting of political privileges to relatively harmless, but very unpopular, radical or reactionary groups generates little enthusiasm.

It should be quite clear by now that if Americans are being socialized to be good citizens of a democratic form of government, it is an electoral competition democracy form of government that is most congruent with this political socialization. This is not to argue that what currently exists is an electoral competition democracy. As stated earlier, we are not claiming that the socialization process determines the form of adult political life. Incongruities can exist between existing political patterns and what citizens are predisposed toward though we would expect that in the long run there would be a strain toward consistency. The question of whether or not the United States functions as an electoral competition democracy can only be answered by examining the political process, not by making inferences from the socialization process. We cannot reject the possibility that some other form of democracy exists despite the pattern of political socialization.

Recall from our discussion of electoral competition democracy that the main citizen burden was selecting leaders and the criteria employed in this selection process were essentially irrelevant. Going beyond the election process to meddle in government affairs while not legally prohibited, is neither encouraged nor necessary for democratic government. As we have already seen in our discussions of participa-

tory democracy and representative democracy, the participatory training received by citizens adequately fulfills these modest, though
hardly unimportant, requirements. Virtually all citizens are strongly
disposed toward voting and elections and only minimal pressure exists
for citizens to meddle in politics once the question of who is to rule has
been decided. There is no question that most Americans are willing and
able to choose their leaders (even though sizeable numbers do not
exercise their voting options).

Moreover, the relatively low levels of knowledge and sophistication that ran contrary to the requirements of our other two forms of
democracy present no problems for electoral competition democracy.
To vote on the basis of personality rather than issue position, to be
ignorant of public affairs, and to misunderstand government actions
does not make politics undemocratic. Efficiency and effectiveness are
relevant for leadership, not average citizens, and to make choices
poorly does not make these choices meaningless or a violation of
democracy. Hence, from the perspective of electoral competition
democracy arguments that only a competent, informed citizenry can
hold leaders to their promises and thus keep the government democratic are essentially irrelevant. The quality of participation has nothing to do with democracy; the only thing that matters is whether a
certain kind of activity, i.e., choosing between competing candidates,
occurs.

The only demand of electoral competition that appears to be met
less than satisfactorily by the political socialization process is in toleration for a variety of political viewpoints. However, since this demand
is not absolute—not every opinion must be tolerated and every interest
allowed to compete—low levels of support for democratic values has
less significance than for participatory democracy and representative
democracy. We could even go so far as to argue that as long as most
preadults are willing to allow *some* opportunity for political diversity,
no matter how narrow the range of diversity, this demand is satisfied.
Insofar as children seem largely uninterested in vehemently stamping
out all but the politically orthodox, this more modest version of the
demand is probably fulfilled.

Finally, when we turn to attitudes toward political authority we
find that what were defects from the perspective of our other forms of
democracy become virtues in the content of electoral competition
democracy. Recall that leaders of an electoral competition democracy
are to be perceived as highly regarded, competent experts, who are to
be trusted at their jobs. Without such positive evaluations leaders
might find it difficult to perform their proper functions in an electoral
competition democracy, namely, ruling. As we have already discussed,

Americans are eminently well trained to provide this highly positive support. Though dissatisfaction with particular officials is occasionally shown, it is obviously clear that young citizens acquire a variety of attitudes and beliefs allowing leaders considerable freedom to maneuver.

CONCLUSION: POLITICAL SOCIALIZATION AND DEMOCRATIC GOVERNMENT

Our analysis has proceeded by seeking the best fit between the existent political socialization process and a number of alternative democratic theories. This approach differs substantially from the one taken by some writers who assume that a democratically socialized citizenry remains to be achieved (and hence, the purpose of analysis is to criticize existing nondemocratic outcomes).[8] Instead, our argument suggests that we are indeed educating our children to be good democrats provided one is willing to accept electoral competition democracy as a valid concept of democracy.

No doubt this approach may be considered an implicit glorification of a rather modest level of citizen competence and exercise of political power. Indeed, some critics would probably argue that even attaching the label democratic to present socialization products is a perversion of the classical notion of democracy with its emphasis on active citizens directly governing their lives. Perhaps in some ways our analytical strategy is reminiscent of the archer who shot his arrows first and then pointed the target around each arrow to guarantee himself a bullseye each time. Thus, by shifting the definition of a highly valued term like democracy it is possible to judge almost any socialization practice as consistent with democratic government.

Such criticism is, at least in part, valid. Since we have shown that we are training children to be good democratic citizens we can perhaps congratulate ourselves on this effort. After all, the goal of training citizens for democracy has always been given the highest priority by educators. At the same time, however, our analysis can be construed in a very different way. Because we have considered the degree of fit between the socialization process and alternative democratic theories, we have also shown where the existing socialization process is seriously defective from the perspective of different conceptions of a demo-

[8]See, among others, Robert E. Cleary, *Political Education in the American Democracy* (Scranton, Pa.: Intertext Educational Publishers, 1971).

cratic citizenry. By no means have we asserted that electoral competition democracy is the one and only true democracy and hence the socialization process should remain untouched. The unsatisfied demands of participatory democracy and representative democracy provide a clear and systematic program of reform or even radical change. Rather than abstractly demand education for democracy with no particular concrete program, our analysis provides specific points in need of change if one desires a citizenry trained for participatory or representative democracy.[9]

By way of illustration consider our description of children's attitudes toward political authority and existing institutions. From the perspective of an advocate of representative democracy the highly positive orientations described in Chapter Three should be an object of reform. As we saw in the preceding section of this chapter, such benevolent images provide leaders with enormous latitude of action which runs contrary to the demand that citizens keep close reins on those governing them. Advocates of participatory democracy will also desire to change these orientations though perhaps to a greater extent than the representative democrat and for somewhat different reasons. To the extent that each of these democratic theories has a number of unsatisfied requirements, we are confronted with an enormous agenda for change. In this sense, our analysis of the congruence between socialization and democracy is much closer to a radical critique than a glorification of the status quo.

As a concluding note, one last, if somewhat tangential, question should be raised: What are the costs and benefits to be gained by moving toward representative or participatory democracy via changes in socialization? All save the most ardent democrats, however, would acknowledge that democracy (however defined) is not the only political condition to be maximized. There are other values such as decent living conditions, freedom from anomic violence, and rational economic production also worth pursuing; and it is not altogether obvious that a redirection of the socialization process toward deglorification of constituted authority, would be consistent with other values held by a representative or participatory democrat. Existent research is not clear, for example, on what would happen if children were socialized to meet the demands of the two unfulfilled versions of democracy. That we would have a democratically disposed citizenry is obvious, but

---

[9]It should also be added that our analysis of manipulation of the political socialization process provides a guide for such radical change.

what else would we obtain? For example, would a whole population of highly active, competent citizens make any process of governance impossible? Would life become so politicized that nothing was beyond the direct control of one's community? These and many other unanswered questions should caution us from assuming that to maximize more and more demanding conceptions of democracy represents automatic progress of some sort.

10

Conclusion:
Continuity and Change

Our analysis of early political learning suggests that despite some talk about fundamental upheavals, the crisis of the system, or even revolution, the future pattern of American politics will remain broadly consistent with the past. Future choices—insofar as they are influenced by the mass public—will continue to be dominated by existent givens that shape political outcomes, but are not themselves part of daily political conflict. To those taking the existing structure of American politics for granted, this conclusion may appear self-evident and hardly in need of varification. Nevertheless, as even the most cursory review of the rise and fall of governments and institutions demonstrates, this persistence is by no means an ordinary historical occurrence. Much more typical has been the inability of political patterns to sustain themselves over long periods of time.

This tenacity of the broad contours is displayed even in the radical rhetoric espoused by critics of the status quo. With few exceptions, the core features of political life are ignored: thus, for example, there is no call for abolishing America as the primary political unit and little thought given to restructuring institutions such as Congress or altering reliance on elections as the legitimate method of leadership selection. If we can momentarily remove ourselves from the heat of particular political battles over air pollution, racial injustices, government supported medical coverage, and other great issues of the day, it is clear that conflicts rage over relative details, not the basic rules and patterns themselves. No doubt even many of the radicals who warn against working within the system and reject the establishment accept virtually all the core features of the system or at least can conceive of no viable alternative to existent givens.[1]

The imposition of imposed major policy constraints through the political socialization process is not without considerable advantage. True, one may argue that every important choice should be made consciously and with due consideration for the costs and benefits, but the elimination of competing alternatives on fundamental issues obviously makes existing conflict more manageable. Consider the nature of political life where no item of business were beyond the reach of daily decision-making. Without minimum agreement on what was momentarily beyond contention, politics would become an exhaustive, chaotic, and probably inefficient process. Save perhaps the most parochial societies, where the impact of government were minimal, few people could survive under such conditions of fluid, all-encompassing political choices. That stability should be maximized at the expense of everything else is infrequently argued, but neither should we disregard the advantages of some degree of political inertia and having some issues off-limits.

At the same time, as we have argued in previous chapters, political stability via the socialization of alternatives into nondecisions is not without real costs to certain interests. Political socialization is not a neutral process: the acceptance of some givens but not others means

---

[1]This acceptance by radical, even "counter-cultural" activists, of the basic political structures is made clear in Flacks' sympathetic description of the social changes brought about by these youthful activists. Almost all the changes Flacks attributes to these activists are in the realm of popular culture, e.g., music, life style, *etc.* More significant, nowhere in this description of youthful revolt is evidence presented of an alternative set of political rules and structures. At best, Flacks discerns some opposition to such institutions as large, bureaucratic corporations, but such general antagonism hardly represents a full-blown counter-politics. Richard Flacks, *Youth and Social Change* (Chicago, Ill.: Markham, 1971), especially Chapters 4 and 5. Other data on the nonradical nature of contemporary American youth are described in Seymour Martin Lipset, "Youth and Politics," in Robert K. Merton and Robert Nisbet, *Contemporary Social Problems*, 3rd ed. (New York: Harcourt Brace Jovanovich, 1971).

that certain interests are likely to win and others likely to be defeated. Unthinking rejection of criteria other than geographical proximity as the basis for political unity, beliefs in the inevitability and correctness of present authority patterns, distaste for nonelectoral political action, and intolerance for unconventional views to mention but a few consequences of political learning do not add up to a political system giving equal weight to everyone. Under these particular givens, for instance, a large permanent minority seeking extensive changes must operate under inherently unfavorable circumstances. It is only by strenuous effort that such a disadvantaged group can compete equally. Such efforts can be compared to the abilities of a person of normal height who must compete against much taller basketball players—the basic rules of basketball place the shorter person at an inherent disadvantage even if the rules are enforced without bias.

Though we have thus far emphasized continuity and stability, it would be a grievous mistake to conclude that the political socialization process forever turned out generation after generation all embracing the status quo as beyond reproach. Such a situation is perhaps only possible in small, highly traditional societies. Moreover, such a claim is clearly contradicted by the changes in the range of acceptable policy alternatives within the last twenty or thirty years. Many political actions once out of bounds now appear to be an integral and normal part of American life. Witness, for example, changes made by blacks and women in their fight for equality. Whereas legal exclusion of blacks from politics was only relatively recently deemed normal in many states, it is now difficult to imagine how such a condition was tolerated for so long. The same could be said for many government programs once judged too radical for the public to accept (e.g., improving relations with Red China). No doubt many possibilities currently viewed as too far out will soon become part of the normal political landscape.

To understand how the contours of the normal range of choices can shift over time, let us briefly consider some general factors encouraging discontinuities in the political learning process. By discontinuities we mean deviations from previously accepted orientations about what constitutes the acceptable range of alternatives. Some of these forces for discontinuity are inherent; others are common only in modern industrial societies, but each contributes to the possibility of new alternatives becoming part of the reasonable array of choices. Analytically, we can distinguish five such pressures:

1. *Changing adult maturational experiences.* Though many important political dispositions are formed before adulthood, the adult years nevertheless provide considerable opportunity for change. In

particular, maturity brings a succession of problems and events that must be confronted and somehow solved.[2] Getting married, finding employment, raising a family, acquiring property, and growing older are situations faced by nearly everyone. It is unlikely that except in the most tradition bound societies these experiences are the same situations faced by the previous generation. For example, getting a job today may require more education than thirty years ago and the process of acquiring this additional education can open up new perspectives. Similarly, health care for the aged is not the same set of problems it once was, and these new problems may require different solutions. In a sense, personal survival requires adaptation and the acceptance of new ideas.

These new adult experiences can not only affect adult attitudes, but may spill over into child rearing. Consider, for example, the consequences of gradually rising educational requirements for many jobs. A father who himself faced this problem may make his children more education minded so they will be better prepared for future requirements. If this were a pervasive phenomena, the net effect might be a new generation quite different from their parents.[3] Moreover, children via their parents can experience these new situations and the socialization process is thus affected with no conscious parental effort. It is even possible that in some situations the deepest impact of adulthood experiences would be not on the parent, but on the more impressionable child. It has been noted, for example, that children of the Great Depression display greater antipathy toward the Republican Party than those who were adults during this period.[4]

2. *Significant unique events.* Not only does each generation pass through numerous routine and potentially learning-laden experiences, but dramatic occurrences can also have a transforming impact on previously acquired political orientations.[5] Major economic depressions,

[2]This process of adult socialization is more fully described in Orville G. Brim, Jr., "Adult Socialization," in John H. Clausen, ed., *Socialization and Society* (Boston: Little, Brown and Company, 1967).

[3]This process of adults consciously changing traditional socialization practices to help their children better survive the future also takes explicit political forms. Inkeles, for example, shows that in the past Soviet revolution period parents socialized in traditional values redirected their children toward newer collectivist goals. Alex Inkeles, "Social Change and Social Character: The Role of Parental Mediation," *Journal of Social Issues* 9 (1955), 12–23.

[4]Angus Campbell, *et. al.*, *The American Voter*, pp. 153–56.

[5]Individuals who share a common political experience that substantially affects their future political orientations are sometimes described as belonging to a "political generation." This phenomenon of a politically distinctive age cohort is further elaborated in Karl Mannheim, "The Problem of Generations," in *Essays on the Sociology of Knowledge*, edited and translated by Paul Kecskemeti (London: Routledge & Kegan Paul, 1952).

outbreaks of war, military defeats, assassinations, runaway inflations, and other important events can resocialize people away from long standing notions of what is reasonable. No doubt the experiences of widespread unemployment and general economic stagnation during the 1930s made people more willing to think about programs once considered beyond the realm of possibility. The launching of Sputnik in 1957 also caused people to view established beliefs in a new light. A more recent phenomenon that may have moved the boundaries of reasonable and unreasonable alternatives was the Vietnam War. Though it is perhaps too soon to say exactly what the war's long-term impact will be, it is more than likely that many citizens and leaders were permanently affected by events both at home and in Vietnam.

3. *Long-term societal changes.* Less dramatic than sudden depressions or widespread outbreaks of domestic violence, but certainly no less important, are the pressures exacted by long-term gradual changes occurring within modern nations. Such pressures can emanate from a variety of changes: a rise in economic mobility, increases in overall educational levels, a trend toward urbanization and industrialization, the development and dissemination of new technologies, the growth of communication networks, shifts in demographic patterns, and changes in forms of ownership are but a few of the types of changes generally occurring in modern societies.[6] Consider, for example, the impact of automation on comtemporary American society. The sheer existence of methods of production not requiring extensive manpower allows a rethinking of previously unquestioned views on the necessity of the work ethic, the content of education, and the eradicability of poverty. Similarly, in some developing nations sharp increases in population and decreasing economic capacity can create an environment conducive to the consideration of policies once rejected as inconceivable (e.g., land reform, democratization, centralized planning). In many instances the range of available choices is enlarged when societies face problems for which the usual responses are totally irrelevant.

4. *Leadership innovation.* Any review of history will indicate that leaders can also affect the line separating reasonable and unreasonable political choices. Particularly in the United States where authorities are given extensive leeway in doing what they consider best for the country, dramatic actions can raise possibilities once considered beyond the political pale. Consider, for example, Roosevelt's radical (for

[6]This type of change is well illustrated in Converse's analysis of the consequences of rising educational levels within the American electorate. See Philip E. Converse, "Change in the American Electorate," in Angus Campbell and Philip E. Converse, eds., *The Human Meaning of Social Change* (New York: Russell Sage Foundation, 1972), pp. 322–37.

its time) New Deal legislation. As previously suggested, acceptance of these departures was encouraged by new conditions, but it is also likely that Roosevelt himself was partly responsible for the inclusion of new alternatives in the existing repertory of choices. Nixon's overtures and visits to Red China suddenly made certain policies much more reasonable. In a similar sense Martin Luther King and his philosophy of militant nonviolence increased the conceivable options available to dissatisfied blacks. As the vast array of ignored crackpot political innovations attests, however, it is unlikely that any leader can singlehandedly alter the boundaries of givens unless many supportive conditions are present.

5. *Breakdowns and changes in socializing agencies.* Since much of what children learn is transmitted through agencies such as the family and the school, it is obvious that where these agencies undergo substantial change, the likelihood increases that new alternatives will become available. For example, if due to war or economic dislocation the American family is seriously weakened, we would also expect that the basic loyalties transmitted through the family would also change. In many instances the weakening of transmission agencies is the result of conscious decisions. Particularly within developing nations, manipulating the socialization process by undermining the family's influence is a key mechanism to accelerate modernization. Within the United States there are frequent attempts to increase the socializing impact of the schools and, in the case of programs like Head Start, conscious efforts are made to give the school environment an advantage over family life (through not for explicitly political reasons). The introduction of new socializing agents, for example television or youth groups such as the Boy Scouts, also provides new opportunities for discontinuities even though existent agencies may remain intact.

Though we have analytically distinguished five conditions encouraging discontinuities in the socialization process, many of these conditions are closely interrelated and likely to occur together. For example, during periods of rapid social change we are likely to find leaders venturing into new areas in search of solutions, shifts in the relative impact of political socialization agencies, and an occasional dramatic crisis like a runaway inflation or an outbreak of domestic violence. Moreover, it also seems likely that some of these discontinuities encourage other discontinuities, so that disturbances in the socialization transmission process spill over and snowball into greater and greater possibilities of change. Consider, for instance, the introduction of television which resulted from long term technological development, but whose potential for affecting the socialization process is multitudinous. Not only can TV affect the pattern of family personal interaction (and thus the family's political role), but television's capacity to link individuals to the outside world may make dramatic events, charismatic leadership, and pressing social problems a reality to be confronted. Hence, the post-TV-child not only grows up in a different family environment, but in a world of richer and more fluid stimuli as well. The rapid industrialization and urbanization during the nineteenth century probably also triggered off a series of interrelated disruptions in the socialization process.

It should also be apparent that most, if not all, of these five conditions are present in contemporary American society. That Americans must face situations unknown fifty years ago is virtually self-evident. Even in the most isolated rural areas it is unlikely that parents can socialize their offspring to embrace all the values of the previous generation. Moreover, the development of mass communications and universal literacy bring citizens in much closer touch with the crises and dramatic events continually occurring in modern society. Thus, even isolated individuals can be shocked and disturbed by urban riots or stories of epidemic outbreaks of crime. Expectations of proper leadership behavior have also changed as the government becomes more and more responsible for regulating society. The era of Calvin Coolidge politics of doing very little is over and from the president on down there is now an emphasis on programmatic innovation rather than normalcy. In short, conditions are fluid in contemporary America and events and long-term forces act like shock waves buffeting the orderly transmission of values via the socialization process.

Given all these pressures toward discontinuity it is not unsurprising that both the political climate of opinion and the repertory of reasonable public policies have shifted in many areas. Consider, for example, the swelling of support for preservation of the environment, toleration for liberalized abortion, the less puritanical regulation of the arts, changes in discrimination against women and minorities, and shifts in public views on drugs to mention only a few issue areas in which major redefinition of the normal range policies have occurred. For example, ten years ago the idea of banning automobiles from the cities would have been dismissed as hairbrained. The same was true for the legalization of marijuana. Though both of these policies are not yet law, they are now at least considered reasonable alternatives. No doubt an American of the 1950s would be shocked by some of the choices now debated if he were to find himself in the 1970s.[7]

[7]For additional data on attitudinal change see Stuart Chase, "American Values: A Generation of Change," *Public Opinion Quarterly* 29 (1965), 357–67; Elmo Roper, "The Politics of Three Decades," *Public Opinion Quarterly* 29 (1965), 368–76; Fred I. Greenstein, *Children and Politics* (New Haven: Yale University Press, 1965), Chapter 7. Also, the *Public Opinion Quarterly* regularly presents collections of opinion data containing over time comparisons.

Despite the existence of powerful forces disturbing the maintenance of the boundaries between unthinkingly accepted givens and debatable issues, and evidence of shifts toward previously unconsidered options, fundamental political upheaval is not likely to be at hand. This is not to say that great changes are impossible; but rather, the likelihood of change increases as we move away from more basic issues and toward the more day to day types of conflict. Almost all the opinion shifts we have mentioned (and there are many more besides these) involve relatively specific policy changes, and though these shifts receive the bulk of our attention, they represent only the tip of the political iceberg.[8] Gyrations of opinions aside, the basic constitutional order remains largely unquestioned, the structure of authority is still legitimate, and the role of the citizen in the political process continues largely unchanged.[9] To continue our analogy with sports—new players have entered the game, the score has changed, and numerous exciting moments have transpired, but the game itself remains the same. Those with the advantage retain their advantage, and given what we know about the political socialization of future citizens, this advantage is likely to persist.

[8]Moreover, as Philip Converse has argued, much of this attitude shift may be random change of causually held preferences. For example, Converse found that over a six-year period people's attitudes on government economic policy changed randomly each time they were interviewed. These and other data suggest that many dramatic fluctuations on specific policy alternatives are highly superficial. Philip E. Converse, "The Nature of Belief Systems in Mass Publics," in *Ideology and Discontent* edited by David E. Apter (New York: The Free Press, 1964) and Philip E. Converse, "Attitudes and Non-Attitudes: Continuation of a Dialogue," in *The Quantitative Analysis of Social Problems* edited by Edward R. Tufte (Reading, Pa.: Addison-Wesley Publishing Company, Inc., 1970).

[9]The more general question of a supposed participation explosion is discussed in greater detail in Robert Weissberg, "The Political Activity of Americans and Democratic Citizenship," in *American Democracy: Theory and Reality* ed. Robert Weissberg and Mark V. Nadel (New York: John Wiley and Sons, Inc., 1972), especially pp. 128–33.

Index